The Faustian Pact in International Law

Titles available in the series:

Visit the **Edinburgh Critical Studies in Law, Literature and the Humanities** website at http://edinburghuniversitypress. com/series-edinburgh-critical-studies-in-law-literature-and-the-humanities

The Faustian Pact in International Law

Literature, Jurisprudence, and Giorgio Agamben's Critical Theory

Edwin Bikundo

EDINBURGH
University Press

Dedicated to the memory of my late mother,
Agnes Osanya Makori Bikundo,

Lux æterna luceat eis.

Edinburgh University Press is one of the leading university presses in the UK. We publish academic books and journals in our selected subject areas across the humanities and social sciences, combining cutting-edge scholarship with high editorial and production values to produce academic works of lasting importance. For more information visit our website: edinburghuniversitypress.com

Edinburgh University Press Ltd
13 Infirmary Street
Edinburgh EH1 1LT

First published in hardback by Edinburgh University Press 2024

Typeset in 11/13pt Adobe Garamond Pro
by Manila Typesetting Company

A CIP record for this book is available from the British Library

ISBN 978 1 4744 5566 4 (hardback)
ISBN 978 1 4744 5567 1 (paperback)
ISBN 978 1 4744 5568 8 (webready PDF)
ISBN 978 1 4744 5569 5 (epub)

Contents

Acknowledgments

This book would not have been possible without the guidance and generosity of my esteemed colleagues over the years. In particular, Wouter Werner, Fleur Johns, Daniel McLoughlin, Fréderic Mégret, Sinja Graf, Patricia Kameri-Mbote, Kojo Koram, Mark Antaki, Maria Elander, Sundhya Pahuja, Tim Peters, Simon Bronitt, Kanyiri Kariuki, Souheir Edelbi, Bryan Mukandi, Marco Wan, William MacNeil, Desmond Anderson, Rebecca Wallis, Lorenzo Verancini, Peter D. Rush, Janice Sim, Nicholas Heron, Daniel Hourigan, and Kieran Tranter have all read either the whole or parts of the manuscript and given valuable feedback, or at any rate provided their insights at conference or seminar presentations. I remain eternally grateful. Early versions of essays in this book have previously appeared elsewhere. Chapter 1 in *Pólemos: Journal of Law, Literature and Culture*, Chapter 2 in *Law and Literature,* Chapter 3 in *Law, Technology and Humans,* Chapter 4 in *The International Criminal Law Review*, Chapter 6 in the *Asia Pacific Journal of Ocean Law and Policy*, Chapter 7 in *Law, Culture and the Humanities*, Chapter 8 in *The Griffith Journal of Law & Human Dignity* and Chapters 5 and 9 in *The Netherlands Yearbook of International Law*

Introduction: Goethe's *Faust*, Giorgio Agamben, and International Law

Why the Faustian pact? Why international law? Why now? Inquiring into whether international law is quintessentially Faustian and how to deal with that – as this book seeks to do – does not necessarily explain and justify itself. To start with, Johann Wolfgang von Goethe's *Faust* dangles the tantalising possibility of frustrating Faustian pacts, and two lines from it sparked and have spurred and sustained this project on. The first was Mephistopheles' description of himself as:

> A part of that force
> Which, always willing evil, always produces good.[1]

where he represented himself – and indeed was presented – as somehow a servant of God or at the very least as doing God's work for Him. The second, and related to this, was Mephistopheles' sly and ironic observation to God that Faust 'serves You in a curious way',[2] which may well have been simultaneously description and self-description. Whether taken together or separately, these lines say a good deal about the Mephistophelean character and role, which claims to bring good and evil together in some sort of productive and somehow mutually reliant relationship, all the while couched in a consciously bottomless ironic register.

Consequently, the Faustian pact or literary (it could never be literal – could it?) deal with the devil at its heart rests on the claim that out of evil, good *will* nevertheless arise. This trope utilises false hope by invoking real desire and relates good and evil with the latter somehow producing the former – that is, it explains away evil by invoking good, and is consequently a lay theodicy. When we use this framing of theodicy and turn to the field of law, we find law itself is public, or secular, or perhaps more inclusively, political theodicy.

A Faustian temptation offered to unmet claims premised on justice is to have them enforced by law through force, with force distinguished from violence only through legal operation. This therefore means that the present justice of the argument is set aside for it to be necessarily enforced through might, which is now difficult to distinguish from right. This is because that immediacy of justice is set aside perpetually for the enforceability of the justice claim. The politically arcane fact, that the chamber-of-justice-according-to-law admits supplicants only at the price of giving up whatever was actively sought purely on the basis of justice in the first place, is generally obscured from view. Recall, political arcana are secret modes of the exercise of political power, ordinarily either hidden or obscured – or, at any rate, veiled from full public view.[3] No wonder then that Ernst Kantorowicz[4] used political theology as virtually synonymous with mysteries of state or *arcana imperii*, associating him not only with his contemporary Carl Schmitt[5] and Giorgio Agamben[6] in their wake but, according to Donaldson,[7] to Niccolò Machiavelli before all of them.

The deeply ambiguous and consequently ambivalent role of the law in perpetuating the conceptualisation and running of the concentration camps (both real and virtual – that is, both literally and literarily) is considered an anomaly when it is not glossed over or ignored in conventional treatments of the subject. This book instead takes that marginalised topic as its focus, using the ambiguity of the Faustian pact to explain the absolute ambiguity and consequent ambivalence of resorting to law as an instrument of justice and for emancipation. It then, in turn, uses law's absolute ambiguity to elucidate the absolute ambiguity and ambivalence of the contractual elements on the Faustian pact and wager. The impetus behind the book (and its cover illustration) was drawn from two instances of the concentration camp's spatial arrangement. The first is illustrated best by Primo Levi's account of a football match between the SS and concentration camp inmates that took place at the centre of Auschwitz.[8] The second is the symbolic, legendary oak of Buchenwald – the only tree left standing in the centre of that concentration camp;[9] supposedly Goethe had sat there with his lover[10] and is even believed to have written poetry in its shade. While the Nazis preserved the tree to associate themselves with High German culture, the prisoners looked to it as a reminder of the other Germany that – just like them – was taken hostage by the Nazi regime. Goethe would probably recognise these moments of contrived normality within the horrors of the camp as exemplifying two hearts beating within modernity's breast. The role of law in this, and how culture as expressed in and by literature shapes it, are this book's preoccupations. The law being ambiguous is always on all sides of any dispute and international law itself is a prime example of this: 'given that the self-interest of states is built into international law, the language and legislation of human rights have historically been ambivalent, constituting both a discourse of rebellion and of state legitimacy'.[11] This ambivalence of human rights is what Ben Golder discerns from the fact that legally enforceable rights are 'both emancipatory and regulatory'.[12] Golder notes that, while rights 'can enlarge, expand, or protect the sphere of action of subjects (as well as performatively bring new worlds and communities into being)', they simultaneously 'can also be the conduit, or the vehicle, for relations of power that constitute those very subjects and communities in particular ways and hence reinscribe them within existing forms of power, often recuperating and domesticating the political challenges they might pose'.[13]

The book proceeds on the broad thesis that Westphalian law generally, and international law in particular, are the product of secularisation while secularisation is merely the shifting of what was once based on God, the devil and religion onto to the action of humans upon humans. Given that these shifts leave everything else more or less intact, this is a secular and thus non-salvific religion in all but name. After all, 'Obedience to legal rules to which we would have consented relieves us of the task of evaluating the morality and prudence of our actions' (West 1985), notwithstanding that the consent is always strictly manufactured.

From the perspective of religion, not only is this self-evidently the work of the devil, but there are other associations with the devil, hell and Faustian pacts of one sort or the other that this book will explore. Given the importance of poetry, the centrality of theology and explicit references in his work,[14] it is surprising that more has not been made of Goethe's epic poem *Faust* in relation to Agamben's work. This becomes even more curious in light of the theodicy he outlines at several points with regard to law's justification of violence. This book aims to partially address that puzzle.

This book therefore quite unexpectedly gradually developed into a meditative survey of the power of irony and punning words like 'humanity', 'order', 'crisis', 'contract', 'necessity', 'force of law', 'experiment' etc. in law. Indeed, for Agamben, 'poetry lives only in the tension and difference (and hence also in the virtual interference) between sound and sense'.[15] Surely, then, the literary pun binds us to the apparatus of law through language just as it could hopefully unbind us from that same apparatus of law. Indeed, Agamben points out that Plato was fond of punning.[16] Notable Agamben translator Adam Kotsko notes, in passing, Agamben's 'untranslatable puns'.[17]

Both the Faustian pact and the law thus give what one asks for only at the expense of what they actually want in a similar way through the apparatus of language. This linguistic mechanism is that of the 'pun' or play on words, which draws attention to the unbridgeable divide between signs and signification or semiotics and semantics. This is sometimes expressible as an opposition between say legal positivism and natural law theory, making the devil as a trope an arch positivist always acting in completely bad faith but nevertheless still themselves bound within the literal strictures of language. Indeed, if this book is correct, the law's justifications and rationalisations are merely a subset of the broader category of Faustian pact. International law, as we shall see below, is replete with examples of this theodicy of violence (where might and right coincide in the enforceability of law), which are justified by a claimed necessity that can never be proven nor disproven; hence it is not a brute empirical fact that can be proven as either true or false on the basis of evidence but is merely a mystification that must be true in order for inter-national law to make coherent sense. Which is to say, the necessity of law as such is itself a legal fiction that the law must assume to be true in the face of all and any evidence in order to remain coherent. Although many of the examples of Faustian pacts chosen in this book are drawn from international criminal law, this is particularly in its role of enforcing breaches of adjacent areas of public international law including but not limited to the law of the sea, international humanitarian law, international human rights law, state and individual responsibility for internationally wrongful acts and the law on the use of force – at a minimum.

More could be made of the mystery as to why the influence of Johann Wolfgang von Goethe's *Faust* on Italian philosopher Giorgio Agamben's body of work is not more prominent. After all, as a great philosophical poet, who was tremendously concerned with language, Goethe's work could not have failed to capture Agamben's attention, especially given his early and sustained interest in poetry. Indeed, Agamben cites Goethe in at least twelve of his works, including *The Use of Bodies, Creation and Anarchy, Pilate and Jesus, The Kingdom and the Glory, Homo Sacer, The Signature of All Things, Stanzas, The End of the Poem, Potentialities, Karman, Adventure* and *Infancy and History*. Crucially, the last five reference Goethe's *Faust* directly. Thus, Chapter 1 of this book sets out the clear, persistent influence of Goethe's *Faust* upon Agamben's philological and philosophical approach to explicating law's foun-dational riddles – which is for this book legal punning. Chapter 1 'Behold, I tell you a mystery' seeks to demonstrate that Goethean influence, ironically enough through a close examination of both Faust's and Agamben's attempts at partially translating a biblical phrase: 'in the beginning was the word'.

References to the devil in international criminal justice are various and varied, and tap into a rich vein of allusion, association and meaning. These range from the simple, where the term is used metaphorically, to the more complex, referencing Faustian pacts of one form or another, to the downright esoteric encompassing the arcane origins of the immunity afforded official acts.

Chapter 2, 'Reading Faust into International Criminal Law's Metaphorical References to the Devil', therefore examines the varied and persistent references to the devil prevalent throughout international criminal law, citing examples as diverse as Romeo Dallaire's *Shake Hands with the Devil* and the trial of Rudolf Kastner, demonstrating how literary and theological imagery profoundly shapes law. Kenyan President Uhuru Kenyatta's statement 'That devil shall be defeated' as well as Canadian General Romeo Dallaire's 'Shake hands with the devil' are two examples respectively resisting and promoting international individual criminal liability. That Carl Schmitt was asked by his interrogator at Nuremberg 'When did you renounce the devil?' and that defence counsel at the International Criminal court in the Kenyan Situation analogised the Kenyan government as being accused of entering into 'a deal with the devil', and the judge at Rudolf Kastner's case in Israel referred to Nazi-era crimes describing him as having 'sold his soul to the devil' all cut across perpetrators and victims, and speak of compacts with absolute evil in order to produce good. They are all political theodicies explaining away evil by linking it in some causal way to good. It must be said that these examples are not literal but only literary. They nonetheless go beyond rhetorical flourishes that lose neither efficacy nor effect even by being used by opposed parties for opposed reasons.

Experiments abound in philosopher of language Agamben's work. This is particularly so when he explicitly addresses questions and criticisms surrounding his own methodology. Chapter 3, 'What is Real about Experimental Norms?', turns its attention to Agamben's use of experiments throughout his body of work, drawing parallels with Faustian logic to illustrate how, rather than only being in the pursuit of demonstrable knowledge, the purpose of experiments is always accompanied by the highest expression of power over human beings. Humans experimenting on other humans sits precisely at the junction of law, technology and the humanities, synthesising as it simultaneously does descriptive, normative and creative elements in relation to reality. Experiments describe reality, normalise shared conceptions of reality and create their own reality. These utilise different inflections of 'norm' as a pattern, or a model, or a standard to be met or fulfilled.

Chapter 4, 'Carl Schmitt as a Subject and Object of International Criminal Law', addresses why Nazi Crown jurist Carl Schmitt was not prosecuted. Aspects of his work expressed avowedly anti-Semitic sentiments while some of his intellectual concepts could be deployed to support National Socialist territorial expansion or *Lebensraum* ('living space'). Schmitt's explicit self-comparison with Niccolò Machiavelli is in many ways completely apt, given their mutually 'devilish' associations. This comparison is instructive, inviting as it does ambiguous readings or ironical inflections of their works.[18]

Chapter 5, 'Saving Humanity from Hell', touches upon how and why individual criminal responsibility, in the absence of state intervention, demonstrates a globalising political power conjoined to a universalising legal glory. The chapter argues that crises – a medical term that has made its way into the heart of law[19] – enable a negative grounding of legal and political jurisdiction that relies on a legitimation, which requires confirmation by judicial bodies. The analysis outlines the institutionalisation of an exceptional legal mechanism in the International Criminal Tribunal for the former Yugoslavia (ICTY), its proliferation to the International Criminal Tribunal for Rwanda (ICTR) and its normalisation in the ICC. The purpose of this analysis is neither to parse what the law is and what it should be, nor what the law does versus what it promises, but rather to show how and why individual criminal responsibility in the absence of state intervention demonstrates a globalising political power conjoined to a universalising legal glory.

Chapter 6, 'Artificial Islands, Artificial Highways and Pirates', reviews how the struggle between land and sea encompasses both the law of the sea and international criminal law. Drawing on Carl Schmitt's *Land and Sea*, in light of Johann Wolfgang Goethe's *Faust*, clarifies issues within this archetypal, geopolitical conflict while providing insights into the current, cyclical iteration: the Sino-American battle for global naval supremacy. The links between building and opposing artificial islands on the South China Sea and international efforts to combat piracy off the Somali coast are not immediately apparent. However, while the United States promotes freedom of navigation, China constructs artificial islands bolstering its territorial claims. Both utilise their navies similarly but for opposed reasons. This reflects a strategic antagonism with the United States championing a sea open to global navigation and commerce while China builds a primarily land-based 'New Silk Road' linked to critical markets and natural resources. This struggle between land and sea encompasses both the law of the sea and international criminal law. Reading Carl Schmitt's *Land and Sea* in light of Johann Wolfgang Goethe's *Faust* provides the opportunity to evaluate whether it may clarify issues at stake that Schmitt himself did not have the opportunity to consider, including the Faustian characteristics of the dispute and consequently of each of the parties.

Chapter 7, 'Follow your Leader – I Prefer Not to', considers Giorgio Agamben's models for non-violent resistance, demonstrated through his usage of Hermann Melville's character of Bartleby, to address the opposing strategies of non-cooperation and violent resistance underlying the images of slave and free human in liberal democratic thought. Giorgio Agamben relies on Bartleby from Hermann Melville's short story of the same name as a model of political resistance. Agamben proffers Bartleby's phrase 'I prefer not to' as a model for paralysing apparatuses of power. Benito Cereno is the central figure in a Melville story, again of the same name. He was the captain of a slave ship taken over by the slaves whose leader Babo forced him to act as the master while they feigned the condition of slaves in order to get provisions. Babo's signature phrase was 'follow your leader'. This chapter compares the opposed strategies of non-cooperation versus violent resistance that are embodied in each of these phrases to argue that because the slave-figure is the shadow image of the free human in liberal democratic thought, violence is an illusory basis for emancipation. Such violence would be mimicry of the oppressor by the oppressed.

Chapter 8, 'The President's Two Bodies', examines the medieval doctrine of the 'King's two bodies', played out before the International Criminal Court (ICC) in the trial of the President of the Republic of Kenya, Uhuru Kenyatta. The medieval distinction between the official and the personal bodies of the state sovereign played out before the ICC. This scenario involved the President of the Republic of Kenya willingly submitting to the jurisdiction of the ICC but only in his personal capacity and not as president. Essentially, this argument is based on the medieval doctrine of the 'King's two bodies'.[20] This examination will follow Kantorowicz and Agamben in relating how two bodies united as one (or two lives sharing one body or two parts of one body) in its origins can sit with law at the crossroads of political theory and political theology. It draws from a rich heritage of these traditions that are of necessity developed through reconciling pressing practical imperatives to the subtlest theoretical niceties.

Although democracy and democratic practices, in the form of both direct and indirect public participation in governance are axiomatically a cherished value of liberal democratic principles, populism is nevertheless treated with wariness because of its potential to come into conflict with other cherished values of liberal democratic principles such as human rights and the rule of law. The 'people' as such have a limited direct role ascribed in public international law. Therefore, in Chapter 9, 'People, Politics and Populism in International Criminal Law', populism references a crisis of political representation where a schism between a people and its representatives is detected, or claimed or exploited. That so-called democratic deficit makes international criminal law practitioners on the one hand particularly vulnerable to demagogic speech challenging their legitimacy and on the other particularly tempted to counter demagoguery by asserting themselves as being more legitimate representatives of a victimised people than their oppressive rulers. This chapter consequently argues that in international criminal law the people is metaphorically explicable as an optical illusion appearing and disappearing at crucial moments in different guises. In the Kenyan case study selected, these contested guises include victims and popular mandates. The people as such are never present and yet remain politically as well as legally indispensable as a rhetorical claim to ground concrete action oriented towards justice.

Chapter 10, 'War! What is it Good For?', observes that whereas both law and music have provided justification for war as a necessary evil, the two are seldom considered together in that regard. Although they have both provided an explaining away of the evil of war (a lay theodicy), this remains unexplored and under-theorised. Consequently, the chapter asks what utility there could possibly be in war, what the law has to say about it and why music is relevant. The discussion examines and stages encounters between war, law and music using examples ranging from 'The Laudes Regiae' medieval acclamatory hymn and George Frideric Handel's 'The Lord is a Man of War' to Bob Marley's 'War' speech set to reggae and Edwin Starr's 'War' in relation to the international law on the use of force. In this vein, a little-known war casualty was Starr's 1969 Vietnam-era protest song 'War', which gives this chapter its full title. Along with Culture Club's 1984 ironically titled 'War Song', among others, it was banned from radio playlists in the lead-up to the First Gulf War. With lyrics like 'War . . . What is it good for? . . . Absolutely nothin'', '(War) friend only to the undertaker/Oh, war it's an enemy to all mankind' in the case of Starr and 'war is stupid and people are stupid' in the case of Boy George, these songs were deemed not particularly good for morale – either civilian or military – and were viewed as dangerously off message in an era of ever-tightening control over messaging during times of war.

It has been justly noted that, 'as long as our culture continues to struggle between religious and scientific conceptions of its own existence Faust will continue to represent our own modernity'. Faust's continuing relevance is based partly on the fact that it 'is a comprehensive synthesis of European culture and, as such, is largely responsible for the widespread perception that Germany in the nineteenth and early twentieth centuries had reached the pinnacle of cultural development'.

Harold Bloom notes that, of 'all the strongest Western writers, Goethe now seems the least available to our sensibility'.[21] For Bloom:

> Goethe's daemon or daemons – he appears to have commanded as many as he wanted – is always present in his work, aiding the perpetual paradox that the poetry and prose alike are at once exemplary of a Classical, almost universal *ethos*, and a Romantic, intensely personal *pathos*. The *logos*, or in Aristotelian terms the *dianoia* (thought content) of Goethe's work, is the only vulnerable aspect, since the Goethean Science of Nature today seems an inadequate conceptualizing of his formidable daemonic apprehension of reality. That hardly matters, for Goethe's literary power and wisdom survive the evaporation of his rationalizations.[22]

Not only is *Faust* influential, but it profoundly influenced the Western literary canon. As Bloom notes, '*Faust* cannot be truly Shakespearean, but it almost incessantly parodies Shakespeare.'[23] He continues, 'Faust doesn't have a human spirit or personality, but Mephistopheles delightfully does. When he wrote of Mephistopheles, Goethe was a true poet, and of the Devil's party while knowing it, because Goethe seems to have known everything.'[24] This is fairly ironic in the context of Mephistopheles' comment that, 'I may not be omniscient, but I do know quite a lot.'[25] The variety and scope of the chapters in this book attempt to provide examples of Faust's continued relevance to our time and the space of international law generally.

Notes

1. J. Goethe, *Faust Volumes 1 and 2: Goethe's Collected Works* (Princeton, NJ: Princeton University Press, 2014), 108, lines 1335–6.
2. Goethe, *Faust Volumes 1 and 2*, 108, line 300.
3. P. S. Donaldson, *Machiavelli and Mystery of State* (Cambridge: Cambridge University Press, 1988), 227.
4. E. Kantorowicz, *The King's Two Bodies* (Princeton, NJ: Princeton University Press, 1957), 65.
5. C. Schmitt, *The Concept of the Political* (Chicago: University of Chicago Press, 1996a); C. Schmitt, *Dialogues on Power and Space* (Cambridge: Polity Press, 2014); C. Schmitt, *Land and Sea: A World-Historical Mediation* (New York: Telos, 2015).
6. Giorgio Agamben (2005a).
7. Donaldson, *Machiavelli and Mystery of State*.
8. P. Levi, *The Drowned and the Saved* (New York: Summit Books, 1988), 54–5.
9. E. Kogon, *A Theory and Practice of Hell: The German Concentration Camps and the System Behind Them*, trans. H. Norden (New York: Octagon Books, 1979), 49.
10. S. Farmer, 'Symbols That Face Two Ways: Commemorating the Victims of Nazism and Stalinism at Buchenwald and Sachsenhausen', *Representations* 49 (1995), 97–119.
11. J. R. Slaughter, *Human Rights, Inc: The World Novel, Narrative Form, and International Law* (New York: Fordham University Press, 2007), 88.
12. B. Golder, *Foucault and the Politics of Rights* (Stanford, CA: Stanford University Press, 2015), 91.
13. Golder, *Foucault and the Politics of Rights*, 91.
14. G. Agamben, *Infancy and History: The Destruction of Experience* (New York: Verso 1993), 14, end of poem IX at 52; G. Agamben, *The End of the Poem: Studies in Poetics* (Stanford, CA: Stanford University Press 1999), 286; Agamben, *The Adventure* (Cambridge, MA: MIT Press, 2018), 13–14.
15. Agamben *The End of the Poem*, 109.
16. G. Agamben, *What is Philosophy?* (Stanford, CA: Stanford University Press, 2017), 73, 95.
17. G. Agamben, *Karman: A Brief Treatise on Action, Guilt, and Gesture* (Stanford, CA: Stanford University Press, 2018b).
18. L. Strauss, *Thoughts on Machiavelli* (Glencoe, IL: The Free Press, 1958).

19. R. Koselleck, 'Crisis', trans. Michaela W. Richter, *Journal of the History of Ideas* 67 (2006) 397–400.
20. E. Kantorowicz, *The King's Two Bodies* (Princeton, NJ: Princeton University Press, 1957).
21. H. Bloom, *The Western Canon: The Books and School of the Ages* (New York: Harcourt Brace, 1994), 190.
22. Bloom, *The Western Canon*, 191.
23. Bloom, *The Western Canon*, 195.
24. Bloom, *The Western Canon*, 197.
25. Goethe, *Faust Volumes 1 and 2*, line 1582.

1

'Behold, I tell you a mystery': Tracing *Faust's* Influences on Giorgio Agamben to and from International Law

Behold, I tell you a mystery;
we shall not all sleep,
but we shall all be changed in a moment,
in the twinkling of an eye, at the last trumpet.
> George Frideric Handel: Messiah (HWV 56), 47. Accompagnato Bass
> (I Corinthians 15, 51–52)

O death, where is thy sting? O grave, where is thy victory?
The sting of death is sin, and the strength of sin is the law.
> George Frideric Handel: Messiah (HWV 56), 50. Duet Alto & tenor
> (I Corinthians 15, 55–56)

I've studied now, to my regret,
Philosophy, Law, Medicine,
and – what is worst – Theology
. . .
That is why I've turned to magic,
in hope that with the help of spirit-power
I might solve many mysteries,
so that I need no longer toil and sweat
> Johann Wolfgang von Goethe: *Faust*, lines 354–56 and 277–380

Introduction

This chapter makes the claim that Giorgio Agamben's *Homo Sacer* project is suffused with explicit and implicit references to Johann Wolfgang von Goethe's *Faust*. It begins by locating Agamben's task within and from international law, then relates how the mysteries that he seeks to unravel therein are central to his concerns generally and not just specifically to *Homo Sacer*. It then proceeds to further demonstrate this point by relating how both Faust and Agamben go about translating the same biblical passage, beginning with 'in the beginning' to relate origins to commandments. It concludes that international law is central to Agamben and that his approach to expounding upon it is profoundly marked by Goethe's *Faust*.

Unveiling the Mysteries of International Law and 'the bloody mystification of a new planetary order'

At the beginning of his nine-book project, philosopher of language Giorgio Agamben introduces its protagonist of the same name as the title of the series and the first book in the series: *Homo Sacer*, the sacred man who may be killed but, paradoxically, may not be sacrificed.[1] Crucially, Agamben offers the paradigm of *Homo Sacer* as 'the key by which not only the sacred texts of sovereignty but also the very codes of political power will unveil their mysteries'.[2] Moreover, Agamben introduces the origin of the book, and hence of the project, 'as a response to the bloody mystification of a new planetary order'.[3] Eric Meyer's reading substitutes 'world' for 'planetary'.[4] Doing that places Agamben as responding to a very specific context: that of then US President George W. Bush's speech at the beginning of the first Gulf War:

> Out of these troubled times, our fifth objective – a new world order – can emerge: A new era – freer from the threat of terror, stronger in the pursuit of justice and more secure in the quest for peace. An era in which the nations of the world, east and west, north and south, can prosper and live in harmony . . . Once again, Americans have stepped forward to share a tearful goodbye with their families before leaving for a strange and distant shore. At this very moment, they serve together with Arabs, Europeans, Asians and Africans in defense of principle and the dream of a new world order.[5]

This 'new world order' theme was important enough to merit returning to in a speech made following the war:

> Twice before in this century, an entire world was convulsed by war. Twice this century, out of the horrors of war hope emerged for enduring peace. Twice before, those hopes proved to be a distant dream, beyond the grasp of man.
>
> Until now, the world we've known has been a world divided, a world of barbed wire and concrete block, conflict and cold war.
>
> And now, we can see a new world coming into view. A world in which there is the very real prospect of a new world order. In the words of Winston Churchill, a 'world order' in which 'the principles of justice and fair play . . . protect the weak against the strong.' A world where the United Nations, freed from cold war stalemate, is poised to fulfill the historic vision of its

founders. A world in which freedom and respect for human rights find a home among all nations . . . It is a victory for the rule of law and for what is right.[6]

By the last book in the *Homo Sacer* series, *The Use of Bodies*, Agamben can state that mystery spans not just metaphysics and law but also politics, both practical and philosophical:

> Just as the tradition of metaphysics has always thought the human being in the form of an articulation between two elements (nature and logos, body and soul, animality and humanity), so also has Western political philosophy always thought politics in the figure of the relation between two figures that it is a question of linking together: bare life and power, the household and the city, violence and institutional order, anomie (anarchy) and law, multitude and people. From the perspective of our study, we must instead attempt to think humanity and politics as what results from the disconnection of these elements and investigate not the metaphysical mystery of conjunction but the practical and political one of their disjunction.[7]

More to the point, Agamben sees his task as enabling the disjunction between, among others, 'violence and institutional order, anomie (anarchy) and law'.[8] We can see clearly then in the background to *Homo Sacer* a certain preoccupation with mystery, and especially legal mystification encompassing the use of force or violence, human rights and the violent making and unmaking of universalising legal orders – whether global or planetary. It should therefore, to say the least, be rewarding to pay closer attention to the role of mystery and especially legal mystification in Agamben's work.

Mystery in Agamben as Esoteric Doctrine, Drama, Practice or Form of Life

Unravelling mystery in one form or the other is clearly therefore an abiding concern of Agamben's work. He does this principally in engagement with Odo Casel, but also touches on two other important interlocutors of his, Carl Schmitt and Ernst Kantorowicz, who link this ongoing engagement with mystery to his writings on law and to, as we shall see below, *Faust*. Agamben uses mystery in more than just the sense of something difficult or impossible to understand or explain, but also as secret rites of Greek and Roman religion to which only initiates were admitted, along with their practices, knowledge or lore, and additionally the Christian Eucharist and drama. This last sense of drama (and more besides, as we shall see below) as a mystery play links his oeuvre to Goethe's *Faust*, which was framed as an ironic mystery play.[9] The thing to note here is that for Agamben the Christian liturgy contains all of these senses as simply different facets of the same phenomenon which has now been secularised into politics. Agamben makes the case for this in dialogue with Casel at numerous points, including:

> Christianity – such is the thesis that summarizes Casel's thought – is essentially 'mystery,' a liturgical action that each time renders present in ritual form the salvific praxis of Christ, and the worshiping community obtains salvation by entering into contact with this praxis.[10]

For Agamben, as for Casel, Christianity is a historical religion; thus, the 'mysteries' of which it speaks are 'also and above all historical facts, so are taken for granted'.[11] Also, 'Mystery originally does not mean "secret and ineffable doctrine" but "sacred drama"'.[12] Agamben notes that

> the ancient world interprets this mysterical infancy as a knowledge which cannot be spoken of, as a silence to be kept. So, as they appear in Gianblico's *De Mysteriis*, the mysteries are now a '*teurgia*', essentially a skill, a 'technique' for influencing the gods. Here the *pathema* becomes *mathema*, the un-speakable of infancy, a secret doctrine weighed down by an oath of esoteric silence.[13]

When it comes to the law, Agamben finds that:

> The ultimate end of the juridical regulation is to produce judgment; but judgment aims neither to punish nor to extol, neither to establish justice nor to prove the truth. Judgment is in itself the end and this, it has been said, constitutes its mystery, the mystery of the trial.[14]

However, by the end of *The Kingdom and the Glory*, Agamben can confidently assert that:

> What our investigation has shown is that the real problem, the central mystery of politics is not sovereignty, but government; it is not God, but the angel; it is not the king, but ministry; it is not the law but the police – that is to say, the governmental machine that they form and support.[15]

In coming to this conclusion, Agamben draws partly from, 'The celebrated passage in I Corinthians 15, 35–55 [which] . . . in truth says nothing more than this: that the bodies of the just will be resurrected in glory and will be transformed into glory and into the incorruptible spirit.'[16] Part of that celebration of the passage, of course, includes George Frideric Handel's oratorio *Messiah*, partly reproduced in the epigraph above, from which this chapter partially draws its title.

In *The Mystery of Evil*, Agamben notes that:

The *mysterium inquitatis* . . . is a historical drama (*mystērion* in Greek means 'dramatic action'), which is underway in every instant, so to speak, and in which the destiny of humanity, the salvation or the fall of human beings, is always at stake.[17]

Agamben points out that:

Casel shows than in Greek *mystērion* does not designate a secret doctrine which could be formulated discursively but which it is prohibited to reveal. There the term *mystērion* indicates a praxis, an action or a drama in the theatrical sense of the term as well, that is, a set of gestures, acts, and words through which a divine action or passion is efficaciously actualized in the world and time for the salvation of those who participate in it.[18]

In *Creation and Anarchy*, Agamben works through the public function of liturgy in the following way, which centralises the role of mystery:

At the basis of Casel's doctrine in fact stands the idea that the liturgy (it is well known that the Greek term *leitourgia* means 'public work or performance,' from *laos*, 'people,' and *ergon*) is essentially a 'mystery.' Yet mystery does not in any way signify, according to Casel, an unknown teaching or secret doctrine. Originally, as in the Eleusinian mysteries that were celebrated in classical Greece, mystery signified a practice, a sort of theatrical action, made up of gestures and words that are carried out in time and in the world, for the salvation of human beings. Christianity is not therefore a 'religion' or a 'confession' in the modern sense of the term, an ensemble of truths and dogmas that it is a question of recognizing and professing: it is rather a 'mystery,' that is, a liturgical *actio*, a 'performance,' whose actors are Christ and his mystical body, namely, the Church. And this action is, of course, a specific praxis, but at the same time, it defines the most universal and truest human activity, in which what is at stake is the salvation of those who carry it out and of those who participate in it.[19]

In *Opus Dei*, Agamben offers a more sustained engagement with Casel in explicating mystery in a way that leads us step by steady step inexorably towards the role of the devil in providence, including

that the pagan mysteries (Eleusian, Orphic, and Hermetic) must not be seen as a secret doctrine, which one could pronounce in words but that one is prohibited to reveal. Such a meaning of the term *mystery*, according to Casel, is late and derives from the influence of the Neopythagorean and Neoplatonic schools. Originally, *mystery* designates a praxis, that of the *dromena,* the gestures and acts by means of which a divine action is accomplished in time and in the world for human salvation: *silentium mysticum non qualecumque theologiam, sed actiones ritusque sacros texisse* (mystical silence does not conceal any kind of theology, but sacred actions and rites).[20]

Opus Dei once again relies on Casel to explain that mystery is a participatory cultic action uniting a community of believers:

> For Casel, *mystery* means essentially 'cultic action.' Defining Christianity as a mystery is therefore equivalent for him first of all to affirming that the Church is not simply a community of believers, defined by sharing a doctrine crystallized in a set of dogmas. The Church is defined rather through participation in the mystery of the cultic action.[21]

Opus Dei, while still engaging Casel, elucidates the point that liturgy and mystery are two sides of the same coin linking the action of Christ to the action of the church:

> Evoking the originary political meaning of the term *leitourgia,* Casel affirms that the two terms *mystery* and *liturgy* mean the same thing but from two different points of view: '*mystery* means the heart of the action, that is to say, the redeeming work of the risen Lord, through the sacred actions he has appointed; *liturgy,* corresponding to its original sense of "people's work," "service," means rather the action of the church in conjunction with this saving action of Christ's'.[22]

In *Opus Dei,* this unity of action of the church/action of Christ effectively creates a reality of the faithful participants being saved in Christ:

> According to Casel, the term *effectus* names this effective unity of image and presence in the liturgical mystery, in which the presence is real in its operativity, that is, as *Heilstat,* salvific action: 'mystery-presence means a real presence, but a reality of a special type. A reality, to the extent to which it corresponds solely to the goal of the sacrament, which is that of permitting the faithful to participate, for their salvation, in the life of Christ as savior.[23]

Consequently, for *Opus Dei* mystery is the effectiveness of the cultic action whose public work makes Christ's action real: 'the mystery is the effect; what is mysterious is effectiveness, insofar as in it being is resolved into praxis and praxis is substantiated into being. *The mystery of the liturgy coincides totally with the mystery of operativity.*'[24] For Agamben, 'Magical and sacramental operations correspond to each other term for term.'[25]

Carl Schmitt, a key interlocutor of Agamben's elsewhere, is in no way explicitly cited in *Opus Dei*; however, his famous notion that 'All significant concepts of the modern theory of the state are secularized theological concepts'[26] was definitely the kind of thinking against which Casel was writing, as Agamben documents:

> Our time, writes Casel, is witnessing the decline of individualism and humanism, which by stripping nature and the world of the divine had believed themselves to have forever dispelled the obfuscation of mystery. In this way, by means of the collapse of rationalist humanism, our time has opened up 'a new turning to the mystery' . . . The world 'becomes for him once more a stage on which God's drama is being carried out . . . God's mystery once again inspires dread, attracts and calls us' . . . With a barely veiled allusion to so much that was happening in those years in the secular sphere and, in particular, to the rediscovery of ceremonials and liturgies in the political sphere, Casel can thus write: 'Today the world outside Christianity and the church is looking for mystery; it is building a new kind of rite in which man worships himself. But through all this the world will never reach God.'[27]

After all, Schmitt did write about how a human sovereign became a god to humans, *homo homini deus*, as distinct from the state of nature where humans were wolves to human, *homo homini lupus*.[28] Montserrat Herrero points out that Schmitt 'attests to the possibility of new forms of political theology emerging from the Trinitarian dogma, as can be perceived in Goethe's motto *"nemo contra deus nisi deus ipse"*'.[29] Herrero even concludes that Kantorowicz's work constitutes a 'defence of Schmitt's political theology against [Erik] Peterson'.[30]

Furthermore, Brian J. Fox demonstrates that Schmitt's political theology was more politics than theology – more the papal states than the papacy as the ideal political community. This approach to the Church is found as early as 1912, in a diary entry where Schmitt reflects upon Faust's 'solution' as referring 'to the state, which is also an overcoming of temporality. The ideal is of the Papal States.'[31] Schmitt's allusion to Faust cannot be coincidental, given that for Schmitt, 'Even Satan's power is . . . as such from God and not evil.'[32]

Ernst Kantorowicz, another key interlocutor of Agamben's, speaks of jurists, lawyers and judges as engaged in a 'ministry (mystery) of "the cult of justice"':

> The emperor's [Frederick II] antiphrastic formula ['father and son of Justice'] belonged to a different world of thought. It fell in with the intellectual climate of the 'Jurists' Century' in general, and in particular with that of Frederick's *Magna Curia* where the judges and lawyers were expected to administer Justice like priests; where the High Court sessions, staged

with a punctilio comparable to Church ceremonial, were dubbed 'a most holy ministry (mystery) of Justice' (*Iustitiae sacratissimum ministerium [mysterium]*); where the jurists and courtiers interpreted the 'Cult of Justice' in terms of a *religio iuris* or of an *ecclesia imperialis*, representing both a complement to and an antitype of the ecclesiastical order; where, so to speak, the robe of the law clerk was set over against the robe of the ordained cleric; and where the emperor himself, 'whom the Great Artificer's hand created man,' was spoken of as *Sol Iustitiae*, the 'Sun of Justice,' which was the prophetic title of Christ.[33]

Not only does Kantorowicz engage with Fredrick II in all three of his monographs, *Frederick the Second*, *The King's Two Bodies* and *Laudes Regiae*, but he notes in passing Frederick II being associated with a 'pact with the devil'.[34] Part of the reason why that monarch was such an object of fascination for Kantorowicz is that he was a banned and excommunicated emperor who crowned himself without a coronation mass in Jerusalem as King of Jerusalem precisely because he was banned and excommunicated, and consequently had no need for the church as an intermediary between him and God.[35] He could consequently approach God directly 'as a triumphant conqueror'.[36] Furthermore, 'since as a priest he knew all mysteries no mystery was safe from his fearless mocking attack'.[37] Additionally, 'The only limits he could recognise were those he set himself.'[38]

Agamben points out that, 'according to Christian theology there is only one legal institution which knows neither interruption nor end: hell. The model of contemporary politics – which pretends to an infinite economy of the world – is thus truly infernal.'[39] Furthermore, 'The principle according to which the government of the world will cease with the Last Judgment has only one important exception in Christian theology. It is the case of hell.'[40] Agamben cites Hannah Arendt's statement that, 'The concentration camps are the laboratories in the experiment of total domination, for human nature being what it is, this goal can be achieved only under the extreme circumstances of human made hell.'[41]

Adam Kotsko, translator of Agamben's *The Sacrament of Language*, *The Highest Poverty*, *Opus Dei*, *The Use of Bodies* and *The Kingdom and the Glory*, notes that:

> Secular modernity has remained fascinated by the devil. Even as his theological role grew more and more marginal in mainstream churches, encounters with the devil proved formative for the modern world. This holds above all for the Romantics' embrace of Milton's Satan as the true hero of *Paradise Lost* and for the decisive influence that Goethe's *Faust* would have on the milieu that produced German idealism. The devil has had a prolific career

in literature, opera, and film, in addition to enjoying a theological resurgence among more marginal and populist religious groups in the late twentieth century.[42]

Agamben relies on Warburg's description of the symbol and the image as 'the crystallization of an energetic charge and an emotional experience that survive as an inheritance transmitted by social memory. For Warburg, this was true for artists, historians and scholars, who were akin to '"necromancers" who consciously evoke the spectres threatening them.'[43] In *The Signature of All Things*, Agamben makes the point that 'conjurer . . . encompasses two opposite meanings: "to evoke" and "to expel"'.[44] Or, he suggests, 'perhaps these two meanings are not opposites, for dispelling something – a specter, a demon, a danger – first requires conjuring it'.[45] The extensive footnote Agamben appends to that Warbugian analysis shows the analysis heavily relies on Faust:

> Thus he conjured up spectres which quite seriously threatened him. He evaded them by erecting his observation tower. He is a seer such as Lynkeus (in Goethe's Faust); he sits in his tower and speaks . . . he was and remained a champion of enlightenment but one who never desired to be anything but a simple teacher.[46]

In *Infancy and History*, Agamben reproduces a dialogue between Walter Benjamin and Theodor Adorno:

> Your idea of providing in the *Baudelaire* a model for the *Arcades* study was something I took very seriously, and I approached the satanic scene much as Faust approached the phantasmagoria of the Brocken mountain when he thought that many a riddle [translated as mystery in the Oxford version] would now be solved. May I be excused for having had to give myself Mephistopheles' reply that many a riddle poses itself anew?[47]

Benjamin responds with, 'Philology is the examination of a text which proceeds by details and so magically fixates the reader on it. That which Faust took home in black and white.'[48] Agamben states that:

> Adorno has approached his friend's text like Faust at the 'satanic scene' of the phantasmagoria on the Brocken mountain. Benjamin is accused of allowing the pragmatic content of his topics to conspire 'in almost demonic fashion' against the possibility of its own interpretation, and of having obscured mediation by 'materialist-historiographic invocation'. This language reaches its culmination in the passage where Benjamin's method is described in terms of a spell: 'If one wished to put it very drastically, one could say that your study is located at the crossroads of magic and positivism. That spot is bewitched Only theory could break the spell . . .'[49]

In *Karman,* Agamben relies on a 'Treatise on Satan' (the subtitle to *Karman* is *'A Brief Treatise on Action, Guilt and Gesture'*, analysing Satan's role as accuser:

> In a midrash that bears the title 'Massekhta Satan' ('Treatise on Satan'), God has Satan appear before him on the last day to judge him. The accusation that he directs at him is accusation itself: Satan is accused of having constantly accused humanity and, in this way, the works of creation.[50]

This passage is so close to one in the opening scene of Faust's 'The Prologue in Heaven' that it could not possibly be coincidence where the Lord speaks to Mephistopheles in what can only be a paraphrase of the midrash:

> LORD. Do you have nothing else to tell me?
> Do you ever come except to criticize?
> Is nothing ever right for you on earth?[51]

God, for Agamben in dialogue with Casel, works in mysterious ways. What role, then, is detailed to the devil? As we have seen above, 'mystery' links international law to *homo sacer* and to *Faust*; as we shall see below, this is principally through the formula of *sacer esto* included in the people and the law as a curse. The link to Faust is no accident, but is actually important. Agamben notes that: 'By itself *sacer* has its own proper value, one of mystery.'[52] In the first section of the first chapter, 'Homo Sacer' of the second part of *Homo Sacer*, Agamben translates the phrase *sacer esto* as 'May he be sacred.'[53] After extensive analysis, he concludes that '*Sacer esto* is . . . the originary political formulation of the imposition of the sovereign bond.'[54] It is 'to be treated as the production of a taboo but as the sanction that defines the very structure of law, its way of referring to reality'.[55] Agamben notes that:

> The nature of office . . . is strikingly illuminated if one puts it in relation with the sphere of command, . . . the imperative defines the proper verbal mood of law . . . *sacer esto,* . . . insofar as the decree of the norm, otherwise void in itself, always has as its object the behavior or action of an individual external to it.[56]

Furthermore:

> The imperative defines the verbal mode proper to law and religion, which have a performative character. This is to say that words and phrases in those discourses do not refer to being but to having-to-be. Because their mere utterance actualizes their own meaning.[57]

For Agamben, the declaration *sacer esto* unites mystery to *homo sacer* to command, to office, to conjuration, to law's linking of consequences to action, and in all those ways, as we saw above and shall see below, to *Faust*.

Faust and Agamben Translate the Bible: 'in the beginning'

Jacques Derrida, to his eternal credit, said of Agamben that, 'each time the author of *Homo Sacer* is, apparently, the first to say who will have been first'.[58] As we shall see when describing Agamben, this is apt given Agamben's observation that:

> The moment of arising, the arche of archaeology is what will take place, what will become accessible and present, only when archaeological inquiry has completed its operation. It therefore has the form of a past in the future, that is, a future anterior.[59]

It was not only accurately diagnostic of Derrida but was also fairly prescient, given that evidence for his claim is able to be found in Agamben's subsequent writings. In *Creation and Anarchy*,[60] for example, we find Agamben linking origin and command to a play on words.[61] Indeed, Agamben points out Plato punning. Kotsko notes Agamben's 'untranslatable puns':

> In our culture, the *archē*, the origin, is always already the command; the beginning is always also the principle that governs and commands. It is perhaps through an ironic awareness of this coincidence that the Greek term *archos* means both 'commander' and 'anus': the spirit of language, which loves to play, transforms into a play on words the theorem according to which the origin must also be 'foundation' and principle of governance.[62]

That link is via Agamben of biblical origin (pun unintended):

> In the Greek translation made by the rabbis of Alexandria in the third century BC, the book of Genesis opens with the phrase '*en archē*, in the beginning God created the heavens and the Earth'; but as we read immediately afterward, he created them by means of a command, which is to say an imperative: *genēthētō*, 'And God said: let there be light.' The same thing happens in the Gospel of John: '*en archē*, in the beginning was the logos, the word.' But a word that is in the beginning, before everything, can only be a command. Thus I believe that perhaps the most correct translation of this famous incipit should be not 'in the beginning was the word' but 'in command – that is, in the form of a command – was the word.' If this translation had prevailed, many things would be clearer, not only in theology, but also and above all in politics.[63]

In *Karman,* while analysing the link that law fashions between actions and consequences, Agamben[64] notes that Goethe's *Faust* as 'tragedy' resolutely assigns the primacy to 'action and praxis' as opposed to 'knowledge and contemplation': 'it is significant that the "tragedy" of Faust resolutely assigns

the primacy to action: *Am Anfang war der Tat'*, translated as, 'In the beginning was the Act.'[65] Reading *Karman* and *Creation and Anarchy* side by side
reveals that in setting out to translate the Gospel of John's 'in the beginning',
Agamben is doing almost the exact same thing as Goethe's Faust does in his
attempts at interpreting '*Logos*' successively as 'Word', 'Mind', 'Power' and
then 'Act' in the first Study Scene in Part I of the tragedy:

> It is written, 'In the beginning was the *Word*.'
> How soon I'm stopped! Who'll help me to go on?
> I cannot concede that *words* have such high worth
> and must, if properly inspired,
> translate the term some other way.
> It is written: 'In the beginning was the *Mind*.'
> Reflect with care upon this first line,
> and do not let your pen be hasty!
> Can it be *mind* that makes all operate?
> I'd better write: 'In the beginning was the *Power*!'
> Yet, even as I write this down,
> Something warns me not to keep it.
> My spirit prompts me, now I see a solution
> and boldly write: 'In the beginning was the *Act*.'[66]

The key difference here is that Agamben focuses on '*en archē*' 'in the beginning' which Faust – while reciting it four times in attempting to translate
'*Logos*' – does not shift from the standard translation of the rest of the phrase.

There is a further textual link here between Agamben and Faust as seen
in the allusion to and reference to the Christian theological dispute over
Arianism named after an Alexandrian priest named Arius (*c.* 250–*c.* 336),
who maintained that the son of God was created by God the father and
as a consequence was neither coeternal nor consubstantial with the father.
In *Faust* we see Mephistopheles disguised as Faust in dialogue with a fresh
undergraduate student, who is unsure of what exactly to study and insists that
words must have a fixed meaning – which is ironical not least because of the
problems Faust has just had in translating *Logos*:

> STUDENT. But there must be ideas behind the words.
> MEPHISTOPHELES. That's true, but do not fret too much about it,
> since it's precisely when ideas are lacking
> that some word will appear to save the situation.
> Words are perfect for waging controversies,
> with words you can construct entire systems,

in words you can place perfect faith,
and from a word no jot or tittle may be taken.[67]

The 'jot or tittle' referencing the Greek letter *iota* is an allusion to the conflict between the Homoiusians and Arian Homoousians centring on the 'i',[68] which was resolved in declaring Arianism as a heresy given that it denied the divinity of Christ. Agamben traces this debate as it culminated 'in the elaboration of the doctrine of the single substance in three different hypostases that was finally established at the Council of Constantinople in 381'.[69] In his introduction to Erik Peterson's *Theological Tractates*, Michael Hollerich notes that, 'Arianism was a cipher for the political theology of Christians who had been bewitched by Hitler and his regime in its early days.'[70] Montserrat Herrero, for one, concludes that Kantorowicz's work was defending Schmitt's political theology against Peterson.[71] Agamben, who elsewhere engages substantially with Peterson (he spells his name as Erik Peter*sen*) sets out the stakes of this debate and how they relate, beginning with anarchy:

> what is in question here is not really a chronological precedence (time does not exist yet), or just a problem of rank (many anti-Arians share the opinion that the Father is 'greater' than the Son); it is rather a matter of deciding whether the Son – which is to say, the word and praxis of God – is founded in the Father or whether he is, like him, without principle, *anarchos,* that is, ungrounded.[72]

We find *The End of the Poem* engaging with this point directly as well:

> In the prologue to the Gospel of John, the interlacement of life (*zoē*) and speech (*logos*) is expressed in the following formula: 'Everything was made by him [the Logos] and without him nothing of what was made was made. Life was in him, and life was the light of men.' But until the fourth century, when the text was altered to combat the Arian heresy, and in the commentaries of the first Church Fathers and the Latin version that precedes the Vulgate, the text appeared in a different form, one that noticeably changes its meaning: 'Everything was made by him, and without him nothing was made, and what was made in him was life, and life was the light of men.'[73]

For Agamben, if we do not understand the original 'anarchic' vocation of Christology, it is not even possible to understand Christian theology, or even the history of Western philosophy:

> The fact that Christ is 'anarchic' means that, in the last instance, language and praxis do not have a foundation in being. The 'gigantomachy' around

being is also, first and foremost, a conflict between being and acting, ontology and economy, between a being that is in itself unable to act and an action without being: what is at stake between these two is the idea of freedom.[74]

In *The End of the Poem*, Agamben references Faust's descent 'into the Reign of the Mothers, the goddesses who shelter "what has not existed for a long time" and in whom we must see a figure of mother tongues', which for Agamben makes it

> necessary also to pose a question that must remain provisionally unanswered here: can there be an experience of speech that is not an experience of the letter in the sense that we have seen? Can there be speech, poetry, and thought beyond the letter, beyond the death of the voice and the death of language?[75]

For Agamben, Goethe 'devoted his life' to 'the cult of the demon'.[76] Furthermore, 'The demon with whom Goethe made an informal deal, one that is yet no less firm than Faust's, is the ambiguous power that guarantees success to the individual on condition of renouncing every ethical decision'.[77]

> Law plays a key role here in the notion of legal personality:
> Persona names not a physical subject, but the mask or pretense by means of which he becomes the subject of law, who can bring into being with his or her own will juridically valid actions and, consequently, be obligated to answer for them.[78]

The way to arrest this, according to Agamben, is via inoperativity:

> inoperativity is . . . the space . . . that is opened when the apparatuses that link human actions in the connection of means and ends, of imputation and fault of merit and demerit are rendered inoperative. It is, in this sense, a politics of pure means.[79]

Agamben describes law as a realm where words have a magico-juridical aspect – where 'words and deeds, linguistic expression and real efficacy, coincide'.[80]

Franz Kafka provides the epigraph for Giorgio Agamben's *Karman* and in many ways its central animating inquiry, which is: 'How can a human being be guilty?'[81] Agamben goes on to observe: 'But it is above all in the novel *The Trial* that Kafka reflected on the mystery of imputation, from which there seems to be no way out.'[82] In *The Coming Community*, while exploring the 'demonic element' in Kafka, Agamben cites Spinoza: 'the devil is only the weakest of creatures' who 'is essentially impotent' and 'nothing other than divine impotence'.[83] In this context even '[Adolf] Eichmann, an absolutely banal man who was tempted to evil precisely by the powers of right and law, is the terrible confirmation through which our era has revenged itself on their [Kafka's and Walser's] diagnosis'.[84]

The devil is also mentioned, according to Agamben.[85]

It is, however, another German intellectual – Max Weber – with whom Agamben seems to be in subterranean conversation. Weber is nowhere mentioned in *Karman*; however, right from the title itself down to determining how guilt is determinable, there are certain intriguing allusions to Weber's *Politics as a Vocation* strewn through Agamben's text, as is elaborated upon below. Agamben also references 'politics as a vocation' elsewhere in his work.[86] Something about this period made Weber go on to twice quote the same passage of Goethe's *Faust*: 'Reflect, the Devil is old, so become old if you would understand him' in *Politics as a Vocation* as well as in *Science as a Vocation*.[87] This reaching out for a religio-literary figure was no mere aberration, given that Weber too said that, 'Anyone who wishes to engage in politics at all . . . is entering into relations with satanic powers that lurk in every act of violence.'[88]

Chapter 1, '*Causa* and *Culpa*', opens with the observation that both *causa* as either cause or case or both and *culpa* as culpability or imputability 'lack an etymology'.[89] It engages explicitly with, among others, Yan Thomas, Carl Schmitt and Hans Kelsen to uncover 'the bond that ties agents to their action'[90] and in that way links choices to consequences. Agamben notes in this regard that 'the law is defined as an articulation of violence and justice'.[91] It reads like the Weberian statement that 'the law is defined as an articulation of violence and justice is an obvious fact'.[92] Agamben positions this definitive aspect of the law as a political theodicy – a justification of evil – asserting that 'the law consists of essentially in the production of a permitted violence, which is to say in a justification of violence'.[93] He even mentions Kelsen's reference to the Sermon on the Mount.[94] He notes that this link of the law and sanction was considered 'less than perfect' in Roman jurisprudence.[95] This approach is comparable to Weber's question, 'Can the ethical demands made on politics really be quite indifferent to the fact that politics operates with a highly specific means, namely, power behind which *violence* lies concealed?'[96] In this, Weber includes the startling observation that 'the politician must abide by the opposite commandment ["resist not him that is evil with violence"]: "You shall use force to resist evil, for otherwise you will be *responsible* for its running amok".'[97] Weber arrives at this conclusion by identifying and distinguishing an ethic of responsibility vs an ethic of conviction. In the former, 'a Christian does what is right and leaves the outcome to God'; in the 'latter you must answer for the (foreseeable) consequences of your actions'.[98]

He summarises this as '*karman* means *crimen*, which is to say that there is something like an imputable action that produces consequences'.[99] In this regard, Agamben notes two paradigms in Western ethical and political thought: a 'tragic' model based on action and an anti-tragic one founded on knowledge and contemplation. He notes that, as tragedy, Goethe's *Faust* resolutely assigns the primacy to action.[100] Weber makes the profoundly Mephistophelean observation that:

> No ethic in the world can ignore the fact that in many cases the achievement of 'good' ends is inseparable from the use of morally dubious or at least dangerous means and that we cannot escape the possibility or even probability of evil side effects.[101]

He then points out that, 'The history of every religion on earth is based on the conviction that the reverse [nothing but good can come from good and nothing but evil from evil] is true.'[102] Weber would include Agamben's *Karman* in this process, saying, 'the Indian doctrine of *Karma* etc., grew out of this experience'.[103] Weber speaks in a register strongly grounded on theodicy: 'The early Christians, too, were well aware that the world was governed by demons and that whoever becomes involved with politics, that is to say, with power and violence as a means, has made a pact with satanic powers.'[104]

Weber doubles down on this: 'I repeat, he is entering into relations with the satanic powers that lurk in every act of violence.'[105] He even goes on to note approvingly that, 'Machiavelli makes one of his heroes praise those citizens who esteemed the greatness of their native city more than the salvation of their souls.'[106] Furthermore, 'These [satanic] powers are inexorable and create consequences for their actions and also subjectively for themselves, against which they are helpless if they fail to perceive them.' For good measure, he directly quotes *Faust*: 'The Devil is old . . . to understand him, best grow older.'[107]

In the third chapter, 'The Aporias of the Will', Agamben traces how Christian theology developed the concept of will in order render human action imputable.[108] It did this by replacing the ancient human subject who *can* with one who *wills*. For Agamben, free will read as freedom is equivocal because the context in which it is used is not political freedom but rather moral and juridical freedom regarding the imputability of actions.[109] The Church Fathers used 'it as a technical term to express the mastery of the will over actions in . . . the origin of evil and responsibility of sin'.[110] In that sense, it was first found 'referring significantly to the devil'.[111] Furthermore, 'will coincides with the creation of hell'.[112]

The final chapter, 'Beyond Action', has Agamben relating how:

> *Persona* names not a physical subject, but the mask or pretense by means of which he becomes the subject of law, who can bring into being with his

or her own will juridically valid actions and, consequently, be obligated to answer for them.[113]

He then states that

> inoperativity is not another action alongside and in addition to all other actions, not another work beyond all works: It is the space – provisional and at the same time non-temporal, localized and at the same time extra-territorial – that is opened when the apparatuses that link human actions in the connection of means and ends, of imputation and fault of merit and demerit are rendered inoperative. It is, in this sense, a politics of pure means.[114]

Agamben's work does delve deeply into theological concepts, but the focus is more on their strategic deployment rather than their systematic development over time.[115] As such, it is always political theology in the Schmittian sense that casts lawyers as the ministers of justice in the role of guardians of the ministry of the mystery, as well as the practitioners of the mystery of the ministry of might and right. In the context of the law's complicity with violence generally and regarding slavery specifically, this political theodicy is seen in his treatments of the Faustian pact, which is located at the intersection of philosophy, law and religion. Resort to violence thus appears as a Faustian pact by way of conceiving violence as inherently evil but nevertheless somehow capable of achieving good. In Goethe's *Faust*, Faust asks Mephistopheles, 'Who are you then?' and is answered perhaps truthfully but not completely honestly, 'Part of that force which would do ever evil, and does ever good.'[116] This is ultimately an illusory hope in that, while the evil is certain, the good is only promised. Moreover, any good that may occur subsequent to the agreement is not causally linked to the agreement as such.

For Agamben, Goethe 'devoted his life' to 'the cult of the demon'.[117] Furthermore, 'The demon with whom Goethe made an informal deal, one that is yet no less firm than Faust's, is the ambiguous power that guarantees success to the individual on condition of renouncing every ethical decision.'[118] For Schmitt, power is never evil but always good, even when held by the devil.[119] Agamben coins a neologism, 'kakokenodicy', to name how, following the two World Wars, philosophers and theologians reached for 'a justification of evil through kenosis', based on an emptying out of the individual will.[120]

It is no wonder, then, that it has been justly noted that, 'as long as our culture continues to struggle between religious and scientific conceptions of its own existence Faust will continue to represent our own modernity'.[121] Faust's continuing relevance is based partly on the fact that it 'is a comprehensive synthesis of European culture and, as such, is largely responsible for the wide-spread perception that Germany in the nineteenth and early twentieth centuries had reached the pinnacle of cultural development'.[122] The unravelling of mystery reveals that political theodicy demonstrates that God works in mysterious ways and that an essential part of the mystery is that the devil is in the detail of that working.

Conclusion

This chapter has amply demonstrated that Agamben's *Homo Sacer* project is suffused with explicit and implicit references to Johann Wolfgang von Goethe's *Faust*. It began by locating Agamben's task within and from international law and then related how the mysteries that Agamben sought to unravel therein were central to his concerns generally and not just specifically to *Homo Sacer*. It then proceeded to further demonstrate this by relating how both Faust and Agamben go about translating the same biblical passage beginning 'in the beginning' to relate origins to commandments. It is now clear that international law is central to Agamben and his approach to explaining it is profoundly marked by Goethe's *Faust*.

Notes

1. G. Agamben, *Homo Sacer: Sovereign Power and Bare Life* (Stanford, CA: Stanford University Press 1998), 8.
2. Agamben, *Homo Sacer*, 8.
3. Agamben, *Homo Sacer*, 12.
4. E. Meyer, 'Philosophy in the Contemporary World: After September 11, a Permanent State of Exception?', blog of the APA (2018), https://blog.apaonline.org/2018/02/01/philosophy-in-the-contemporary-world-after-september-11th-a-permanent-state-of-exception.
5. G. W. Bush, 'Address Before a Joint Session of the Congress on the Persian Gulf Crisis and the Federal Budget Deficit' (1990), https://en.wikisource.org/wiki/Address_Before_a_Joint_Session_of_the_Congress_on_the_Persian_Gulf_Crisis_and_the_Federal_Budget_Deficit.
6. G. W. Bush, 'After the War: The President: Transcript of President Bush's Address on the End of the Gulf War', *New York Times*, 7 March 1991, www.nytimes.com/1991/03/07/us/after-war-president-transcript-president-bush-s-address-end-gulf-war.html.
7. G. Agamben, *The Use of Bodies* (Stanford, CA: Stanford University Press, 2016), 272.
8. Agamben, *The Use of Bodies*, 272.
9. J. Anderegg, 'Unrecognized Modernity: Intertextuality and Irony in Goethe's *Faust*' (2016) *Colloquia Germanica* 39, no. 1 (2016): 32.
10. G. Agamben, *Opus Dei: An Archaeology of Duty* (Stanford, CA: Stanford University Press, 2013), 30.
11. G. Agamben, *Pilate and Jesus* (Stanford, CA: Stanford University Press, 2015).

12. Agamben, *Pilate and Jesus.*
13. G. Agamben, *Infancy and History: The Destruction of Experience* (New York: Verso, 1993), 60.
14. G. Agamben, *Remnants of Auschwitz: The Witness and the Archive* (New York: Zone Books, 2000), 19.
15. G. Agamben, *The Kingdom and the Glory: For a Theological Genealogy of Economy and Government* (Stanford, CA: Stanford University Press, 2011), 276.
16. Agamben, *The Kingdom and the Glory*, 249.
17. G. Agamben, *Mystery of Evil: Benedict XVI and the End of Days*, trans. A. Kotsko (Stanford, CA: Stanford University Press, 2017), 14.
18. Agamben, *Mystery of Evil*, 27–8.
19. G. Agamben, *Creation and Anarchy: The Work of Art and the Religion of Capitalism* (Stanford, CA: Stanford University Press, 2019), 9–10.
20. Agamben, *Opus Dei*, 34.
21. Agamben, *Opus Dei*, 34.
22. Agamben, *Opus Dei*, 35.
23. Agamben, *Opus Dei*, 35.
24. Agamben, *Opus Dei*, 55.
25. G. Agamben, *The Signature of All Things: On Method* (New York: Zone Books, 2009), 53–4.
26. C. Schmitt, *Political Theology: Four Chapters on the Concept of Sovereignty* (trans. G. Schwab), 4th ed. (Chicago: University of Chicago Press, 1985), 36.
27. Agamben, *Opus Dei*, 31–2.
28. C. Schmitt, *The Leviathan in the State Theory of Thomas Hobbes* (Chicago: University of Chicago Press, 1996), 31.
29. M. Herrero, 'On Political Theology: The Hidden Dialogue Between C. Schmitt and Ernst H. Kantorowicz in *The King's Two Bodies*', *History of European Ideas*, 41, no. 8 (2015), 1169.
30. Herrero, 'On Political Theology', 1169.
31. B. J. Fox, 'Carl Schmitt and Political Catholicism. Friend or Foe? *CUNY Academic Works* 47 (2015), http://academicworks.cuny.edu/gc_etds/92947).
32. J. Meierhenrich and O. Simons, *The Oxford Handbook of Carl Schmitt* (Oxford: Oxford University Press, 2016), 162.
33. E. Kantorowicz, *The King's Two Bodies* (Princeton, NJ: Princeton University Press, 1957), 142.
34. E. Kantorowicz, *Frederick the Second: 1194–1250* (New York: Richard R. Smith, 1931), 813.
35. Kantorowicz, *Frederick the Second*, 286–7.
36. Kantorowicz, *Frederick the Second*, 287.
37. Kantorowicz, *Frederick the Second*, 808.
38. Kantorowicz, *Frederick the Second*, 810.
39. G. Agamben, *The Church and the Kingdom* (London: Seagull Books, 2012), 40–1.
40. G. Agamben, *The Kingdom and the Glory*, 163.
41. Agamben, *Homo Sacer*, 120.
42. A. Kotsko, *The Prince of This World* (Stanford, CA: Stanford University Press, 2017), 195.

43. G. Agamben, *Potentialities: Collected Essays in Philosophy* (Stanford, CA: Stanford University Press, 1999), 94.
44. Agamben, *The Signature of All Things*, 83.
45. Agamben, *The Signature of All Things*, 84.
46. Agamben, *Potentialities*, 286.
47. Agamben, *Infancy and History*, 109.
48. Agamben, *Infancy and History*, 114.
49. Agamben, *Infancy and History*, 114.
50. Agamben, *Karman: A Brief Treatise on Action, Guilt, and Gesture* (Stanford, CA: Stanford University Press, 2018b), 7.
51. J. Goethe, *Faust Volumes 1 and 2: Goethe's Collected Works* (Princeton, NJ: Princeton University Press, 2014), 108, line 295.
52. Agamben, *Karman*, 16.
53. Agamben, *Homo Sacer*, 72.
54. Agamben, *Homo Sacer*, 85.
55. G. Agamben, *The Sacrament of Language: An Archaeology of the Oath* (Stanford, CA: Stanford University Press, 2011c), 38.
56. Agamben, *Opus Dei*, 84.
57. Agamben, *Opus Dei*, 119.
58. J. Derrida and G. Bennington, *The Beast and the Sovereign: Seminars of Jacques Derrida, Vol. 1* (Chicago: University of Chicago Press, 2009), 92.
59. Agamben, *The Signature of All Things*, 105–6.
60. G. Agamben, *Creation and Anarchy: The Work of Art and the Religion of Capitalism* (Stanford, CA: Stanford University Press, 2019).
61. G. Agamben, *What is Philosophy?* (Stanford, CA: Stanford University Press, 2017), 73, 95.
62. Kotsko, in Translator's Introduction to Agamben, *Karman*.
63. Agamben, *Creation and Anarchy*, 52.
64. Agamben, *Karman*, 35.
65. Goethe, *Faust Volumes 1 and 2*, line 1237.
66. Goethe, *Faust Volumes 1 and 2*, lines 1224–36.
67. Goethe, *Faust Volumes 1 and 2*, lines 1993–2000.
68. Goethe, *Faust Volumes 1 and 2*, 344.
69. Agamben, *The Kingdom and the Glory*, 12.
70. M. Hollerich, 'Introduction', in *Theological Tractates*, edited by E. Peterson (Stanford, CA: Stanford University Press, 2011), xi–xxxi, xxv.
71. Herrero, 'On Political Theology'.
72. Agamben, *The Kingdom and the Glory*, 57.
73. G. Agamben, *The End of the Poem: Studies in Poetics* (Stanford, CA: Stanford University Press, 1999), 56.
74. Agamben, *The Kingdom and the Glory*, 59.
75. Agamben, *The End of the Poem*, 75.
76. Agamben, *Karman*, 5.
77. G. Agamben, *The Adventure* (Cambridge, MA: MIT Press, 2018), 13–14.
78. Agamben, *Karman*, 77.
79. Agamben, *Karman*, 85.
80. G. Agamben, *State of Exception* (Chicago: Chicago University Press, 2005), 132.

81. Agamben, *Karman*, 7.
82. Agamben, *Karman*, 6.
83. Giorgio Agamben, *The Coming Community* trans. Michael Hardt (Minneapolis: University of Minnesota Press 2007), 31–2. Agamben also mentions the devil in five chapters of, *Stanzas: Word and Phantasm in Western Culture* trans. Ronald S. Martinez (Minneapolis: University of Minnesota Press 1993), 7, 10, 98, 113, 115, 143.
84. Agamben, *The Coming Community* 31–2.
85. G. Agamben, *The Coming Community*, 31–2, in stanzas 7, 10, 98, 113, 115 and 143.
86. See Agamben, *State of Exception*.
87. Agamben, *State of Exception*, 27 n 27, 91 n 87.
88. M. Weber, *The Vocation Lectures*, edited by D. S. Owen (Indianapolis, IN: Hackett, 2004), 90.
89. Agamben, *Karman*.
90. Agamben, *Karman*, 9.
91. Agamben, *Karman*, 20.
92. Agamben, *Karman*, 20.
93. Agamben, *Karman*, 22.
94. Agamben, *Karman*, 20.
95. Agamben, *Karman*, 23.
96. Weber, *The Vocation Lectures*, 81.
97. Weber, *The Vocation Lectures*, 83.
98. Weber, *The Vocation Lectures*, 83.
99. Agamben, *Karman*, 28.
100. Agamben, *Karman*, 35.
101. Weber, *The Vocation Lectures*, 86.
102. Weber, *The Vocation Lectures*, 86.
103. Weber, *The Vocation Lectures*, 86.
104. Weber, *The Vocation Lectures*, 86.
105. Weber, *The Vocation Lectures*, 90.
106. Weber, *The Vocation Lectures*, 91.
107. Weber, *The Vocation Lectures*, 91, citing Goethe, *Faust Volumes 1 and 2*, Part 2, lines 6817–18.
108. Agamben, *Karman*, 44.
109. Agamben, *Karman*, 47.
110. Agamben, *Karman*, 47.
111. Agamben, *Karman*, 47.
112. Agamben, *Karman*, 59.
113. Agamben, *Karman*, 77.
114. Agamben, *Karman*, 85.
115. Agamben, *Karman*, 43–4.
116. J. Goethe, *Faust: A Tragedy: Interpretive Notes, Contexts, Modern Criticism*, 2nd ed. (New York: W.W. Norton, 2001), 36.
117. Agamben, *The Adventure*, 5.
118. Agamben, *The Adventure*, 5.
119. C. Schmitt, *Land and Sea: A World-Historical Mediation* (New York: Telos, 2015), 41.

120. G. Agamben, *Mystery of Evil: Benedict XVI and the End of Days*, trans. A. Kotsko (Stanford, CA: Stanford University Press, 2017), 36–7.
121. J. Brown, *The Cambridge Companion to Goethe* (Cambridge: Cambridge University Press, 2002), 84.
122. Brown, *The Cambridge Companion to Goethe*, 89.

2

Reading Faust into International Criminal Law's Metaphorical References to the Devil

Introduction: 'Make poetry obey your will'

International criminal law is replete with metaphorical references in one form or another to the decidedly non-legal but at once theological and, more to the point, literary devil. This is because the references to the devil are secular appropriations of an originally religious term. In examining this issue, this chapter owes a huge theoretic and methodological debt to Giorgio Agamben's concept of the paradigm, and his take on the theory of signatures, both of which retain a certain 'capacity for elaboration'.[1] Agamben somewhat counter-intuitively makes the point that 'secularization acts within the conceptual system of modernity as a signature, which refers it back to theology'.[2] Agamben's work admittedly does delve deeply into theological concepts, but the focus is more on their decisive deployment in secular contexts rather than their systematic theological development over time.

In that spirit, this chapter advances the 'Faustian pact' as an exemplary paradigm with legal utility, historically borrowed from literature but originating in religion and, as a consequence, still bearing that originally religious signature that the law could never quite eradicate or completely repress, even as it presses that paradigm into service. For Agamben, although

> figures such as *Homo sacer* [the 'sacred man' originating in Roman Law who may be killed but not sacrificed], the *Muselmann* [the concentration camp inmate inured to all suffering], the state of exception, and the concentration camp . . . are all actual historical phenomena . . . [he treats] them as paradigms whose role was to constitute and make intelligible a broader historical-problematic context.[3]

As an exemplar, the 'paradigm is a form of knowledge that is neither inductive nor deductive but analogical. It moves from singularity to singularity.'[4] Agamben indicates that 'the paradigm of every signature' is founded upon language, which is to say the 'originary signature is language'.[5]

Agamben's notion of the 'signature' as something in one sphere (say, the devil in legal contexts), which is marked by its origin from a different sphere (the devil in literature but in turn sourced by literature from theology) is, as a consequence, directly relevant and tied to Agamben's own windingly acknowledged debt, in his most explicitly methodological volume *The Signature of All Things*, with Carlo Ginzburg, Ginzburg's debt to Giovanni Morelli and Sigmund Freud's statement that Morelli's method was 'closely related to the technique of psychoanalysis'.[6] By reading excerpts from Johann Wolfgang von Goethe's *Faust* alongside references to the devil in international criminal law, this approach promises certain insights into some repressed aspects of legality, a method that Freud compared with psychoanalysis in that they both seek 'to divine secret and concealed things from despised or unnoticed features, from the rubbish-heap, as it were, of our observations'.[7] The chapter's approach therefore follows Ginzburg[8] and surveys the available clues that accompany the 'signature' of the devil erupting in international criminal law contexts precisely *because* it does not seem to be *of* law, yet it is *in* law. On that basis, what if we take that marginal topic as our focus? While it is simply not possible to systematically delineate all the possibilities that an exhaustive analysis of the Faustian pact in international criminal law could produce, or even minutely examine the few examples cited here, it would nonetheless be sufficient to illustrate the Faustian pact metaphor's enduring utility, rationality and importance to law. Furthermore, Agamben relies on Aby Warburg's description of the symbol and the image as

> the crystallization of an energetic charge and an emotional experience that survive as an inheritance transmitted by social memory, for Warburg, this was true for artists, historians and scholars, who were akin to 'necromancers' who consciously evoke the spectres threatening them.[9]

Agamben makes the point that 'conjurer . . . encompasses two opposite meanings: "to evoke" and "to expel." Or perhaps these two meanings are not opposites, for dispelling something – a specter, a demon, a danger – first requires conjuring it.'[10] The extensive footnote Agamben appends to that Warbugian analysis shows that the analysis is heavily reliant on *Faust*: 'Thus he conjured up spectres which quite seriously threatened him. He evaded them by erecting his observation tower. He is a seer such as Lynkeus (in Goethe's Faust).'[11] Agamben further cites *Faust* in *The End of the Poem*,[12] *Potentialities*,[13] *Karman*,[14] *The Adventure*,[15] and *Infancy and History*.[16] An additional link is that a key interlocutor of Agamben's in the secularisation stakes is controversial German jurist Carl Schmitt, who not only referred to his own secularisation thesis as 'Faust's solution',[17] but also stated that, 'Even Satan's power is

... as such from God and not evil.'[18] This renders Schmitt's devil a more a literary spectre than a literal one, and consequently more a political and less a theological device. Bloom's observation that Faust's salvation while as he was '[un]nrepentant, unforgiven, after a lifetime in league with the Devil' is 'not Christian in any orthodox sense whatsoever' is quite apposite.[19] Thus, the devil as appropriated by these secular thinkers into secular contexts is lacking in piety, and as a consequence its good faith and fidelity to its origins is not to be assumed in the absence of tangible evidence.

There are four substantive sections to the chapter, which look into, lead to and depart from different and diverse references to the devil, but all with strict relation to international criminal law. The second section looks into whether these ostensibly metaphorical references are possibly no more than a mere rhetorical flourish. It considers international criminal law as an apparatus in which rhetoric plays its part. It seeks to demonstrate that rhetoric is a constitutive part of international criminal law – a crucial limb, not a mere outward flourish. Furthermore, it reveals that when law accommodates reference to the devil as embedded in a rhetorical practice, it remains a practical operation of a performative kind where speaking *is* doing – akin to a magician casting a spell. The third section reads Goethe's (legally informed) take on the Faustian pact as a contract – that is, an archetypical legal document, instrument and relation (but also a wager which is a relatively uncommon species of contract) – in order to use it as a lens to posit legality as an archetypical Faustian pact (or perhaps better, but less innocently, as a Mephistophelean offer to treat), where whatever is achieved is what was asked for but not what was sought and the final outcome of which is dependent upon the open texture of language, specifically in the gulf between expression and intention.[20] It thus should give rise to at best ambivalence, given that it always incorporates a self-aware accommodation of evil. The fourth part considers the notion of 'office' as a hidden in plain sight referent to the devil in international criminal law, specifically as a 'devilish' legal device at the heart of international criminal law's doctrine and practice to a remarkable degree. The conclusion is that that the Faustian pact is a hidden but intimate part of international criminal law and by implication legality generally – but only with the active consent, connivance and cooperation of all those that it would hold in its thrall through its tempting equation of evil with good. Its utility in international criminal law lies chiefly in how it mediates between individual actions and their social consequences. Goethe as a legally sophisticated poet is uniquely valuable because of the shared dependence upon language of poetry and law, both semantically and semiotically, that Agamben amply and repeatedly demonstrates.[21] The mocking words Goethe as a poet-playwright self-reflexively put in the mouth of the Manager speaking to the poet-playwright in *Faust's* Prelude on the Stage scene:

> since you pretend to be a poet,
> Make poetry obey your will.[22]

are a Mephistophelean challenge to the lawyer in their capacity as a lawyer when paraphrased as 'since you pretend to be a lawyer, make law obey your will'. Could rhetorical references to the devil only serve and never overpower law's intended purposes?

Rhetoric and Law: 'You see among Your servants me as well'

In order for the law to hold anyone in its thrall, a set of propitious words – either oral or written – is necessary; when moulded into a formulary, these words work as an incantation once they are effectively enunciated. In other words, figuratively speaking, a spell is required. James Boyd White makes the point that, 'law is in the first place a language, a set of terms and texts and understandings that give to certain speakers a range of things to say to each other'.[23] He vigorously asserts that 'language does much to shape both who we are – our very selves – and the ways in which we observe and construe the world. There is no non-linguistic observer, no non-linguistic observed'.[24] Agamben concurs that there is no non-linguistic point from which to observe language when citing Jean-Claude Milner saying linguistics is 'an experimental science without an observation post . . . a science that has the example as its proper mode of experimentation'.[25]

Agamben further traces two rhetorical aspects relevant to this discussion, which bring law and magic into close proximity precisely because of their mutual relation to language. The first rhetorical aspect is the assertion, which is in the indicative mood; the second is the commandment, which is in the imperative mood. One refers to what 'is' or exists; the other refers to 'be' or shall exist. One belongs to science and philosophy, the other to politics, law, religion and magic.[26] The imperative defines the verbal mode proper to law and religion, which have a performative character. Words and phrases in those discourses do not refer to being, but to having-to-be.[27] It is no wonder that Agamben, building on Aristotle, John L. Austin and Emile Benveniste, proposes a definition of law as a realm where words have a magico-juridical aspect, where 'words and deeds, linguistic expression and real efficacy, coincide'.[28] Hence, in law, *saying* something is and cannot be distinguished from *doing* that same thing.[29] Likewise, invoking the devil even as a rhetorical device nonetheless has consequences for law, which is of course why the invocation is made in the first place. In *Faust*, we first meet Mephistopheles in the

'Prologue in Heaven' scene. His first words are spoken with deep irony to the Lord:

> *Enter* MEPHISTOPHELES.
> MEPHISTOPHELES. Since, Lord, You once again are come
> to ask us how we're getting on,
> and before have often welcomed me,
> You see among Your servants me as well.[30]

Angels are also present in the scene, and Mephistopheles's words could be taken to mean that he who is not a servant of God is seen among God's servants the angels, or that he – like them – is truly seen as a servant of God. Rhetorical references to the devil can also be seen in the same ambiguous light in terms of its service to legal ends.

Aristotle defined rhetoric as 'the faculty of observing in any given case the available means of persuasion'.[31] For him – as it is for present purposes – it is a method for analysing the contextually constrained ways in which an audience is brought to a particular view by a speaker. Aristotle classified rhetoric in three ways (only one of which directly concerns international criminal law). The first is the *political*, which looks to the future and encourages or motivates to action. The second is the *legal* or forensic, which looks at the past in making judgements. The last is the *ceremonial*, which focuses on the present.[32] Clearly, in this schema, the ceremonial mediates between the legal (our immediate focus) and the political moving on a temporal line from past to present to future. It must be said, however, that the moments of advocacy, law-making and judgement unite all three of these rhetorical varieties.

For Aristotle, rhetoric was a counterpart to dialectic or argumentative discourse, and therefore not quite the same thing. The rhetorical form of demonstration was the enthymeme, a syllogism differing from the dialectical syllogism in that its demonstration was not based on logical proof as such, but instead either on what was probable, or taken from indicative signs of what was sought to be proven. Importantly, in Aristotelian terms, legal rhetoric in particular was more amenable to deception than even political rhetoric.[33] This vulnerability notwithstanding, the possible abuse of rhetoric was not an argument against 'its proper use on the side of truth and justice'.[34] That end-justifies-the-means theodicy was despite the intriguing fact that the honest rhetorician had no separate name distinguishing them from the dishonest rhetorician.[35] In other words, a rhetor was a rhetor and *truth* as such, whether relative or absolute, has no place in the discussion. What matters instead is the efficaciousness of the pronouncement in question – that is, the *effect* that the rhetorical speech produces in its audience. What, then, is the effect of reaching for the borrowed theological concepts of 'devil' or 'hell' in international criminal law beyond using rhetorically striking language to attract the attention and sway the minds of the audience? If rhetoric here serves the law's purposes, then it does so 'in a curious way' (Goethe 2014, line 300), as we shall see below.

Hell and the Devil in International Criminal Law: 'Fear neither hell nor its devils'

When German jurist Carl Schmitt memorably wrote in his *Political Theology* that all 'significant concepts of the modern theory of the state' are secularised theological concepts because of their 'historical development' and 'systematic structure', he accounted for God as analogous to the omnipotent lawgiver, and even for miracles as reappearing in the exception.[36] He did not, however, account for what the equivalent of the devil actually was – even though, as Adam Kotsko notes, 'it appears that the devil has served as a privileged conduit for that conceptual transfer' he was referencing.[37] This would seem to be a curious omission to say the least, except that he elsewhere engaged with and conflated the devil, Satan and the demonic in his *The Leviathan in the State Theory of Thomas Hobbes*.[38] Schmitt was intimately familiar with *Faust*[39] and in his treatment of Hobbes's famous depiction of the sovereign state as a Leviathan made up of individuals with a head bearing the crown, hands bearing a sword on the right and sceptre on the left all looming over the city from the sea, Schmitt recalls that, 'In *The Book of Job*, Chapters 40 and 41, it is depicted as the strongest and most tremendous sea monster. Portrayed in vivid detail beside him is a land animal, the behemoth.'[40]

It bears recalling here that *Faust*'s the 'Prologue in Heaven' scene renders a conversation between God and the devil as 'a quite decent . . . chat . . . with the very devil'[41] to set up the entire tragedy as a play within a play or even as a gloss on *The Book of Job*. For Schmitt, moreover, the Leviathan and its associations lead (without Hobbes's knowledge or intention) to a vague association of the state with the devil or the demonic – or indeed Satan himself.[42] On a cautionary note, therefore, he cites Johann Georg Hamann, noting that 'the distance "from transcendental ideas to demonology is not great"'.[43] Agamben, too, concurs with the view that the Leviathan is indeed loosely associated with symbolising the devil or Satan in Christian theology and Jewish mysticism.[44] Further he insists that Hobbes's 'great metaphor' Leviathan inaugurates a 'new political body of the West' based on the 'absolute capacity of the subject's bodies to be killed'.[45] Furthermore, this Leviathan is 'not a reality, however artificial, but an optical illusion'.[46]

Franz Neumann (who in 1928 attended Schmitt's seminars),[47] a member of the prosecution staff at the International Military Tribunal sitting in Nuremberg after World War II, states in his *Behemoth: The Structure and Practice of National Socialism*, by way of explaining its title:

> *Note on the Behemoth*
>
> In the Jewish eschatology – of Babylonian origin – Behemoth and Leviathan designate two monsters, Behemoth ruling the land (the desert), Leviathan the sea, the first male, the second female. The land animals venerate Behemoth, the sea animals Leviathan, as their masters, Both are monsters of the Chaos. According to the apocalyptic writings, Behemoth and Leviathan will reappear shortly before the end of the world. They will establish a rule of terror – but will be destroyed by God. In other versions Behemoth and Leviathan will fight each other incessantly, and finally will destroy each other. The day of the righteous and just will then come. They will eat the meat of both monsters in a feast which announces the advent of a realm of God. Jewish eschatology, the Book of Job, the prophets, the apocryphal writings are full of references to this myth, which is often differently interpreted and often adapted to political circumstances. St. Augustine saw in the Behemoth the Satan.
>
> It was Hobbes who made both the Leviathan and the Behemoth popular. His Leviathan is the analysis of a state, that is a political system of coercion in which vestiges of the rule of law and of individual rights are still preserved. His Behemoth, or the Long Parliament, however, discussing the English civil war of the seventeenth century, depicts a nonstate, a chaos, a situation of lawlessness, disorder, and anarchy.
>
> Since we believe National Socialism is – or tending to become – a nonstate, a chaos, a rule of lawlessness and anarchy, which has 'swallowed' the rights and dignity of man, and is out to transform the world into a chaos by the supremacy of gigantic land masses, we find it apt to call the National Socialist system *The Behemoth*.[48]

Curiously enough, this explanatory note was completely and silently omitted from the subsequent edition of the work, perhaps as a marker of the aforementioned marginality of the trope of the devil in international criminal law. Importantly, in terms of the historical context of international criminal law, Ian Kershaw's definitive biography of Adolf Hitler notes numerous instances where its subject reaches for the devil as a figure of speech, including 'I'll brew them [the British for their support of Poland] a devil's potion', and that the ethnic cleansing they were engaged in involving both 'cleverness and hardness' was 'the devil's work', necessary because it 'must save us from again having to enter the fields of slaughter on account of this land'.[49] Hitler even tried to explain away the Molotov-Ribbentrop pact as 'a pact with Satan to cast out the Devil'.[50] Ironically, an early supporter of Hitler's, Georg Schott, represented Faust as 'Goethe's ideal of the Fuhrer',[51] As Weisberg points out, 'There is a direct line between the Gospel writer John's portrait of unyielding Jewish loyalty to previously received traditions of meaning and morality and the conclusion reached in that text by Jesus himself (as so reported) that those Jews who resisted his messianic message were the sons of "the devil".'[52] Given this ample historical allusion, we would therefore need to unpack elements of what makes Faust's pact with the devil Faustian in order to approach more contemporary references to the devil with a clearly developed analytic framework that is up to that task.

In Goethe's *Faust*, we first encounter a scholarly and world-weary Faust in his narrow Gothic chamber of a study fearing 'neither hell nor its devils' in a scene titled: 'Night *A high-vaulted, narrow Gothic room. FAUST, sitting restless at a desk*'.[53] This scene follows on from the three introductory scenes before the tragedy proper begins of the 'Dedication', the 'Prelude on the Stage' and the 'Prologue in Heaven'. Prior to the pact, Faust is already unusually steeped in learning: philosophy, law, medicine and theology. In his own words:

> I've studied now, to my regret, Philosophy, Law, Medicine,
> and – what is worst – Theology
> from end to end with diligence.
> Yet here I am,
> a wretched fool and still no wiser than before.
> I've become Master, and Doctor as well,
> and for nearly ten years I have led my young students a merry chase,
> up, down, and every which way –
> and find we can't have certitude.
> This is too much for heart to bear!
> I well may know more than all those dullards,
> those doctors, teachers, officials, and priests,
> be unbothered by scruples or doubts,
> and fear neither hell nor its devils –
> but I get no joy from anything, either,
> know nothing that I think worthwhile,
> and don't imagine that what I teach
> could better mankind or make it godly.[54]

Already we can see that Faust is an uncommonly successful man with more talent than most, even before the deal with the devil is entered into. Given Faust's demonstrated gifts, the pact does not seem necessary. This apparent *unnecessariness* is an initial identifiable element of the Faustian pact. Nonetheless, the world-weariness of this gifted but dissatisfied academic drives him to conjure up the 'earth spirit' but, as will become clear, his amateurish attempt in no way allows Faust to keep the spirit after summoning them:

> *He takes the book and mysteriously utters the sign of the spirit. In a flash of reddish flame the EARTH SPIRIT appears.*

SPIRIT. Who calls to me?
FAUST (turning away). A fearful apparition!
SPIRIT. You've used great efforts to attract me,
have long exerted suction on my sphere,
and now –
FAUST. Alas, I lack the strength to face you!
SPIRIT. You beg and pant to see me,
to hear my voice, to view my face;
your urgent prayer has made me well disposed,
so here I am! What paltry fear
now cows a demigod! Where is the summoning soul,
the breast that in itself conceived a world
it bore and cherished, the breast that swelled
in trembling joy to reach our spirit-plane?
Where are you, Faust, whose ringing voice I heard,
who strove with all his faculties to reach me?
Can he be you who in my aura
tremble in all your depths of being –
a worm that writhes away in fright?
FAUST. I stand my ground before you, shape of flame!
I am that Faust, I am your peer!
SPIRIT. In the tides of life, in action's storm,
I surge and ebb, move to and fro!
As cradle and grave,
as unending sea,
as constant change,
as life's incandescence,
I work at the whirring loom of time
and fashion the living garment of God.
FAUST. How close I feel to you, industrious spirit,
whose strands encompass all the world!
SPIRIT. Your peer is the spirit you comprehend;
mine you are not! [*Disappears.*]

FAUST (collapsing). Not yours?
Whose then?
I, made in God's image,
not even your counterpart![55]

This ability to invoke but inability to bind is similar in theme to that covered by Goethe in the poem 'The Sorcerer's Apprentice', where the apprentice, while being able to enchant a broom to fetch water, is quite unable to stop it from hauling water from the stream until his master comes along and voices the requisite spell. This theme caught the attention of not just Walt Disney, who memorably adapted it for his 1940 animated film *Fantasia*, but also Karl Marx,[56] who spoke of the capitalist as being 'Like the sorcerer who is no longer able to control the powers of the netherworld whom he has called up by his spells'. In this, Marx – who was familiar with and quite fond of quoting *Faust*[57] – shared common ground with Schmitt who, while speaking of Hobbes's use of the image of the Leviathan in the frontispiece of the book of the same name, stated:

> Whoever utilises such [demonic] images easily, glides into the role of a magician who summons forces that cannot be matched by his arm, his eye, or any other measure of his human ability. He runs the risk that instead of encountering an ally he will meet a heartless demon who will deliver him into the hands of his enemies.[58]

This is a second identifiable element of the Faustian pact – its *uncontrollability* – in that it is always beyond the control of whomever enters into it. Before Schmitt[59] memorably wrote in his *Political Theology* that all 'significant concepts of the modern theory of the state' are secularised theological concepts because of their 'historical development' and 'systematic structure', Marx wrote 'We do not turn secular questions into theological questions. We turn theological questions into secular questions.'[60]

The scene above and two subsequent ones in the same setting, both titled Faust's Study, are required to set out the immediate terms and context for the pact (which incorporates a contractual wager) at least as laid out in the first part of the tragedy. In the first study scene, the Earth Spirit 'devil' gets away with a mocking 'Not I'. Faust's situation is similar in outlook and effect to 'The Sorcerer's Apprentice', in that while it was well within their amateurish powers to voluntarily invoke the magical powers, both were unable to control them just like the capitalist in Marx's terms or Hobbes over Leviathan according to Schmitt. This inability to either keep them or dispel them demonstrates agency on the part of the magical powers so invoked, and thus enables a contractual relationship based on mutual consent to be entered into.

Both also run the risk of a present evil in order to produce some claimed future good. In Faust's Study I, Faust asks of Mephistopheles:

> The essence of such as you,
> good sir, can usually be inferred from names
> that, like Lord of Flies, Destroyer, Liar,
> reveal it all too plainly.
> But still I ask, who are you?[61]

Mephistopheles's arch response is:

> A part of that force
> which, always willing evil, always produces good.[62]

This third and most critical identifiable element of the Faustian pact is its studied *ambiguity* in purporting to produce good through enacting evil. What about its relation to law and legality?

Concentration Camps as 'hell unto itself': 'So even hell is bound by laws?'

A fourth identifiable element of the Faustian pact is its *legality*, made clear where Faust – quite by accident – binds the devil through the workings of a law about which he had no clue:

> FAUST. Why don't you go through the window, then?
> MEPHISTOPHELES. For demons and for spectres there's a rule:
> where they've got in is where they must go out.
> The former's up to us,
> the latter's not in our control.[63]

This essential legality of the contractual relationship fascinates Faust and he inquires of the devil:

> FAUST. So even Hell is bound by laws?
> I like your implication that one could
> safely make contracts with you gentlemen![64]

Mephistopheles responds with an entreaty:

> MEPHISTOPHELES. You can be sure of getting all we promise,
> without a single niggardly deduction.
> But it takes time to work out such arrangements,
> so let's discuss the matter fairly soon.
> Right now, however, I urgently request
> that this one time you give me leave to leave.

Legality also stretches to concentration camps, which were frequently seen as hell on earth.[65] Holocaust survivor Olga Lengyel describes Auschwitz as an 'antechamber to hell', Birkenau as 'a hell unto itself' and an SS guard as a 'blonde devil'.[66] Another survivor account reaching for the 'hell' metaphor is *A Theory and Practice of Hell: The German Concentration Camps and the System Behind Them*, based on the experience of its author and Holocaust survivor, Eugen Kogon,[67] at Buchenwald. Agamben relies on Kogon's analysis of the *Muselmann*.[68] Standard international criminal law texts, at least in modern times, typically orient their discipline's history to the trial of the Nazis following World War II.[69] The Nuremberg trials were a response to the Nuremberg laws. The central event in this is the Holocaust. The deeply ambiguous role of the law in perpetuating the conceptualisation and running of the concentration camps (and other machinery necessary for perpetrating mass international crimes) is nevertheless considered an anomaly when it is not glossed over or ignored. There are two instances of the concentration camp's normative spatial arrangement that may be taken as a conceptual starting point for legality and the Faustian pact. The first is best illustrated in Holocaust survivor Primo Levi's recounting of a football match between the SS and inmates that took place at the centre of Auschwitz.[70] The second is the intriguing fact that the only tree left standing in the centre of Buchenwald was an oak, where according to legend Goethe had sat with his lover and written poetry beneath its shade. While the Nazis preserved the tree to identify themselves as part of high High German culture, the prisoners saw it as a reminder of the other Germany, which – like them – had been taken hostage by the Nazi regime.[71] Goethe would probably see both these moments of contrived normality within the horrors of the camp as exemplifying two hearts *still* beating within modernity's breast. No wonder, then, that Agamben's *Homo Sacer* uses a photograph of 'the second master plan for Auschwitz' on its cover. His entire *Homo Sacer* or 'Sacred Man' nine-book project can viably be read as the patient explication of the Faustian pact at the heart of international law in that he develops two paradigms regarding legal personality and political territoriality that are of particular relevance here. The first is that human rights are founded on the banning of 'bare' or natural life from politics; the second is that 'the camp' is the political space where power confronts pure biological life. For Agamben, the camp and its inmates (rather than the city with its citizens) is the paradigmatic modern spatial and temporal political practice.[72] Agamben notes that in this regard, 'the law is defined as an articulation of violence and justice'.[73] He positions this definitive aspect of the law as a political theodicy – a justification of evil – stating that 'the law consists of essentially in the production of a permitted violence, which is to say in a justification of violence'.[74] His analyses therefore demonstrate that the law, both in the positive presence and in the negative absence, remains stubbornly indispensable to the conception, setting up and running of concentration camps.

'That Devil will be defeated': 'A devil in hand is well worth keeping'

A fifth identifiable element of the Faustian pact is its *voluntariness*. James Boyd White illustrates the necessary voluntariness of the Faustian pact.[75] Interestingly, Perry Bechky argues that in James Boyd White's discussion, while violence or cunning might have their place in effecting a willed intention, cooperation can only be achieved through rhetorical discourse.[76] The voluntariness of both parties is made clear when Faust fails to keep the devil ensnared in the inadvertent trap seen above where Faust is disinclined to let the evil spirit go and a back-and-forth dialogue ensues along the following lines:

> FAUST. Do stay another moment and, before you go,
> let me hear more of your fine stories.
> MEPHISTOPHELES. It's time you let me go!
> I'll call again soon,
> and then you can ask any question you wish.
> FAUST. I didn't lay a snare for you!
> You put yourself into the trap.
> A devil in hand is well worth keeping:
> it takes a good while to catch one again.
> MEPHISTOPHELES. If it's your wish, of course I'm glad to stay
> and keep you company – but only if
> you'll let me use the arts in which I'm skilled
> to entertain you in a proper way.
> FAUST. I've no objection, and leave the choice to you.
> Just see to it your arts are entertaining![77]

Faust, however, is tricked into falling asleep, after which Mephistopheles makes good his escape. Upon waking:

> FAUST (*awakening*). Have I been duped once more? Are life-giving forces
> so quickly spent – did a lying dream invent my devil, and did a poodle
> simply run away?[78]

On Wednesday, 5 February 2014, Mr Fergal Gaynor, then the Legal Representative of Victims at the International Criminal Court (ICC), alerted the court to and took issue with the accused, Uhuru Kenyatta, President of the

Republic of Kenya, as having obliquely and derogatively referred to the ICC as, 'That devil will be defeated, and Kenya shall move forward'.[79] Although the victims' representative saw fit to call attention to this, it must be said the court did not appear to do anything with this information. Furthermore, Kenyatta's statement, even if taken in precisely the sense proffered by the victim's representative, did not appear to affect the victims directly, but seemed to attack the prestige or – perhaps better – the legitimacy of the court. In any event, not even the prosecutor deemed it necessary to take this discussion any further. Gaynor not only introduced the devil into the courtroom, but also in his (but not only his) official capacity in a sense represents a rather more esoteric aspect of the Faustian paradigm. Let us for a moment look at the key characteristics of victimhood as enumerated by the ICC, starting with the aforesaid voluntariness:

> **Victim as a participant**[80]
> Participation is voluntary
> Communicating to the Court their own interests and concerns
> It is up to the victims to decide what they want to say
> Participation is possible at all stages of proceedings when considered appropriate by the Judges
> Always entitled to be represented before the ICC by a legal representative
> Normally participates via a legal representative, and need not appear in person

Clearly, in order to participate at any stage of the proceedings and in order to be heard, voluntariness is front and centre for victims. The main point, focusing particularly upon the fifth and sixth characteristics of victimhood, is that victims are an abstraction that is or are *only* present in court through their representative. To reinforce this point, their representative has even been known to produce a 'representative sample' of the victims, thus further highlighting the victim's presence by their very absence.[81] This is partly why Agamben can say that

> humanitarian organizations . . . can only grasp human life in the figure of bare or sacred life, and therefore, despite themselves, maintain a secret solidarity with the very powers they ought to fight.[82]

This inclusion by exclusion partly helps to explain that victims are represented in the adversarial trial process as neither prosecution nor defence at the expense of not being actually present, and this can only be done through and by their consent. Furthermore, victims at international criminal law are very often perpetrators and victims and witnesses, and at least in the Kenyan case, apparently all three at once.

'When did you renounce the Devil?': 'Oh no! The devil is an egoist'

In September 1945, Schmitt was arrested by the Americans and held in internment until March 1947, during which time they brought him to Nuremberg as a potential defendant in the ongoing international criminal trials.[83] At his interrogation, on being asked when he had renounced 'the devil' [the Nazi Party], Schmitt responded with a terse '1936'.[84] Quite ironically, Schmitt himself was described as 'a strong spirit of a satanic kind'.[85] More crucially for our purposes, he has also been described as 'an author of Faustian temperament' (Sartori 1989). It is no wonder, then, that Schmitt 'had something about him that led some to compare him to . . . Mephistopheles.'[86]

Although, as seen above, Faust was tricked into falling asleep, all was not lost because in the second study scene the devil's representative comes back of his own volition. Faust has to repeat the invitation three times; while further demonstrating the voluntary nature of the pact, this highlights the mutual distrust between the parties where bad faith is substituted for the usual good faith in contracts:

> FAUST. A knock? Come in! Who bothers me this time?
> MEPHISTOPHELES. It's me.
> FAUST. Come in!
> MEPHISTOPHELES. That must be said three times.
> FAUST. Come in, then!
> MEPHISTO (*entering*). Now you've done it right![87]

The Mephistophelean invitation to treat is explicitly one of enslavement:

> I'll gladly place myself at your disposal
> here and now.
> I will be your companion
> and, if I suit you,
> become your servant and your slave!
> FAUST. And in return for this, what am I to do?
> MEPHISTO. You've lots of time until that needs to be
> considered.[88]

Lengyel[89] and Kogon[90] both experienced the Nazi concentration camps as enslavement. Faust's hesitation and distrust at the offer to have Mephistopheles as his slave for life on earth coupled with Mephistopheles' coyness about what he would require in return brings us to a sixth identifiable element of the Faustian pact: because of the mutual bad faith it is inherently and mutually *antagonistic*:

> FAUST. Oh no! The devil is an egoist
> and is not apt, for love of God,
> to offer anyone assistance.
> State in clear terms what you expect –
> there's trouble in the household otherwise.[91]

'Shake Hands with the Devil': 'I will bind myself to your service'

A seventh identifiable element of the Faustian pact is that once it is entered into, it is a contract of *servitude*. That is to say it is contracting out of freedom through the exercise of freedom:

> Mephistopheles. I'll bind myself to serve you here,
> be at your beck and call without respite;
> and if or when we meet again beyond,
> then you will do the same for me.[92]

There is at least one good example of the devil in the context of servitude deployed in the international criminal law process. To start with, Bruno Stagno Ugarte, President of the Assembly of States Parties of the ICC from 2005 to 2008, cited Romeo Dallaire's memoir *Shake Hands with the Devil* as stating precisely the purpose of the ICC and the commitment of its State Parties:

> We need to study how the genocide happened not from the perspective of assigning blame – there is too much to go around – but from the perspective of how we are going to take concrete steps to prevent such a thing from ever happening again. To properly mourn the dead and respect the potential of the living, we need accountability, not blame.[93]

This accountability referred to a criminal process holding perpetrators accountable, while blame referenced the perceived failings of the international community to prevent the Rwandan genocide. Dallaire provides two instances referencing the devil: one a simple simile; the other a more complex metaphor of making a deal with the devil. To start with the first:

> I know there is a God because in Rwanda I shook hands with the devil. I have seen him, I have smelled him and I have touched him. I know the devil exists, and therefore I know there is a God.[94]

The second instance describes his first meeting with members of the *Interahamwe* militia responsible for acts of genocide – not just key leaders like Augustin Bizimungu and Théoneste Bagosora, but also important actors such as Robert Kajuga, Bernard Mamiragaba and Ephrem Nkezabera. These named individuals were the personification of the very devil for the then general. This is more than just a description by simile, however: it goes beyond that to actually doing business with this devil. Dallaire states that he had to anaesthetise himself to the ethical and moral dimensions of meeting with génocidaires in order to negotiate transfers of displaced persons. It was on the way back to his headquarters after the meeting when he felt he 'had shaken hands with the devil' that they 'had exchanged pleasantries'. He continued: 'I felt guilty of evil deeds myself since I had actually negotiated with him.'[95] This key episode gives the book its title and arguably its central premise. For our purposes, it is important to note that the only justification proffered for dealing with the devil was transferring displaced persons and orphans out of harm's way. The evil of dealing with the devil is rendered necessary by the indisputably good imperative of saving lives. It is consequently, in its way, trying to justify or at least explain the presence of evil that is a patently lay theodicy.

'A deal with the devil': 'I'll give you things no mortal's ever seen'

An eighth identifiable element of the Faustian pact is its combined danger and risk, its *hazardousness*. Mephistopheles urges Faust to 'take the risk':

> MEPHISTOPHELES. You can, on these conditions, take the risk.
> Commit yourself, and you'll soon have the pleasure
> of seeing here what my skills are;
> I'll give you things no mortal's ever seen.[96]

Faust is not taken in by this given that the devil's reputation precedes him:

> FAUST. And what have you to give, poor devil!
> Has any human spirit and its aspirations
> ever been understood by such as you?
> Of course you've food that cannot satisfy,
> gold that, when held, will liquify
> quicksilver like as it turns red,
> games at which none can ever win,
> a girl who, even in my arms, will with her eyes
> pledge her affections to another,
> the godlike satisfaction of great honor
> that like a meteor is gone at once.
> Show me the fruit that, still unplucked, will rot
> and trees that leaf each day anew![97]

There are two senses to 'deal with the devil'. The first involves entering into a contractual relationship, while the second is the opposite in seeking to cope with, control or even overcome the infamous deity. *Faust* as the passage above makes clear combines both.

On 23 September 2011, during Francis Muthaura's pre-trial hearing for crimes against humanity before the ICC, his legal counsel Karim Khan said:

> Your Honours, another essential plank of this Prosecution's case is what can only be described as an unholy alliance, a deal with the devil, between the government and [sic] Kenya and a criminal, a lamentable, an invidious criminal group called the Mungiki.[98]

Given that this purported deal led to trial before the ICC after Kenyatta became president, it would not quite have met expectations given that, strictly speaking, the Mungiki's violence did not lead to his election.[99] His political alliances with would-be rivals did swell his vote; however, those alliances would probably not have been entered into but for the looming trials at the ICC. Ironically, therefore, the ICC in spectacularly unintended ways contributed to Kenyatta's ascension to the presidency.

'Sold his soul to the devil': 'Blood is quite a peculiar sort of juice'

A ninth identifiable element of the Faustian pact – despite its inherent risks, or hazardous nature given that it is a wager and consequently no ordinary agreement – is its bindingness to the strict letter of the agreement, which is to say it is completely *literal* and tied to language as expression but not as meaning let alone intention:

> FAUST. If on a bed of sloth I ever lie contented,
> may I be done for then and there!
> If ever you, with lies and flattery,
> can lull me into self-complacency
> or dupe me with a life of pleasure,
> may that day be the last for me!
> This is my wager!
> MEPHISTOPHELES. Here's my hand!
> FAUST. And mine again!
> If I should ever say to any moment:
> Tarry, remain! – you are so fair!
> then you may lay your fetters on me,
> then I will gladly be destroyed!
> Then they can toll the passing bell,

your obligations then be ended –
the clock may stop, its hand may fall,
and time at last for me be over!
MEPHISTOPHELES. Consider well your words – we'll not forget them.
FAUST. Nor should you! What I've said
is not presumptuous blasphemy.
If I stagnate, I am a slave –
why should I care if yours or someone else's?[100]

We see this bindingness to the letter when Mephistopheles insists upon a contract in writing with blood as the ink:

Any small scrap of paper is all right.
A tiny drop of blood will do to sign your name.
FAUST. If this is all that you require, we may as well go through with the
tomfoolery.
MEPHISTOPHELES. Blood is a very special juice.[101]

Ironically, at the end of the second part of *Faust*, part of the reason why Faust ultimately wins over the devil is precisely because his actions (completely inadvertently) cleave more closely to the letter of the agreement than Mephistopheles's. Thus, the literal terms of the agreement replace the intention behind the agreement. Fidelity to the words expressing the intent supplanted the intent itself and, in that way, Mephistopheles failed to get his end of the bargain: Faust's soul. These difficulties in the way of judgement are amply demonstrated in the case of Rudolf Kastner, a Hungarian Jew who entered into a deal with the Nazis to facilitate the escape of some Jews while abandoning the rest to their fate. For this act, a judge in Israel described him as having 'sold his soul to the devil'.[102] Pnina Lahav renders it as 'sold his soul to Satan'.[103] Leora Bilsky examines the Kastner trial though narrative theory, developed through the field of law and literature, to explore the difficulties and ambiguities surrounding the judgment of evil.[104] Bilsky identifies the phrase 'sold his soul to the Devil' as not only based on Faust but also as linked to the better known international trial of Adolf Eichmann.[105] Edwin Black provides another example of reaching for the Faustian pact metaphor to make meaning of the same context when he narrates the:

Story of a negotiated arrangement in 1933 between Zionist organisations and the Nazis to transfer some 50,000 Jews, and $100 million of their assets, to Jewish Palestine in exchange for stopping the worldwide Jewish-led boycott threatening to topple the Hitler regime in its first year.

. . .

> Only supported by the underpinnings of America's economic might was Hitler able to squeeze the Jews, confronting the Zionists with the painful necessity of engineering heartbreaking trade mechanisms with the Devil.[106]

And according to Black:

> motivated by the desire to save both the threatened community and future communities, the Zionists had to coldly assume the distasteful, gun-to-the-temple responsibilities of standing up to the Devil in his own lair and negotiating a way out. That way was the Transfer Agreement.[107]

The principal utility of the citing of the devil in the examples above is to enable the shifting of responsibility and blame from oneself to another, for more or less compelling reasons. Desmond Manderson (2005) notes this longstanding aspect of the criminal law. This division between the act and the actor in terms of attribution is not exhausted by these examples. The identical logic of the devil usefully shifting blame elsewhere or attributing agency to actors external to oneself goes even further, deeper and more obscure. Robert Jay Lifton articulates the concept of 'doubling', or the Faustian bargain, as a psychological principle that divides the 'self' as a means of adapting to extreme environments.[108] One of these selves can then unrestrainedly embrace evil. This doubling of the persona as we see below enables the notion of having an 'office', which ostensibly separates an individual from their actions.

The Notion of the Office: 'He serves you in a curious way'

A tenth identifiable element of the Faustian pact is its presuppositional *irony* in purporting to link good and evil productively. Goethe puts the following words in the mouth of God regarding why he uses the devil as his agent for his own purposes:

> Human activity slackens all too easily,
> and people soon are prone to rest on any terms;
> that's why I like to give them the companion
> who functions as a prod and does a job as devil.[109]

This use of the devil as an agent for God is at the root of the notion of 'office', which distinguishes an action and an actor in terms of both efficacy and responsibility. In looking at official acts, Agamben introduces a crucial distinction between an act in its effective reality and an action insofar as an agent carries it out:

> The first articulation of the doctrine has to do with the theory of the action of demons. The devil serves God and God approves the works that he has

done, but not the way in which he has done them: the works done, but, not the doing of the works.[110]

Agamben then traces the distinction to the theory of the action of the devil within the providence.[111] In it, the devil serves God and God approves his work, but not the way in which he has worked.[112] Furthermore, this religious paradigm of *Opus Dei* or God's work provides the secular West with the term 'office', which 'is more effective than any ordinary human action because it acts *ex opere operato*, independently of the qualities of the subject who officiates it'.[113] Agamben then traces the doctrine to the theory of the action of the devil within the providential economy.[114] In it, the devil serves God and God approves his work, but not the way in which he has worked. When Mephistopheles speaks of Faust to the Lord in the Prologue in Heaven as: 'He serves You in a curious way',[115] he quite possibly is slyly and ironically describing himself.

When we look to the trials under the Nuremberg Charter, we find its principal innovation, procedurally speaking, was that official positions were not only no longer a defence, but conversely were now a basis for criminal responsibility.[116] Indeed in the *Justice Case,* the military tribunal pointed out that because governmental participation was actually a material element of the crimes charged, it could scarcely be said that it could also be a defence to the charges.[117]

Consequently, international criminal law was in this way at the vanguard of demonstrating the Mephistophelean aspects of the law transmuting official acts from a complete defence to an actual element of the crime.

Conclusion

This chapter began by looking at the law's spellbinding effect, the apparatus of which at crucial junctures engenders rhetorical references to the devil embedded in a practice of a performative kind, where speaking *is* doing. It demonstrated the chapter's overall argument that the devil is part of international criminal law, but only with the consent and cooperation of those it would hold in its thraldom of evil posing as good. All the examples surveyed were political theodicies explaining away evil by linking it in some causal way to good. Reading *Faust* alongside references to the devil in international criminal law reveals how the power of both poetry and law is linked to the power of language itself in the space opened up in language between meaning and expression or between semantics and semiotics. Reaching for the law and poetic expression alike promises power through language but only at the price of being bound voluntarily by the strictures of language to language both felicitous and infelicitous.

Notes

1. G. Agamben, *The Signature of All Things: On Method* (New York: Zone Books, 2009).
2. Agamben, *The Signature of All Things*, 8.
3. Agamben, *The Signature of All Things*, 9.
4. Agamben, *The Signature of All Things*, 31.
5. Agamben, *The Signature of All Things*, 35.
6. Agamben, *The Signature of All Things*, 68–70.
7. S. Freud, 'The Moses of Michelangelo'. In *The Standard Edition of the Complete Psychological Works of Sigmund Freud* (London: Hogarth Press, 1953), 222.
8. C. Ginzburg, *Clues, Myths, and the Historical Method* (Baltimore, MD: Johns Hopkins University Press 1989), 106.
9. G. Agamben, *Potentialities: Collected Essays in Philosophy* (Stanford, CA: Stanford University Press, 1999), 94.
10. Agamben, *The Signature of All Things*, 83–4.
11. Agamben, *Potentialities*, 286.
12. G. Agamben, *The End of the Poem: Studies in Poetics* (Stanford, CA: Stanford University Press, 1999), 53.
13. Agamben, *Potentialities*, 286.
14. G. Agamben, *Karman: A Brief Treatise on Action, Guilt, and Gesture* (Stanford, CA: Stanford University Press, 2018), 35.
15. G. Agamben, *The Adventure* (Cambridge, MA: MIT Press, 2018), 5.
16. G. Agamben, *Infancy and History: The Destruction of Experience* (New York: Verso, 1993), 109, 114.
17. C. Linder, 'Carl Schmitt in Plettenberg'. In *The Oxford Handbook of Carl Schmitt*, edited by J. Meierhenrich and O. Simons, 147–70 (Oxford: Oxford University Press, 2016), 162.
18. B. J. Fox, 'Carl Schmitt and Political Catholicism: Friend or Foe?' (2015) 47 *CUNY Academic Work*s. http://academicworks.cuny.edu/gc_etds/929.
19. H. Bloom, *The Western Canon: The Books and School of the Ages* (New York: Harcourt Brace, 1994), 219.
20. R. Safranski, *Goethe: Life as a Work of Art* (New York: W.W. Norton, 2017), 19.
21. Agamben, *The End of the Poem*, 77, 80, 81; Agamben, *The Signature of All Things*, 60–1, 80.
22. J. Goethe, *Faust Volumes 1 and 2: Goethe's Collected Works* (Princeton, NJ: Princeton University Press 2014), lines 220–1.
23. J. B. White, *Heracles' Bow: Essays on the Rhetoric and Poetics of the Law* (Madison, WI: University of Wisconsin Press, 1985), xi.
24. White, *Heracles' Bow*, xi.
25. Agamben, *Potentialities*, 68.
26. G. Agamben, *Creation and Anarchy: The Work of Art and the Religion of Capitalism* (Stanford, CA: Stanford University Press, 2019), 59.
27. G. Agamben, *Opus Dei: An Archaeology of Duty* (Stanford CA: Stanford University Press, 2013), 84, 119.
28. G. Agamben, *The Time That Remains: A Commentary on the Letter to the Romans* (Stanford, CA: Stanford University Press, 2005b), 132.

29. J. Austin, *How to Do Things with Words*, 2nd ed. (Cambridge, MA: Harvard University Press, 1975); J. Butler, *Excitable Speech: A Politics of the Performative* (New York: Routledge 1997); M. Constable, *Just Silences: The Limits and Possibilities of Modern Law* (Princeton, NJ: Princeton University Press, 2005); M. Constable, *Our Word is Our Bond: How Legal Speech Acts* (Stanford, CA: Stanford University Press, 2014).
30. Goethe, *Faust Volumes 1 and 2*, lines 271–4.
31. W. R. Roberts, *The Rhetoric and the Poetics of Aristotle* (New York: Random House, 1984), 24.
32. Roberts, *The Rhetoric and the Poetics of Aristotle*, 32.
33. Roberts, *The Rhetoric and the Poetics of Aristotle*, 3.
34. Roberts, *The Rhetoric and the Poetics of Aristotle*, 3.
35. Roberts, *The Rhetoric and the Poetics of Aristotle*, 3.
36. C. Schmitt, *Political Theology: Four Chapters on the Concept of Sovereignty*, trans. G. Schwab, 4th ed. (Chicago: University of Chicago Press, 1985), 36.
37. A. Kotsko, *The Prince of This World* (Stanford, CA: Stanford University Press, 2017), 195.
38. C. Schmitt, *The Leviathan in the State Theory of Thomas Hobbes* (Chicago: University of Chicago Press. 1996), 6–7, 22–34.
39. C. Schmitt, *Dialogues on Power and Space* (Cambridge: Polity Press, 2014), 82.
40. Schmitt, *The Leviathan*, 6.
41. Goethe, *Faust Volumes 1 and 2*, lines 353–4.
42. Schmitt, *The Leviathan*, 6.
43. Schmitt, *The Leviathan*, 81.
44. G. Agamben, *Mystery of Evil: Benedict XVI and the End of Days*, trans. A. Kotsko (Stanford, CA: Stanford University Press, 2017), 6–7.
45. G. Agamben, *Homo Sacer: Sovereign Power and Bare Life* (Stanford, CA: Stanford University Press, 1998), 125.
46. G. Agamben, *Stasis: Civil War as a Political Paradigm (Homo Sacer II, 2)* (Edinburgh: Edinburgh University Press, 2015b), 125.
47. F. Neumann, H. Marcuse and O. Kirchheimer, *Secret Reports on Nazi Germany: The Frankfurt School Contribution to the War Effort* (Princeton, NJ: Princeton University Press, 2013), xviii.
48. F. Neumann, *Behemoth: The Structure and Practice of National Socialism 1933–1944* (Chicago: Ivan R. Dee, 1943), 5.
49. I. Kershaw, *Hitler, 1936–1945: Nemesis* (London: Allen Lane, 2000), 254–5.
50. Kershaw, *Hitler*, 230.
51. D. B. Dennis, *Inhumanities: Nazi Interpretations of Western Culture* (Cambridge: Cambridge University Press, 2012), 195.
52. R. H. Weisberg, *In Praise of Intransigence: The Perils of Flexibility* (Oxford: Oxford University Press, 2014).
53. Goethe, *Faust Volumes 1 and 2*, lines 352–3.
54. Goethe, *Faust Volumes 1 and 2*, lines 354–73.
55. Goethe, *Faust Volumes 1 and 2*, lines 483–517.
56. K. Marx, *The Communist Manifesto: A Road Map to History's Most Important Political Document* (London: Haymarket Books, 2005), 47.
57. T. M. Kemple, *Reading Marx's Writing: Melodrama, the Market and the 'Grundrisse'* (Stanford, CA: Stanford University Press, 1995); S. Prawer,

'Mephisto and Old Nick' *Publications of the English Goethe Society* 45, no. 1 (1975): 23–63.

58. Schmitt, *The Leviathan*, 81–2.
59. Schmitt, *Political Theology*, 36.
60. Marx, *The Communist Manifesto*, 410.
61. Goethe, *Faust Volumes 1 and 2*, lines 1331–4.
62. Goethe, *Faust Volumes 1 and 2*, lines 1335–6.
63. Goethe, *Faust Volumes 1 and 2*, lines 1409–12.
64. Goethe, *Faust Volumes 1 and 2*, lines 1413–15.
65. For example, see G. Steiner, *In Bluebeard's Castle: Some Notes Towards the Redefinition of Culture* (New Haven, CT: Yale University Press, 1971), 54.
66. O. Lengyel, *Five Chimneys: A Woman Survivor's True Story of Auschwitz* (New York: Howard Fertig, 1995), 107, 116, 200, 213.
67. E. Kogon, *A Theory and Practice of Hell: The German Concentration Camps and the System Behind Them,* trans. Heinz Norden (New York: Octagon Books, 1979).
68. G. Agamben, *Remnants of Auschwitz: The Witness and the Archive* (New York: Zone Books, 2000), 43.
69. I. Bantekas and S. Nash, *International Criminal Law* (London: Routledge, 2007), 139; A. Cassese and P. Gaeta, *Cassese's International Criminal Law*, 3rd ed. (Oxford: Oxford University Press, 2013), 109; R. Cryer, *An Introduction to International Criminal Law and Procedure*, 2nd ed. (Cambridge: Cambridge University Press, 2010), 205; G. Werle and F. Jessberger, *Principles of International Criminal Law*, 3rd ed. (Oxford: Oxford University Press, 2014), 131, 289.
70. P. Levi, *The Drowned and the Saved* (New York: Summit Books, 1988), 54–5.
71. Kogon, *A Theory and Practice of Hell*, 48.
72. Agamben, *Homo Sacer*, 171; Agamben, *Remnants of Auschwitz*, 21, 41.
73. Agamben, *Karman*, 20.
74. Agamben, *Karman*, 22.
75. White, *Heracles' Bow*, xi.
76. P. Bechky, 'Lemkin's Situation: Toward a Rhetorical Understanding of Genocide' *Brooklyn Law Review* 77, no. 2 (2012): 551–624.
77. Goethe, *Faust Volumes 1 and 2*, lines 1422–35.
78. Goethe, *Faust Volumes 1 and 2*, lines 1526–9.
79. *The Prosecutor v. Uhuru Muigai Kenyatta* (ICC-01/09-02/11), Trial Chamber V, Status Conference, 5 February 2014, pp. 23–4. www.legal-tools.org/doc/7e6374/pdf.
80. Lifted verbatim from: Booklet: *Victims Before the International Criminal Court: A Guide for the Participation of Victims in the Proceedings of the Court* (Geneva: International Criminal Court, n.d.), p. 10. www.icc-cpi.int/NR/rdonlyres/8F-F91A2C-5274-4DCB-9CCE-37273C5E9AB4/282477/160910VPRSBook-letEnglish.pdf.
81. 'Victims' Request for Review of Prosecution's Decision to Cease Active Investigation', International Criminal Court, 7. www.icc-cpi.int/iccdocs/doc/doc2027787.pdf#search=%22representative%20sample%22.
82. Agamben, *Homo Sacer*, 133.
83. J. W. Bendersky, 'Carl Schmitt at Nuremberg' *Telos* 22 (1987): 91–6.

84. R. Kempner, *Interrogation of Carl Schmitt (III)* (New York: Telos, 1987); R. Mehring, *Carl Schmitt: A Biography* (Cambridge: Polity Press, 2014), 420.
85. Mehring, *Carl Schmitt*, 445.
86. J. Müller, *A Dangerous Mind: Carl Schmitt in Post-War European Thought* (New Haven, CT: Yale University Press, 2003), 91.
87. Goethe 2014, lines 1530–6.
88. Goethe, *Faust Volumes 1 and 2*, lines 1644–8.
89. Lengyel, *Five Chimneys*, 33, 37, 39, 44.
90. Kogon, *A Theory and Practice of Hell*, 100, 320.
91. Goethe, *Faust Volumes 1 and 2*, lines 1649–55.
92. Goethe, *Faust Volumes 1 and 2*, lines 1656–9.
93. R. Dallaire, *Shake Hands with the Devil: The Failure of Humanity in Rwanda* (Toronto: Random House, 2003); see also B. Oomen, 'Justice Mechanisms and the Question of Legitimacy: The Example of Rwanda's Multi-layered Justice Mechanisms'. In *Building a Future on Peace and Justice: Studies on Transitional Justice, Peace and Development. The Nuremberg Declaration on Peace and Justice*, 2nd ed., edited by K. Ambos, J. Large and M. Wierda, 175–202 (Dordrecht: Springer, 2009), 186.
94. Dallaire, *Shake Hands with the Devil*, xviii.
95. Dallaire, *Shake Hands with the Devil*, 347.
96. Goethe, *Faust Volumes 1 and 2*, lines 1671–4.
97. Goethe, *Faust Volumes 1 and 2*, lines 1675–87.
98. *The Prosecutor vs Francis Kirimi Muthaura, Uhuru Muigai Kenyatta, and Mohammed Hussein Ali*, ICC Pre-Trial Chamber II, Confirmation of Charges Hearing, ICC-01/09-02/11, Court Transcript at 67.
99. J. Verini, 'The Prosecutor and the President'. *New York Times*, 26 June 2016. www.nytimes.com/2016/06/26/magazine/international-criminal-court-more-no-ocampo-the-prosecutor-and-the-president.html.
100. Goethe, *Faust Volumes 1 and 2*, lines 1691–1711.
101. Goethe, *Faust Volumes 1 and 2*, lines 1736–9.
102. See Bechky, 'Lemkin's Situation'; Bilsky, 'Judging and Understanding', *Law and History Review* 19(1) (2001): 183; E. Christodoulidis and S. Veitch, *Lethe's Law: Justice, Law and Ethics in Reconciliation* (Oxford: Hart, 2001), xv, 235; L. Douglas, 'Language, Judgment and the Holocaust' *Law and History Review* 19(1) (2001): 177–82; D. Hawkes, *The Faust Myth: Religion and the Rise of Representation* (New York: Palgrave Macmillan, 2016), 247; Israel Security Agency, 'The Kastner Affair' (n.d.). www.shabak.gov.il/SiteCollectionImages/english/Moreshet/kastnerAffair_en.pdf; Luban, 'A Man Lost in the Gray Zone', *Law and History Review* 19(1) (2001): 161–76. See Cr.C. 124/53 *Attorney General v. Gruenwald*, 44 P.M. 3 (1965); Cr.A. 232/55 *Attorney General v. Gruenwald*, 12(3) P.D. 2017 (1958).
103. P. Lahav, *Judgment in Jerusalem: Chief Justice Simon Agranat and the Zionist Century*. Berkeley, CA: University of California Press, 1997), 125.
104. L. Bilsky, 'Judging Evil in the Trial of Kastner', *Law and History Review* 19(1) (2001): 117–60, 156.
105. Bilsky, 'Judging Evil in the Trial of Kastner', 156. Cr.C. 40/61 *Attorney General v. Adolph Eichmann*, 45 P.M. 3 (1965); Cr.A. 336/61 *Eichmann v. Attorney General* 16(3) P.D. 2033 (1962).

106. E. Black, *The Transfer Agreement: The Dramatic Story of the Pact Between the Third Reich and Jewish Palestine* (New York: Dialog Press, 2008), xvi.

107. Black, *The Transfer Agreement*, 382.

108. R. J. Lifton, *The Nazi Doctors: Medical Killing and the Psychology of Genocide* (New York: Basic Books, 1986).

109. Goethe, *Faust Volumes 1 and 2*, lines 340–3.

110. Agamben, *Opus Dei*, 25.

111. Agamben, *Opus Dei*, 23.

112. Agamben, *Opus Dei*, 23.

113. Agamben, *Opus Dei*, 23.

114. Agamben, *Opus Dei*, 23.

115. Goethe, *Faust Volumes 1 and 2*, line 300.

116. United Nations, *Charter of the International Military Tribunal – Annex to the Agreement for the Prosecution and Punishment of the Major War Criminals of the European Axis ('London Agreement')*, Article 6 (8 August 1945), subsequent trials in Control Council Law No. 10, *Punishment of Persons Guilty of War Crimes, Crimes Against Peace and Against Humanity*, 20 December 1945, *Official Gazette of the Control Council for Germany*, 3, 31 January 1946: 50–5.

117. *Case No. 3, United States v. Altstoetter et al. (The Justice Case)*, Opinion and Judgment and Sentence, Green Series, Vol. 3 at 954 (Mil. Trib. No. 31947-12-04) [ILDC]. www.worldcourts.com/ildc/eng/decisions/1947.12.04_United_States_v_Altstoetter.pdf#.

3

What is Real about Experimental Norms? Thinking with Giorgio Agamben about Medical Trials

Introduction: Experiments as Enacting Power/Knowledge

Human medical experimentation is profoundly haunted by moral ambiguity. On the one hand, prominent Nazi doctor Eduard Pernkopf's book of anatomy based on unlawful experimentation on concentration camp inmates – despite being out of print and commanding thousands of pounds sterling in price – is still in current use by surgeons.[1] On the other hand, although the scientific utility of the knowledge gleaned might well be clear, it nonetheless depended upon utterly dehumanising its subjects due to the absolute power that was wielded over them. Thus, human experimentation sits right at the junction of Michel Foucault's inseparable power/knowledge dyad.[2] Indeed, Holocaust survivor Olga Lengyel observed first hand that 'Since they [Nazi doctors] were free to do whatever they wished, they decided to experiment on these [human guinea pigs at Auschwitz Birkenau] people'.[3] As will become increasingly clear below, these two competing axes invariably coincide in unlawful experimentation, and law is at a loss to sever them. Xavier Aurey notes law's failure 'to address one of the most difficult issues in clinical trials and human experimentation: the almost unavoidable context of exploitation of any situation where a person is used as an object for the good of others'.[4]

In plain English, trials and experiments overlap in sense and meaning. Not only does an 'experiment' refer to a 'trial'; it also denotes trying anything, or putting something to proof or a test. Its horizon of meaning includes a tentative procedure, or an unproven method or an uncertain course of action embarked upon to confirm whether (or not) it will suit a specified purpose. It is thus an action, or indeed an operation, that is undertaken strictly to discover something unknown or to test a hypothesis – or even to establish, or perhaps illustrate, something already known.

Likewise, 'trial' refers to an 'experiment' as well as to an action, investigation, method or treatment that is adopted to ascertain a result by means of experiential knowledge. Of course, it also refers to the examination and determination of a cause by a judicial tribunal generally or, with respect to criminal law specifically, to the determination of guilt or innocence (strictly speaking, innocence is never in issue in a criminal trial because of the rebuttable presumption of innocence) of an accused person by the court. Following from the above identification of experimentation as being more to do with the amenability of the experimental subjects to the will of the experimenter as opposed to, say, the inherent scientific value of the inquiry, this chapter quite by accident discovered that the verb 'try' links medical trials, legal trials and political trials; it is a link that yields three distinct but related meanings of the word 'experiment' in a way that is reliant on the literary trope of the pun:

1. medical trials experimenting on prisoners
2. the concentration camps as a political experiment in totalitarianism
3. the Nuremberg trials as an experiment in international criminal justice.[5]

Consequently, this chapter argues that unlawful human experimentation is not only about extending the boundaries of human knowledge by expanding the scope of objective empirical science, but is also sullied by the expression of political power over human life stripped bare of all legal and political protections. The illegal and illegitimate willingness to do whatever one wishes to another human being, to decide upon experimentation that is then prosecutable as unlawful is the core problem addressed in this chapter.

Not only has Giorgio Agamben's notion of 'bare life' as life denuded of all legal protection and thereby amenable to anything been especially useful in this regard; his less prominent work on experiments has also been very instructive for the project's aims.[6] What roles do experiments play in Agamben's work and why would it matter? 'Experiment' here means the controlled and deliberate verification of experience through repetition in order to produce knowledge – that is, transforming individual subjective experience into general objective knowledge. What is at stake in this inquiry is law's judgement over science and technology. To start us off, in *What is Real*, Agamben makes the counter-intuitive point that 'what is at stake in the experiment is not so much the knowledge of that system as, first and foremost, the modification it undergoes due to the measuring instruments'.[7] Furthermore, not only is there that unavoidable estrangement between the state of what is observed *through* those instruments and that state in *itself*, but also that currently, 'Science no longer trie[s] to know reality but – like the statistics of social sciences – only [to] intervene in it in order to govern it.'[8]

Illuminatingly, in *Infancy and History*, Agamben states: The scientific verification of experience which is enacted in the experiment – permitting sensory impressions to be deduced with the exactitude of quantitative determinations and, therefore, the prediction of future impressions – responds to this loss of certainty [here embodied in Descartes' deceitful demon] by displacing experience as far as possible outside the individual: on to instruments and numbers.[9]

In *Potentialities*, however, Agamben is of the view that: 'One could thus say of philosophy what Milner says of linguistics that it is 'an experimental science without an observation post . . . a science that has the example as its proper mode of experimentation'.[10] In *Means Without End* (Agamben 2000a, 109), politics is not excluded from experimentation for Agamben in that, 'Contemporary politics is this devastating experiment that disarticulates and empties institutions and beliefs, ideologies and religions, identities and communities all throughout the planet, so as then to rehash and reinstate their definitively nullified form.' This point regarding politics being run as an experiment is also present in *The Open*, where Agamben suggests that:

> Perhaps not only theology and philosophy but also politics, ethics, and jurisprudence are drawn and suspended in the difference between man and animal. The cognitive experiment at issue in this difference ultimately concerns the nature of man – or, more precisely, the production and definition of this nature.[11]

In *The Use of Bodies*, Agamben notes, among other things, that for Michel Foucault sadomasochism was 'an experiment in fluidifying power relations'.[12] In *The Kingdom and the Glory*, Agamben highlights the surprising appearance in Linnaeus (given that 'we are accustomed to thinking of [him] as the founder of modern scientific taxonomy') of a familiarly theological paradigm where providence is presented through the presentation of thought experiments in the 1740s and then in 1760: 'in such a way that an apparent evil in reality agrees with the general good'.[13] Troublingly, in *Remnants of Auschwitz*, Agamben notes that, 'Before being a death camp. Auschwitz is the site of an experiment that remains unthought today, an experiment beyond life and death in which the Jew is transformed into a Muselmann and the human being into a nonhuman.'[14] The centrality of the experiment to Agamben's work can therefore hardly be overstated. Central to the present project, however, is where Agamben addresses medical experimentation in concentration and extermination camps in at least two places, making the point that not only did medical experiments occur in those camps, but those camps in themselves were in all probability a political experiment.[15] Further, he pays substantial attention to human experimentation in the chapter title 'VP' (the German for 'Versuchspersonen, human guinea pigs') in Homo Sacer[16] to pose the controversial question:

> If it was theoretically comprehensible that such experiments would not raise ethical problems for officials and researchers inside a totalitarian regime that moved in an openly biopolitical horizon, how could experiments that were, in a certain sense, analogous have been conducted in a democratic country?[17]

His suggested answer is equally, if not more, controversial:

> The only possible answer is that in both contexts the particular status of the VPs was decisive; they were persons sentenced to death or detained in a camp, the entry into which meant the definitive exclusion from the political community. Precisely because they were lacking almost all the rights and expectations that we customarily attribute to human existence, and yet were still biologically alive, they came to be situated in a limit zone between life and death, inside and outside, in which they were no longer anything but bare life. Those who are sentenced to death and those who dwelt in the camps are thus in some way unconsciously assimilated to *homines sacres*, to a life that may be killed without the commission of homicide.[18]

In 'What is a Command?', Agamben traces two linguistic aspects relevant to the real. The first is the assertion, which is in the indicative mood; while the second is the commandment, which is in the imperative mood.[19] One refers to what 'is' or exists, and the other refers to what will 'be' or shall exist. One belongs to science and philosophy, the other to law, religion and magic.[20] For Agamben, 'To this linguistic partition there corresponds the partition of the real into two correlated but distinct spheres: the first ontology in fact defines and governs the sphere of philosophy and science; the second, that of law, religion, and magic.'[21] The imperative defines the verbal mode proper to law and religion, which have a performative character. Words and phrases in those discourses do not refer to being, but to having-to-be.[22] This corresponds to experiments at the junction of power/knowledge in that the scientific knowledge is based upon the indicative mood, whereas the power exercised over the subjects is in the imperative mood. However, as we shall see below, the mere mutual inclusion of the same species in a biological and scientific sense is a necessary but not sufficient element of unlawful human experimentation: it must also be accompanied by a sense of being excluded in some way from the general group to which the experimenter feels they belong. The deep irony here is that the common biological humanity of the experimental subjects with the experimenters was necessary for the experiment's usefulness, but that commonality was effaced by the racial and political dehumanisation of the subjects in order to make the experiments on those human subjects possible and palatable. The victims then were biologically human but considered as sub-human through racial and class-based distinctions – that is, political and not biological justifications – without which the atrocious experiments would not have occurred.

Discrimination as a Core Element of Unlawful Experiments

International criminal law provides two examples of convictions for unlawful human experimentation that occurred in Nazi Germany and Pol Pot's Cambodia, both of which were based on discrimination of race and class respectively. To start with the instance prior in time, although he was never tried, Dr Sigmund Rascher's (also spelt Roscher) name is everywhere in the Nuremberg Military Tribunals Under Control Council Law No. 10's *Medical Case* – and with good reason. The experiments were his brainchild and he would have been tried had he not already met his death, ironically enough in a concentration camp.[23] In that case, tellingly supportive of Agamben's bare life thesis, both the prosecution[24] and the judges cited the instance of an inmate brought in for experimentation 'whose hair and eyes and figure were pleasing to Dr Rascher' but omit not only precisely *what* was pleasing about her hair, eyes and figure and *why* it was pleasing but also that she was actually spared experimentation as a result.[25] Dr Rascher himself was not so coy as his letter partially reproduced below makes plain. He put his feelings over and above the scientific value of the experiment were he to proceed with it:[26]

> It hurts my racial feelings to expose to racially inferior concentration camp elements a girl as a prostitute who has the appearance of a pure Nordic and who could perhaps by assignment of proper work be put on the right road.
>
> Therefore, I refused to use this girl for my experimental purposes and gave the adequate reports to the camp commander and the adjutant of the Reich Leader SS.

The second example occurred on 16 November 2018. Judges Nil Nonn (President), Jean-Marc Lavergne, Ya Sokhan, Claudia Fenz and You Ottara of the trial chamber of the Extraordinary Chambers in the Courts of Cambodia (ECCC) handed down their unanimous decision in Judgement of Case 002/02 against Nuon Chea and Khieu Samphan, convicting them of crimes against humanity, grave breaches of the Geneva Conventions and genocide. This case is important for at least one compelling reason: not only was it the third ever international criminal trial for unlawful experimentation, but it was only the second ever conviction and so warrants attention. In convicting the accused of murder as a crime against humanity, the judges also incorporated unlawful experimentation among the unlawful acts making up that offence as opposed to a standalone offence in its own right.[27] Indeed the Trial Chamber was 'satisfied that the *Medical Case* can be considered as one of several authorities for attributing criminal responsibility for intentional killing even if the perpetrator acted with less than direct intent'.[28] The Trial Chamber found that the available evidence established at least one prominent confirmed victim whose high social status led to squabbling among the perpetrators:[29]

> With regard to medical experiments, the Chamber notes that the available evidence is scarce and does not allow a comprehensive finding on the scope of the practice, both with respect to its duration and frequency. The Chamber finds, however, that THACH Chea's wife was detained at S-21 and was subjected to an experiment to allow the medical unit to study the surgical process on a live body. She died as a result of this experiment and SON Sen blamed Duch and Nat for allowing this to happen to the wife of a famous person, saying that a normal person's wife should have been taken.

This relative lack of value attributed to certain human lives, thereby ascribing those vulnerable humans as being the proper subject of unlawful experimentation, was not unique to *Case 002/02*. Indeed, this point of vulnerable populations being an experimental target precisely because they are vulnerable, and neither for the good of science nor for the advancement of human knowledge necessarily, was not lost on the ECCC Trial Chamber's consideration of the *Medical Case*:[30]

> The factual analysis of the [*Medical*] case shows that while the Nazi doctors had a complete disregard for the life of the individuals subjected to their brutal experiments, or even considered the death of many of them as an expected outcome, in some instances their objective was to assess if it was possible to survive extreme conditions or particularly severe disease. In such situations the intent involved taking the risk of endangering the life of those subjected to the experiments, with the knowledge that this would likely cause their death.

However, in the ECCC case the vulnerability was one based on class whereas in the *Medical Case* the vulnerability as we saw above was on a racial basis. what is more, although the experimental victims' lack of consent was key to the finding of guilt in the *Medical Case*, this did not feature explicitly with regard to unlawful experimentation in *Case 002/02*, even though they looked at consent in the context of forced marriage and enslavement.[31] To be fair, it was implicit in the legal finding that it was murder as a crime against humanity:[32]

> Due to the forced nature of the blood drawing, the fact that these deaths were recorded in S-21 documents, and the nature of the surgical medical experiment, the Chamber finds that the direct perpetrators not only intended to cause serious bodily harm to the victims but acted with the knowledge that the blood drawing and the live surgical experiment could lead to death and accepted such outcome. The fact that the perpetrators repeatedly performed blood drawing and observed the physical effects that the procedure had on the prisoners' bodies and at times their resulting deaths confirms their knowledge and acceptance of the result of their acts.

In any event, it is sufficiently clear that both the *Medical Case* and *Case 002/02 Against Nuon Chea and Khieu Samphan* had unlawful experimentation only occurring on the basis of power over victims who had been denuded of all legal protections.

The Theodicy of Justifying the Evil Effects and Intent of Power by the Value of the Knowledge to be Gained

In the *Medical Case*, the Tribunal noted the defence's argument that, 'The protagonists of the practice of human experimentation justify their views on the basis that such experiments yield results for the good of society that are unprocurable by other methods or means of study.'[33] Yet they opposed that approach by the defence with the imperative 'that certain basic principles must be observed in order to satisfy moral, ethical and legal concepts'.[34] The first, and by far most fully articulated, of these was that, 'The voluntary consent of the human subject is absolutely essential.'[35] This imposed a 'personal' non-delegable 'duty and responsibility for ascertaining the quality of the consent', resting 'upon each individual who initiates, directs or engages in the experiment'.[36] It needs noting, however, that not all but only 'unnecessary physical and mental suffering and injury' were prohibited.[37] The Defence were not alone in justifying the atrocious experiments by recalling their good results, as well as by invoking the need for them. For instance, nerve surgeon Dr Susan Mackinnon is quoted as saying that 'she feels uncomfortable with its [Eduard Pernkopf's book of anatomy] origin, but using the book is a crucial part of being an "ethical surgeon" – and that she could not do her job without it'.[38] The BBC reported that, 'Rabbi Joseph Polak – a Holocaust survivor and professor of health law – believes the book is a "moral enigma" because it is derived from "real evil, but can be used in the service of good".'[39]

These justifications are eerily akin to Mephistopheles' self-description in Johan Wolfgang von Goethe's *Faust* as:

> A part of that force
> which, always willing evil, always produces good.[40]

Nor is this is the sole Faustian referent here. Agamben's analysis of bare life is always heavily reliant on Michel Foucault, who Agamben follows to show how society crosses over the threshold into 'biological modernity', where the life of the human species and individual becomes what is at stake in political calculation – that is, health and biological life become a problem of sovereign power. In a crucial passage, Agamben directly quotes Foucault:

> What follows is a kind of bestialization of man achieved through the most sophisticated political techniques. For the first time in history, the possibilities of the social sciences are made known, and at once it becomes possible both to protect life and to authorize a holocaust.[41]

This quote is simply too redolent of *Faust* to be coincidental, as this dialogue that Goethe puts in the mouth of Mephistopheles would indicate:

> I merely see how mankind toils and moils
> Earth's little gods still do not change a bit,
> Are just as odd as on their primal day.
> Their lives would be a little easier
> If You'd not let them glimpse the light of heaven –
> They call it Reason and employ it only to be more bestial than any beast.[42]

Furthermore, Foucault himself described the articulation of power/knowledge as a 'Faustian pact' 'to exchange life in its entirety for sex itself' and said that 'one would have to speak of bio-power to designate what brought life and its mechanisms into the realm of explicit calculations and made knowledge-power an agent of transformation of human life'.[43] Foucault also notes how the experiment through power/knowledge successfully combines examination with the ceremonial of power and production of truth:

> The examination combines the techniques of an observing hierarchy and those of a normalizing judgement. It is a normalizing gaze, a surveillance that makes it possible to qualify, to classify and to punish. It establishes over individuals a visibility through which one differentiates them and judges them. That is why, in all the mechanisms of discipline, the examination is highly ritualized. In it are combined the ceremony of power and the form of the experiment, the deployment of force and the establishment of truth. At the heart of the procedures of discipline, it manifests the subjection of those

who are perceived as objects and the objectification of those who are subjected. The superimposition of the power relations and knowledge relations assumes in the examination all its visible brilliance. It is yet another innovation of the classical age that the historians of science have left unexplored.[44]

Furthermore, prior to the pact that bears his name, Faust is among others already unusually steeped in learning medicine, in his own words:

> I've studied now, to my regret,
> Philosophy, Law, Medicine,
> and – what is worst – Theology
> from end to end with diligence.[45]

Like his father before him, Faust was a medical experimenter, as the following dialogue illustrates:

> OLD PEASANT. It is indeed appropriate
> that on this festive day you come among us;
> as well we know, when times were bad
> you always were disposed to help us!
> Many a man is here alive
> who, at the time your father stopped the plague,
> was snatched by him at the last moment
> from the burning frenzy of his fever.
> You too – you were a young man then –
> would enter every stricken house
> and yet, although they carried off so many corpses,
> you always would come out unharmed,
> surviving every trial and test –
> by the Helper above our helper was helped.
> VILLAGERS. Good health to one who's tried and true,
> and may he be our help for many years to come!
> FAUST. Offer your homage to the Helper above
> Who teaches that we all should help each other.[46]

Nor is this the only medical experimentation theme in *Faust*. Goethe even paraphrases Hippocrates:

> Life is short,
> and art long,
> opportunity fleeting,
> experimentations perilous,
> and judgment difficult.

into:

> WAGNER. Alas, that art is long,
> and human life so short![47]

Astonishingly, not only do we find Paracelsus cited by the Defence in the *Medical Case* at Nuremberg,[48] but Paracelsus provided Goethe with source material for *Faust*.[49] It is astonishing because, as Hans Binswanger and Kirk R. Smith note of Paracelsus in the *Bulletin of the World Health Organization*:

> 'We shall be like Gods,' he wrote. 'Natural magic will make it possible to see beyond the mountains, to divine the future, to cure all diseases, to make gold, and even to duplicate God's greatest miracle – the creation of man himself.' Many would argue that science has either achieved or will soon achieve most of these things in one way or another, but some would also worry about what Faustian wagers are made in the process.[50]

Like Faust, Goethe was a scientist[51] who, as Thomas Huxley notes in the very first article for *Nature*, 'in 1786, gave himself incredible trouble to get other people to take an interest in his discovery, that man has an intermaxillary bone'.[52] Goethe went through that trouble in order to oppose his contemporaries who argued the opposite in order to distinguish and separate humans from the animal kingdom.[53] This theological defence of human separateness and superiority to other animals is what Goethe sought to refute through scientific demonstration.[54] Unsurprisingly, therefore, Bloom notes that, 'Acclaimed as a literary messiah almost from the start of his career, Goethe shrewdly evaded stultification by becoming an endless experimenter, and *Faust, Part Two* may well be more of an experiment than a poem.'[55] In that way, his contribution was to the definition of humanity as a species as opposed to humanity as a norm or standard of conduct. International criminal law combines both of these poles in the Rome Statute for the International Criminal Court, which refers to 'humanity' in only two contexts.[56] The first is in the preamble, speaking of 'unimaginable atrocities that deeply shock the conscience of humanity', referencing humanity as a standard or norm. The second is always within the context of crimes against humanity in Articles 5 and 7, referencing humanity as a group as well as a norm. Here humanity therefore references not just a biological species – homo sapiens – that is distinguished from the rest of the zoological kingdom due to self-awareness, but also the conduct expected of individual members of that species. Christopher McLeod refers to these as human-kind and human-nature respectively.[57] Giorgio Agamben argues that man [sic] is 'a field of dialectical tensions' separating 'animality and the humanity' which takes bodily form in it.[58] This 'means that man is the being which recognizes itself as such, *that man is the animal that must recognize itself as human to be human*.[59] In that way, for international criminal law, 'humanity' as a term occupies a junction between norm and value, or law and fact.

Although the International Committee of the Red Cross's 2016 *Commentary* on the 1st Geneva Convention of 1949[60] notes the relevance of the International Ethical Guidelines for Epidemiological Studies (CIOMS 2009) and the International Ethical Guidelines for Biomedical Research Involving Human Subjects[61] for the justification of human experiments, none of these instruments mentions criminal culpability at all. Not even the World Medical Association Declaration of Helsinki Ethical Principles for Medical Research Involving Human Subjects does.[62] This leaves the *Medical Case* and *Case 002/02 Against Nuon Chea and Khieu Samphan* as the only exemplars of the law grappling with this difficult area in which medical ethics increasingly supplant international criminal law.

Conclusion

This chapter began by locating human experiment at the intersection of the Foucauldian power/knowledge axis. It then went on to demonstrate that this articulation was theodicean in justifying the power asserted by the knowledge promised. It did this by reading the Faustian pact narrative as already present in human experimentation and demonstrating that both textually and thematically. Clearly, if experiments were solely based within a scientific paradigm, they would not be so legally and politically charged with discriminatory practices. This is why a retreat or displacement of law in favour of individual ethical judgement is to be strenuously resisted.

Notes

1. K. Baker, 'Eduard Pernkopf: The Nazi Book of Anatomy Still Used by Surgeons'. *BBC News*, 18 August 2019. www.bbc.com/news/health-49294861.
2. M. Foucault, *Discipline and Punish: The Birth of the Prison* (New York: Pantheon, 1977), 185.
3. O. Lengyel, *Five Chimneys: A Woman Survivor's True Story of Auschwitz* (New York: Howard Fertig, 1983), 185.
4. X. Aurey, 'The Nuremberg Doctors' Trial: Looking Back 70 Years Later', *International Criminal Law Review* 17(6) (2017): 1049–69, 1054.
5. W. D. Redfern, *Puns* (Oxford: Blackwell).
6. G. Agamben, *Homo Sacer: Sovereign Power and Bare Life* (Stanford, CA: Stanford University Press, 1998), 159.
7. G. Agamben, *What is Real?* (Stanford, CA: Stanford University Press, 2018), 13.
8. Agamben, *What is Real?*, 13.
9. G. Agamben, *Infancy and History: The Destruction of Experience* (New York: Verso 1993), 17.

10. G. Agamben, *Potentialities: Collected Essays in Philosophy* (Stanford, CA: Stanford University Press, 1999b), 68.
11. G. Agamben, *The Open: Man and Animal* (Stanford, CA: Stanford University Press, 2004), 110–11.
12. G. Agamben, *The Use of Bodies* (Stanford, CA: Stanford University Press, 2016), 96–7, 102, 107.
13. G. Agamben, *The Kingdom and the Glory: For a Theological Genealogy of Economy and Government* (Stanford, CA: Stanford University Press, 2011), 279.
14. Agamben, *Remnants of Auschwitz: The Witness and the Archive* (New York: Zone Books, 2000), 52.
15. Agamben, *Homer Sacer*, 154–99; Agamben, *The Open*, 22.
16. Agamben, *Homer Sacer*, 154.
17. Agamben, *Homer Sacer*, 159.
18. Agamben, *Homer Sacer*, 159.
19. G. Agamben, *Creation and Anarchy: The Work of Art and the Religion of Capitalism* (Stanford, CA: Stanford University Press, 2019), 59.
20. Agamben, *Creation and Anarchy*, 59.
21. Agamben, *Creation and Anarchy*, 59.
22. G. Agamben, *Opus Dei: An Archaeology of Duty* (Stanford CA: Stanford University Press, 2013), 84, 119–20.
23. Nuremberg Military Tribunals Under Control Council Law No. 10, *United States v. Karl Brandt, et al.* (Case No. 1) 'The Medical Case' in *Trials of War Criminals Before the Nuremberg Military Tribunals Under Control Council Law No. 10 Volumes I and II Nuremberg*, October 1946–April 1949, Vol. I, p. 38.
24. 'The Medical Case', Vol. II, p. 45.
25. 'The Medical Case', Vol. I, pp. 71, 203.
26. 'The Medical Case', Vol. I, p. 245.
27. Case 002/02 para. 2560, pp. 1296, para. 2564, pp. 1298.
28. Case 002/02 para. 636, p. 346.
29. Case 002/02 para. 2447, pp. 1233–4.
30. Case 002/02 para. 636, p. 345.
31. Case 002/02 para. 267, p. 125 and para. 664, p. 356 respectively.
32. Case 002/02 para. 2565, p. 1298.
33. 'The Medical Case', Vol. II, p. 181.
34. 'The Medical Case', Vol. II, p. 181.
35. 'The Medical Case', Vol. II, p. 181.
36. 'The Medical Case', Vol. II, p. 182.
37. 'The Medical Case', Vol. II, p. 182.
38. Baker, 'Eduard Pernkopf'.
39. Baker, 'Eduard Pernkopf'.
40. J. Goethe, *Faust Volumes 1 and 2: Goethe's Collected Works* (Princeton, NJ: Princeton University Press, 2014), lines 1335–6.
41. Agamben, *Homo Sacer*, 3.
42. Goethe, *Faust Volumes 1 and 2*, lines 280–5.
43. Foucault, *Discipline and Punish*, 143.
44. Foucault, *Discipline and Punish*, 184–5.
45. Goethe, *Faust Volumes 1 and 2*, lines 354–73.
46. Goethe, *Faust Volumes 1 and 2*, lines 993–1010.

47. Goethe, *Faust Volumes 1 and 2*, lines 559–60.
48. 'The Medical Case', Vol. II, pp. 75–7.
49. P. D. Smith, '"Was die Welt im Innersten zusammenhält": Scientific Themes in Goethe's *Faust*'. In *A Companion to Goethe's Faust: Parts I and II*, edited by P. Bishop, 194–220 (Rochester, NY: Camden 2006), 197–98.
50. H. Binswanger and K. R. Smith, 'Paracelsus and Goethe: Founding Fathers of Environmental Health', *International Journal of Public Health* 78(9) (2000): 1162–5, 1163.
51. J. Goethe, *Scientific Studies*, edited by D. E. Miller (Princeton, NJ: Princeton University Press, 1995), 111–16.
52. T. H. Huxley, 'Nature: Aphorisms by Goethe', *Nature* 1 (1869): 9–11, 10.
53. G. A. Wells, 'Goethe and the Inter Maxillary Bone', *The British Journal for the History of Science* 3(4) (1967): 348–61, 350.
54. R. Preece, 'Darwinism, Christianity, and the Great Vivisection Debate', *Journal of the History of Ideas* 64(3) (2003): 399–419, 411.
55. H. Bloom, *The Western Canon: The Books and School of the Ages* (New York: Harcourt Brace, 1994), 198.
56. Rome Statute of the International Criminal Court, 17 July 1998, 2187 UNTS 90, UN Doc A/CONF.183/9 (in force 1 July 2002) Preamble and Arts 5 and 7.
57. C. McLeod, 'Towards a Philosophical Account of Crimes Against Humanity', *European Journal of International Law* 21(2) (2010): 280–308, 283.
58. Agamben, *The Open*, 12.
59. Agamben, *The Open*, 26.
60. Commentary: Convention (I) for the Amelioration of the Condition of the Wounded and Sick in Armed Forces in the Field. Geneva, 12 August 1949 (2016), Article 50. https://ihl-databases.icrc.org/applic/ihl/ihl.nsf/Comment.xsp?action=openDocument&documentId=21B052420B219A72C1257F7D00587FC3.
61. Council for International Organizations of Medical Sciences (CIOMS) in collaboration with the World Health Organization (WHO), *International Ethical Guidelines for Epidemiological Studies* (2009). https://cioms.ch/wp-content/uploads/2017/01/International_Ethical_Guidelines_LR.pdf.
62. World Medical Association, *World Medical Association Declaration of Helsinki Ethical Principles for Medical Research Involving Human Subjects* (1964). www.who.int/bulletin/archives/79%284%29373.pdf.

4

Carl Schmitt as a Subject and Object of International Criminal Law: Ethical Judgement *In Extremis*

Introduction

Carl Schmitt, the well-known German theorist of international law, constitutional law and politics, is a unique figure in the history of international criminal law and worthy of study. Schmitt was associated with the National Socialist regime from 1933 until his ousting in 1936. Schmitt's reputation as 'Crown Jurist' or *Kronjurist* of the Third Reich dogs his legacy to this day.[1] Discerning the precise nature of Carl Schmitt's relationship to National Socialism and National Socialist crimes in his life and work is an open question and by no means a simple one. It is, however, definitely worth the effort – if not almost mandatory – to answer in order to engage with his work. Most of the extant scholarship on Schmitt does not address why he escaped prosecution at Nuremberg.[2] Some authors think his National Socialist associations taint his work, while others see his work as having an intrinsic value separate and apart from the activities of the man himself.[3] The leading works thus tend to discuss Schmitt and his legacy in a more or less binary fashion by separating the two groups of authors and then broadly taking two separate views. Both these opposed poles can then cite examples to bolster their respective positions.[4] Some authors claim that Schmitt was more committed to his ambition than to National Socialism; other scholars maintain that Schmitt's anti-liberal jurisprudence, coupled with his anti-Semitism, made it ethically logical for him to be in favour of the National Socialist regime. What is not in dispute is that Schmitt did not hold any official position in the National Socialist regime. This fact, although neglected, explains why he was not prosecuted. Irrespective of who is (factually) right or wrong, it was the particular interpretation of 'holding an office' that prevailed – to Schmitt's advantage.

This chapter instead uses Schmitt and his work to explore and demonstrate the links between ethical conduct, official duties (in the sense that an office is a separate entity from its holder) and individual liability in international criminal law. The question of legal ethics being applied to official acts in a crisis is not a mere intellectual or historical curiosity unique to the National Socialist period, but a contemporary live issue.[5] The chapter is divided into four parts. The first substantive part introduces Schmitt's interrogation at Nuremberg on the basis of him being the 'Nazi Crown Jurist' as the foundation for the present inquiry. It analyses Schmitt's work and activities in relation to international criminal law as a basis for: (1) criminal charges related to crimes against humanity for anti-Semitic sentiments; and (2) crimes against peace relating to National Socialist territorial expansionism, or *Lebensraum*. The second part relates Schmitt's defence strategy at Nuremberg to his work and the attempt by the Allied Powers to judge his conduct. The third part turns to the concept of 'piracy' as a critical adjunct between Schmitt's work, his personal politics and his trial. It foreshadows the lack of traction of the case against Schmitt by problematising the legal/illegal distinction through an application of Hans Kelsen's legal positivist principles and the ethical/unethical criterion for judgement as per Immanuel Kant's ethics. The fourth and final part turns on the notion of 'office' as conceptually uniting both Kantian ethics and Kelsenian jurisprudence to ground the argument that it was Schmitt's lack of official capacity that above all prevented him from being prosecuted.

That argument develops in dialogue with Giorgio Agamben's 'archaeology of the office', particularly in his singling out of the Nuremberg process's departure from longstanding legal principles regarding official immunity and, related to that, to his reading of Immanuel Kant's ethics in the same context. The conclusion reached is that the best possible refutation of Schmitt – that most acerbic critic of liberal democracy – was to not prosecute him at Nuremberg in a clear affirmation of liberal democratic principles. Indeed, Schmitt referred to these as inaugurating a global legal order of liberal democratic international justice.[6] These principles are a more or less tacit agenda tied to international criminal law right to the present day. Those same principles, moreover, were critiqued in Schmitt's work as linking liberalism to piracy and the imposition of a more or less illegitimate global order.[7]

Certain key components of Schmitt's thought, when viewed in a particular light (a teleological one), would appear to be positively proto-National Socialist or, at the very least, precursors to or enablers of National Socialist legal and political theory and practice. Others would appear to be laudatory of National Socialism itself. In other words, these aspects can be evidence of collusion or participation in crimes against peace and crimes against humanity in the Nuremberg Principles sense. Yet none would appear to be after-the-fact justifications of the National Socialist regime as such. For the sake of brevity, Schmitt's relationships with National Socialism are here presented through his friend/enemy distinction and its relation to his cultural anti-Semitism as well as his *grossraum* or 'great spaces' theory.[8] Those ideas would possibly give rise to individual international criminal responsibility for Schmitt with regard to National Socialism. These are not separate ideas, but are connected in myriad explicit and implicit ways in Schmitt's work. His first idea, the famous friend/enemy distinction, contains existentially belligerent and discriminatory aspects. The distinction would seem to be both a belligerent foreign policy as well as a persecutory domestic policy, together eradicating internal and external enemies of a political movement uniting the state and people of Germany to its leader, who was the legitimating source of all law. All those very National Socialist-like characteristics were thus already unmistakeably present in Schmitt's work prior to him joining the National Socialist Party. They even predated the actual rise to power of the National Socialists. Because these same traits were later to be found in the National Socialist movement itself, they need to be considered carefully.

For a start, Schmitt considered *The Concept of the Political* his best work.[9] In it, he famously wrote that, 'The specific political distinction to which political actions and motives can be reduced is that between friend and enemy.'[10] Furthermore, any universally binding ethical values were excluded because, 'Only the actual participants can correctly recognize, understand, and judge the concrete situation and settle the extreme case of conflict.'[11] External criteria for judgement with a neutral and impartial arbiter independently applying laid-down rules were for him impossible in international law. According to Schmitt, the state as a

> political entity presupposes the real existence of an enemy and therefore coexistence with another political entity. As long as a state exists, there will thus always be in the world more than just one state. A world state which embraces the entire globe and all of humanity cannot exist. The political world is a pluriverse, not a universe.[12]

There is hostility to universal ethical values in more of Schmitt's writing. Schmitt famously sought to challenge the legality of this liberal universal humanitarianism.[13] At least one of Schmitt's biographers notes that his critique of liberalism was already present in his earliest works.[14] It was at its origin not an accommodation of the National Socialists, but his own actual position. During the Weimar period prior to World War II, Schmitt produced a series of devastating criticisms of liberal thought.[15] Schmitt distinguished liberalism from democracy while favouring the latter.[16] The sort of political regime that Schmitt had in mind was not just illiberal in its hostility to, say, the rule of law or minority rights, but also explicitly anti-liberal. For Schmitt, there existed 'absolutely no liberal politics, only a liberal critique of politics'.[17] Liberalism, according to Schmitt, hindered and controlled state power in order to protect 'individual freedom and private property'.[18] Furthermore, liberal concepts typically moved between ethical and economical poles in order 'to annihilate the political as a domain of conquering power and repression'.[19] As explained above, *The Concept of the Political* can therefore be seen as containing trace elements of the offences of which he was accused and – as we shall see below – attacks on his accusers' credibility. That is to say, the most damning parts of his work are more or less inseparable from Schmitt's critique of liberalism.

Schmitt's first edition of *The Concept of the Political* was published in 1927 and went through several editions. It was only in 1933, however, that he included in it a passage from Heraclitus's *Fragmentum* 53, 'War is the father of all things, the king of all things. Some he proves to be gods, others men; some he makes slaves, others free.'[20] The timing of this addition coincided with the National Socialists coming to power and surely cannot be considered accidental. On the contrary, it was a clear instance of accommodation to the National Socialist reality. This turning point was marked as well by Schmitt endorsing Adolf Hitler as the *Nomos* of the German people.[21] He also began to actively seek to rid German jurisprudence of Jewish influence.[22] Schmitt now appeared to have entered into a Faustian pact with the National Socialists.[23] There is no doubt that, at the very least after 1934, Schmitt was fully aware of his allegiance to a murderous regime.[24]

Prior to that pact, if a pact is what it was, Schmitt wrote that it was 'senseless to wage war for purely religious, or moral, or juristic, or economic motives'.[25] This would mean, therefore, that justifying a war in the name of humanity in order to end war 'is then considered to constitute the absolute last war of humanity'.[26] Indeed, 'outlawing war does not abolish the friend–enemy distinction, but, on the contrary, opens new possibilities by giving an international *hostis* declaration new content and new vigor'.[27] This is a point Schmitt belaboured to a certain extent. It has direct relevance both to the idea of 'crimes against humanity' and to the jurisdictional basis for international criminal law overall.[28] Moreover, 'The adversary is thus no longer called an enemy but a disturber of peace and is thereby designated to be an outlaw of humanity.'[29] For all that, there are certain historical details on record that confound a teleological approach in Schmitt's pre-National Socialist period work. There was no actual design or final purpose relating Schmitt's work to bringing about National Socialism. Indeed, if the historical sequence of events is anything to go by, the opposite is true. In 1932 (before joining the National Socialist Party in 1933), Schmitt was fearful of a victory of extremists of either the political left or right, both of whom utilised liberal legality as a temporary expedient to the end of acquiring parliamentary and governmental power in the Weimar state.[30] However, despite Schmitt's pleas, President Paul von Hindenburg – who loathed ruling by decree – permitted even 'negatively inclined parties to operate and compete for power'.[31] Schmitt therefore intended his work to be used against the National Socialists and others – principally the communists. In this, he manifestly failed.

Consequently, Schmitt badly miscalculated the National Socialist take-over.[32] At first he was unable to see the National Socialists as a force of polit-ical renewal;[33] however, he later saw them as a 'perverse resolution' of the main political problems of mass politics.[34] Once it was a *fait accompli*, phi-losopher Martin Heidegger wrote to Schmitt inviting collaboration with the National Socialists.[35] Schmitt, having joined after Heidegger, went on to have a more political role than Heidegger even though he was in a comparatively minor academic role. This change of mind, if not heart, went beyond mere Hobbesian obedience to power to actively seeking to scale the political sys-tem's heights.[36] Schmitt initially met with a certain level of success, with a National Socialist newspaper bestowing on him the rhetorically grand but functionally empty 'Crown Jurist of the Third Reich' honorific.[37] It must be emphasised that this was not an official position with actual power and influence. Schmitt, however, was 'ultimately not adaptable enough to sur-vive' holding onto his position.[38] The available evidence seems to suggest that while he accepted and justified degradation and exclusion of the Jews, he did not conceive of anything like the final solution.[39] These details were not lost on the SS, which denounced Schmitt's dissimulation and warned him not to pretend that his work was compatible with proper National Socialist doctrine.[40] The SS carried out sustained attacks on Schmitt in its official newspaper *Das Schwarze Korps*.[41] Even National Socialist university students were reported to say, 'We don't think much of Carl Schmitt.'[42] Eventually Hermann Goering saved him from further attacks while confirming the fac-tual basis for the attacks.[43] Schmitt was consequently spared a worse fate and allowed to remain a professor in Berlin.[44] The National Socialists therefore did not appear to even need Schmitt. Indeed, Hannah Arendt considered Schmitt as the most interesting example of the fact that, 'Totalitarianism in power invariably replaces all first-rate talents, regardless of their sympathies, with those crackpots and fools whose lack of intelligence and creativity is still the best guarantee of their loyalty.'[45]

Was Schmitt's support for the National Socialist regime solely for self-promotion, or was it at least partly for self-preservation as he insisted after the fact? Perhaps it was a mixture of both, with the emphasis shift-ing from self-promotion in the early years to self-preservation in the latter years of his three-year self-identification with the National Socialists. We can provisionally conclude that it is impossible to completely extricate Schmitt from National Socialism, just as it is impossible to implicate him fully in its excesses. There is a difference, fine though it may be, between proto-fascism and fascism proper. This distinction, as we shall see below, enabled him to escape criminal liability in the historical and political context of the time, but still emphatically leaves him defenceless against unfavourable moral, historical and ethical judgement.

Carl Schmitt's Interrogation at Nuremberg: Crown Jurist of the Third Reich?

In April 1945, following the defeat of the National Socialists, Schmitt was arrested by the Russians in Berlin, interrogated and released.[46] In September 1945, he was arrested by the Americans and held in internment until March 1947, during which period they brought him to Nuremberg as a potential defendant in the ongoing international criminal trials.[47] This was with a view to investigating his alleged participation, either directly or indirectly, in 'the planning of wars of aggression, of war crimes and of crimes against humanity' by providing their 'ideological foundation'.[48] Schmitt was investigated at Nuremberg specifically for his ideas and in his capacity as a prominent legal scholar. He defended himself as being in a position analogous to a hostage caught in a pirate ship. Related to that, the content of his work critiqued global legal jurisdiction as being conceptually aterritorial, as it is organised around the notion of piracy. For Schmitt, invocations of humanity as a basis for jurisdiction were only a dishonest subterfuge to disguise the march to 'global civil war'.[49] According to a consultant for the Legal Division of the United States Office of Military Government for Germany, 'a man of near-genius rating',[50] Schmitt was investigated not for his actions but for his ideas. At the same time, this consultant – who, as it happens, was Schmitt's former student, Karl Loewenstein – found it impossible to separate Schmitt the man from his work.[51] This inseparable conjunction of Schmitt and his work from his interrogator's point of view could, as we shall see, only be possible because he did not occupy an office. He could instead be described as having an academic vocation. That is to say, his dubious political position notwithstanding, there was at least some merit to his work.[52] To further illustrate this point, in an ironic twist of fate yet another of his interrogators, Ossip K. Flechtheim, had had his doctoral thesis previously failed by Schmitt.[53]

Schmitt defended himself on the intriguing basis that his ideas were genuinely misunderstood by both his interrogators and the National Socialists, but for opposing reasons.[54] Somewhat understandably, given the implications for his own guilt, Schmitt resisted his interrogator's characterisation of him as 'one of the leading jurists of the Third Reich'.[55] While disowning such characterisation, Schmitt nevertheless accepted the facts as alleged by his interrogator, only holding that it was 'a question of interpretation and legal evaluation'.[56] Although he did admit writing 'that the administration of justice should be National Socialist', he claimed 'it was a thesis. The National Socialist League of German Jurists extracted it, so to speak, from my mouth. At that time there was a dictatorship with which I was not yet familiar.'[57] Schmitt therefore claimed essentially that his self-damning words were all an act under the constraints of a dictatorship, and thus neither genuine nor actually his own. The abovementioned attacks on Schmitt by the SS in its official newspaper *Das Schwarze Korps* in this way became central to his exculpation.[58]

Schmitt's interrogator, Robert Kempner, remarked that 'reading your writings creates a completely different impression from the one you are now providing'.[59] Kempner further noted the difficulty of rendering a criminal judgment regarding Schmitt's conduct. Thus, given the debates regarding the meaning of his ideas, the interrogations of Schmitt all 'ended in academic discussions'.[60] This is important. Among the writings of Schmitt during the relevant period that could be read as National Socialist inspired propaganda, and which he insisted should be read as an act of resistance to National Socialist ideology, was *Leviathan*, his fairly anti-Semitic work on Thomas Hobbes.[61] Although anti-Semitism only emerged in his published work after 1933 – coincident with the National Socialists coming to power – his diaries document lifelong anti-Semitism, despite intense friendships with and at times financial dependence upon Jews.[62] Furthermore, following the war, Schmitt developed his work to subsequently depict *Leviathan* as a sea monster representing Anglo-American power based on the sea.[63] This Anglo-American power grew at the expense of land-based legal orders and was global in the sense that because the sea has no boundaries, a legal order based on it would view the whole globe as being like the free sea – open to commerce and not closed to jurisdiction, including international criminal jurisdiction. Therefore, the historically enigmatic figure of Schmitt as a person and as a thinker was both a subject – given his ideas regarding international criminal jurisdiction – and an object as a suspect under investigation of international criminal law. Additionally, how to render judgment was a specific difficulty in his particular case because, according to his defence, a genuine appreciation of his ideas was the issue at hand.

Judgment *In Extremis*

Both inside and outside of the interrogation – regarding his central defensive claim of having been driven against his will to state what he did – Schmitt often compared himself with the fictionalised character of Benito Cereno by Herman Melville. Cereno was the captain of a slave ship that was taken over by the slaves, who forced him to act as the master while they feigned the condition of slaves in order to get provisions from an American ship captain who came to their aid.[64] In *Ex Captivitate Salus*, large portions of which had been written during his internment, Schmitt wrote:

> I am the last, conscious advocate of the *jus publicum Europaeum* and, in an existentialist sense, I am its last teacher and researcher, and experience its ending like Benito Cereno experienced the journey of the pirate ship. Hence, silence is now appropriate and timely. It should not worry us. By keeping silent, we reflect upon ourselves and upon our divine origin.[65]

Cereno is used here to symbolise Schmitt as a figure of the intelligentsia taken hostage in a mass system analogous to piracy.[66] At the same time, once 'Schmitt assumes the mask of Benito Cereno, it becomes impossible to ground or establish the sincerity of any of his statements, since each can later be claimed to have been a coerced performance'.[67] This is one challenge that Schmitt poses in terms of judging the authenticity of his conduct under the repressive National Socialist regime, and consequently the depth, breadth and sincerity of his relationship to it. The other challenge is Schmitt's hostile attitude to the post-war legal order built after the defeat of the National Socialists and his ambivalence at best about the global legal order established thereafter under Anglo-American ideals.

Schmitt uses the word *Nomos* to mean at least three things in one composite concept: the ordering of territory; law, regulation or norms; and the concrete form in which a political, economic and social order becomes apparent.[68] All three come together and when a new order is expanding or making an appearance, it destabilises laws based on a rival *Nomos*. Therefore, seen in this light when legality is in dispute – that is, one law is opposed to another law – the answer is not simply making more laws but rather the capacity to judge what is 'really' law. In fact, for Schmitt, globalisation itself can be seen as analogous to the piracy aboard the ship taken over by the slaves (just as the National Socialists could be seen as having taken over Germany).[69] Referencing piracy begins to illuminate how sea power-based free trade and liberal values began to universalise issues of law and right at the expense of the land power-based *jus publicum Europeaum* that had Germany at its geopolitical centre.[70] According to Schmitt, it is at precisely this point that 'the specifically European order dissolved into a spaceless universalism, and no new order took its place'.[71] In this regard, Schmitt states that 'a global universalism lacking any spatial sense' prevailed.[72] For Schmitt:

> The prevailing concept of a global universalism lacking any spatial sense certainly expressed a reality in the economy distinct from the state – an economy of free world trade and a free world market, with the free movement

of money, capital and labor ... over, under and beside the state-political borders of what appeared to be a purely political international law between states spread a free, i.e., non-state sphere of economy permeating everything: a global economy. In the idea of a free global economy lay not only the overcoming of state-political orders, but also, as an essential precondition, a standard for the internal constitutions of individual member states of this order of international law; it presupposed that every member state would establish a minimum of *constitutional* order.[73]

Piracy is a key and recurring motif in this regard in at least three ways. Schmitt deployed it to understand and explain how concrete legal and political orders are won; he also theorised as to how, in its origins, the current globalised legal order was analogous to piracy; and lastly, as is well known, piracy was and is constantly evoked as the beginning of international criminal law. Schmitt later found that treating the perpetrators at Nuremberg as immediate subjects of international law placed them analogously to pirates outside of the legal order and ostracised them as 'enemies of all mankind'.[74] Furthermore, Schmitt posited himself as having been treated just like an outlaw in a similar fashion.[75]

Piracy

The piracy analogy can be seen in a constitutive relationship to a global criminal justice system. Piracy inaugurates international criminal law and the pirate figure is reinvented in order to radically transform the idea of international community that underpins a global legal order.[76] Schmitt and William Schabas agree that piracy, as the basis of universal jurisdiction for international criminal law, is more about jurisdiction, which is to say the expression of power rather than mere criminality.[77] This foundational and originary aspect of piracy, while not exactly a secret, is its under-appreciated role in constituting a so-called international society founded on peace, freedom of commerce and the free seas.[78] This is why, for Schmitt, 'to evoke a united humanity, no name works quite as well as that of the enemy of all'.[79] Furthermore, the concept of piracy was politicised by sea powers as an interim concept between war and peace at the expense of 'continental international law'.[80] The international community thus needed pirates as agents and objects of imperial ambition.[81] There is, therefore, no question that piracy and empire are interconnected. Even though the pirate and the emperor are not the same person, they do have a lot in common (Gould 2013). Legality itself is at stake here – for instance, 'even the English slave traders whose acts of piracy in Africa kept the plantations of America supplied with human cargo believed themselves to be abiding by the rule of law, albeit a law that jurists in England viewed as "odious"'.[82] Paradoxically, universal jurisdiction based on this model of the pirate is attractive for political purposes.[83] Thus it is precisely through its presentation as being universal, neutral and non-political that it finds the logic of the political inescapable.[84] The distinction between a criminal pirate and a legitimate privateer is principally that the latter has the blessing of a state via a letter of marque and therefore acts in some official capacity that the former lacks. Having an official role shields the privateer from having personal responsibility over their actions because they are effectively an instrument of state. In that way, the ethical link between an actor and their action is interrupted by the capacity in which they act. International criminal jurisdiction at Nuremberg put an enduring question mark on the absoluteness of this shield of office.

The Notion of Office and International Criminal Responsibility

According to Agamben, at least up until the Nuremberg trials, someone following an order was not to be held personally responsible for the consequences of their act in obedience to such order.[85] The reasoning behind this was that, 'The goal of an action carried out in order to execute an order is not only that which results from the nature of the act, but it is (or claims to be) also and above all the execution of the order.'[86] What Agamben leaves unsaid is that under the Nuremberg Charter, not only were appeals to domestic law and claims of official immunity excluded, but leaders, organisers, instigators and accomplices participating in the formulation or execution of a common plan or conspiracy to commit any of the listed crimes were responsible for all acts performed by any persons in execution of such a plan.[87] As a consequence, official positions were not only no longer a defence, but conversely became basis for criminal responsibility.

The model that was dethroned, or at the very least watered down or perhaps momentarily excluded, at Nuremberg follows what Agamben refers to as 'acts of office'. In the *Justice Case*, before considering the progressive degeneration of the judicial system under National Socialist rule, the tribunal observed that 'at least on paper the Germans had developed, under the Weimar republic, a civilized and enlightened system of jurisprudence'.[88] Furthermore, it took as true the defendants' contention that under the Third Reich German courts were required to follow German law – which is to say the expressed will of Hitler – even when it was contrary to international law.[89] Nevertheless, the claim that compliance with German law was a defence to the criminal charge was invalid because the tribunal's jurisdiction rested on enforcing the law declared by the International Military Tribunal Charter (IMT) and Control Council Law 10 as superior in authority to any German statute or decree. Furthermore, it pointed out that because governmental participation was actually a material element of the crimes charged, it could scarcely be said that it could also be a defence to the charges:

> The very essence of the prosecution case is that the laws, the Hitlerian decrees and the Draconic, corrupt, and perverted National Socialist judicial system themselves constituted the substance of war crimes and crimes against humanity and that participation in the enactment and enforcement of them amounts to complicity in crime.[90]

Importantly, no defendant was specifically charged in the indictment with the murder or abuse of any particular person. The charge essentially was of the abuse of legality by consciously participating in a

> government-organized system of cruelty and injustice, in violation of the laws of war and of humanity, and perpetrated in the name of law by the authority of the Ministry of Justice, and through the instrumentality of the courts.[91]

All clearly were acts of office holders – judges, prosecutors and the like – standing in for the regime.

In looking at official acts, Agamben introduces a crucial distinction between an act in its effective reality and an action insofar as an agent carries it out.[92] Agamben then traces the doctrine to the theory of the action of the devil within the providential economy.[93] In it, the devil serves God and God approves his work, but not the way in which he has worked.[94] It is perhaps apposite, then, that at his interrogation, on being asked when he had renounced 'the devil', Schmitt responded with a terse '1936'.[95] According to Agamben, such diverse concepts as Kelsen's pure theory of law, Kantian ethics, the political militant and the ministerial functionary are modelled by 'acts of office' – that is, duties.[96] In this model, what a person does and what that person is becomes indistinguishable. Furthermore, ethics in the West are ontologically bound to effectiveness and as a consequence, being and acting 'have no other representation other than effectiveness'.[97] In addition, there is a proximity between the ontology of command and the ontology of office with both being in the imperative mood of having-to-be, which for Agamben defines the ethics, ontology and politics of modernity.[98] Kant was of the view that subjective motive principles did not coincide with objective penal policy standards.[99] Indeed, the administration of punishment was a sovereign right to inflict pain upon a subject on account of a crime committed by that subject.[100] Consequently, judicial or juridical punishment could not be inflicted merely as a means to some other end, either with regard to the criminal or society (Kant 1887, 195). As a result, a criminal *qua* criminal does not have a voice regarding the legislation under which they are punished.[101] The social contract is clearly, then, not the basis for punishment.[102]

Contrast this with Adolf Eichmann, who at his trial in Israel declared that he had lived according to Kantian moral precepts, particularly to the definition of duty as 'that the principle of my will must always be such that it can become the principle of general laws' (Arendt 2006). He explained that he had knowingly and consciously abandoned this 'from the moment he was charged with carrying out the Final Solution', but 'that he had consoled himself with the thought that he no longer "was master of his own deeds", that he was unable "to change anything"'.[103] Arendt adds that in this wartime context,

> all that is left of Kant's spirit is the demand that a man do more than obey the law, that he go beyond the mere call of obedience and identify his own will with the principle behind the law – the source from which the law sprang.[104]

Arendt continues that in Kant's philosophy, that source was practical reason; however, in Eichmann's household use of him, 'it was the will of the Führer'.[105] Further,

> Whatever Kant's role in the formation of 'the little man's' mentality in Germany may have been, there is not the slightest doubt that in one respect Eichmann did indeed follow Kant's precepts: a law was a law, there could be no exceptions.[106]

Should Agamben and Arendt be correct, an ethical imperative to do one's duty has a distinctly Kantian ring. As a deontologist Kant found duties in terms of actions and not their consequences or their virtues or their character. It would not be possible to found a totalitarian system (of which fascism is exemplary) on Kantian thought.[107] Where natural law conflicted with positive law, Kant would favour the former. For him, the fundamental building block of ethics is the actions you take and not the consequences that follow. However, because Kant focuses on duties as actions, Kantian ethics dovetail closely with positive law once a political system is in place but not at the time of its founding. After all, he did write that it was 'the people's duty to endure even the most intolerable abuse of supreme authority'.[108] Consequently, for him the idea of duty involves submission to authority. It is fair to say, then – and the Eichmann example appears to bear this out – that if the political system becomes totalitarian, there is no explicit moral or ethical resource present in Kant to resist that system. In their commitment to positive law, Kantian ethics are designed for normal and not exceptional circumstances *in extremis*.

Schmitt considered Kelsen an exemplary liberal thinker.[109] In a rare instance of mutual agreement with Schmitt, Kelsen explained the matter in an article on the Nuremberg judgment published in 1947, in very similar

terms – that it was contrary to positive law and generally accepted principles of jurisprudence – to deduce that violations of international law entailed
individual criminal responsibility.[110] Kelsen's view was that 'acts performed by
individuals in command or authorized by their government were by that fact
acts of state over which no other state could claim jurisdiction regardless of
the said act being criminal under either international or domestic law'.[111] It
must be said, though, that for Kelsen international criminal law was an exception to the rule in at least two ways. First, barring of national jurisdiction did
not preclude international jurisdiction from coming into play[112] – indeed, it
seemed to demand it. Similarly, exclusion of war/using armed force (as instruments of national policy) did not preclude political violence as an enforcement tool of international law[113] – again, it seemed to imply it. Here the links
between Kant's *Perpetual Peace* and Kelsen's *Peace Through Law* begin to show
themselves beyond the mere continuity of everlasting peace through legal
means.[114] Danilo Zolo demonstrates just how much Kelsen borrowed from
Kant.[115] Not only was Kelsen's central premise of pursuing peace through the
medium of law previously contained in Kant, but their shared coordinates
include a cosmopolitan, universal and legitimate international legal system.[116]
Furthermore, Kant's *Critique of Pure Reason* heavily influenced Kelsen's *Pure
Theory of Law*.[117] However, with a different emphasis from Kelsen, Schmitt
maintained that the viciousness of crimes against humanity was *malum in se*.
Thus, through different routes, Schmitt and Kelsen found that no reference
to pre-existing positive law was necessary to constitute the criminal and sanc-
tionable nature of inhumane atrocities.[118]

Even so, Schmitt could not be held individually responsible on that basis.
Schmitt in the end was neither cleared nor convicted in a court of law and
remained under a cloud of suspicion as a result. This was especially so because
he refused to be de-Nazified right up to his death. The interrogation process
was not and could not be decisive in his case. Only a court would be able to
definitively absolve him. He was not willing to submit to de-Nazification if
that meant disowning his whole life's work – even his opportunism had its
limits.[119] This commitment effectively barred him from a formal academic
career for the rest of his life.

Conclusion

The historical record shows that Schmitt was against the National Socialists
before he was for them, which meant that afterwards he could rely on the
ambivalence of his intellectual disposition and the lack of an official role to
escape criminal sanction. Agamben's archaeology of the office traces a profound shift in role of the office that can be dated to precisely the period
Schmitt was being interrogated. Schmitt's reputation as Nazi Crown Jurist

did not translate to his holding an official position in the Third Reich, for which he could be criminally charged. This conclusion is a tacit indication that the liberal values of Schmitt's interrogators militated against holding him criminally responsible as opposed to morally or ethically responsible. In the final analysis, a liberal-based legal order was either unable or unwilling, or both, to convict this most implacable of enemies, which is in a way the final victory of liberalism (over its most bitter intellectual enemy) by keeping faith in and standing by its values. This is an unmistakeable but nevertheless qualified endorsement of liberalism's enduring utility, credibility and appeal against any other alternatives. However, this moral high ground is in danger of liquefaction given the illiberal acts of liberal democracies in the wake of the 9/11 terrorist attacks in 2001.[120]

Notes

1. C. Burchard, 'The Nuremberg Trial and Its Impact on Germany', *Journal of International Criminal Justice* 4 (2006): 800–29.
2. M. Koskenniemi, *From Apology to Utopia: The Structure of International Legal Argument* (New York: Cambridge University Press, 2005).
3. C. J. Emden, 'Constitutional Theory, 1928: Carl Schmitt and the Rechtsstaat', *Telos* 153 (2010): 159–92.
4. J. W. Bendersky, *Carl Schmitt: Theorist for the Reich* (Princeton, NJ: Princeton University Press, 1983); D. Dyzenhaus, 'The Morals of Modernity', *Canadian Journal of Philosophy* 28(2) (1989): 269–86.
5. See, for instance, the debates around the personal fitness of Professor Harold Hongju Koh (a former legal adviser to the US Department of State in the Obama Administration) to teach human rights at the New York University Law School: see Heller (2015).
6. C. Schmitt, *Writings on War*, trans. T. Nunan (Cambridge: Polity Press, 2011), 39.
7. Schmitt's conditions for legitimacy (*cf.* recognition of the right to engage in just or necessary warfare against the enemy in accordance with internal judgments (which entails normative or prescriptive relativism regarding ethics) and recognition of the co-existence of different groups with self-determination (which entails the Principle of Non-Intervention as an externalist strategy for securing security in terms of stability). The latter is what makes Schmitt a conservative thinker, of course. For the same reason, his approach belongs under so-called narrow stakeholder theory: see Matwijkiw and Matwijkiw, 'Post-conflict Justice: Legal Doctrine, General Jurisprudence, and Stakeholder Frameworks', in *Global Trends: Law, Policy & Justice: Essays in Honour of Professor Giuliana Ziccardi Capaldo*, edited by M. Bassiouni, 345–70 (Oxford: Oxford University Press, 2013), 361).
8. C. Schmitt, *The Concept of the Political* (Chicago: University of Chicago Press, 2007).
9. C. Schmitt, *Dialogues on Power and Space* (Cambridge: Polity Press, 2014), 189.
10. Schmitt, *The Concept of the Political*, 26.

11. Schmitt, *The Concept of the Political*, 27.
12. Schmitt, *The Concept of the Political*, 54.
13. M. Koskenniemi, *The Gentle Civilizer of Nations: The Rise and Fall of International Law 1870–1960* (Cambridge: Cambridge University Press, 2007), 422.
14. R. Mehring, *Carl Schmitt: A Biography* (Cambridge: Polity Press 2014), 44.
15. C. Schmitt, *Political Theology: Four Chapters on the Concept of Sovereignty*, trans. G. Schwab, 4th ed. (Chicago: University of Chicago Press, 1985); C. Schmitt, 'Age of Neutralisations and Depoliticisations' (1993) 96 *Telos* 119; Schmitt, *The Concept of the Political*; C. Schmitt, *Legitimacy and Legality* (Durham, NC: Duke University Press, 2004); C. Schmitt, *Political Theology II: The Myth of Closure of Any Political Theology* (Cambridge: Polity Press, 2008); C. Schmitt and H. Kelsen, *The Guardian of the Constitution* (Cambridge: Cambridge University Press, 2015).
16. Mehring, *Carl Schmitt*, 176.
17. Schmitt, *The Concept of the Political*, 70.
18. Schmitt, *The Concept of the Political*, 70.
19. Schmitt, *The Concept of the Political*, 71.
20. J. C. Donado, 'Heidegger's Letter to Schmitt'. *Telos*, 8 August 2015. www.telospress.com/heideggers-letter-to-schmitt.
21. Mehring, *Carl Schmitt*, 305.
22. Mehring, *Carl Schmitt*, 358–80.
23. Y. Sherratt, *Hitler's Philosophers* (New Haven, CT: Yale University Press, 2013), 302.
24. Mehring, *Carl Schmitt*, 323.
25. Schmitt, *The Concept of the Political*, 36.
26. 'Such a war is necessarily unusually intense and inhuman because, by transcending the limits of the political framework, it simultaneously degrades the enemy into moral and other categories and is forced to make of him a monster that must not only be defeated but also utterly destroyed': see Schmitt, *The Concept of the Political*, 36.
27. Schmitt, *The Concept of the Political*, 51.
28. 'Humanity as such cannot wage war because it has no enemy, at least not on this planet. The concept of humanity excludes the concept of the enemy, because the enemy does not cease to be a human being – and hence there is no specific differentiation in that concept. That wars are waged in the name of humanity is not a contradiction of this simple truth; quite the contrary, it has an especially intensive political meaning. When a state fights its political enemy in the name of humanity, it is not a war for the sake of humanity, but a war wherein a particular state seeks to usurp a universal concept against its military opponent. At the expense of its opponent, it tries to identify itself with humanity in the same way as one can misuse peace, justice, progress, and civilization in order to claim these as one's own and to deny the same to the enemy.' 'The concept of humanity is an especially useful ideological instrument of imperialist expansion, and in its ethical-humanitarian form it is a specific vehicle of economic imperialism. Here one is reminded of a somewhat modified expression of Proudhon's: whoever invokes humanity wants to cheat.' See Schmitt, *The Concept of the Political*, 54–5.
29. 'A war waged to protect or expand economic power must, with the aid of propaganda, turn into a crusade and into the last war of humanity. This is implicit

in the polarity of ethics and economics, a polarity astonishingly systematic and consistent. But this allegedly non-political and apparently even antipolitical system serves existing or newly emerging friend-and-enemy groupings and cannot escape the logic of the political.' See Schmitt, *The Concept of the Political*, 79.

30. Schmitt, *The Concept of the Political*, 14.
31. Schmitt, *The Concept of the Political*, 14.
32. Bendersky, *Carl Schmitt*, 195.
33. J. Müller, *A Dangerous Mind: Carl Schmitt in Post-War European Thought* (New Haven, CT: Yale University Press, 2003), 175.
34. Müller, *A Dangerous Mind*, 177.
35. Müller, *A Dangerous Mind*, 203.
36. Müller, *A Dangerous Mind*, 178.
37. Müller, *A Dangerous Mind*, 182.
38. Müller, *A Dangerous Mind*, 204.
39. Müller, *A Dangerous Mind*, 205.
40. Mehring, *Carl Schmitt*, 347.
41. Mehring, *Carl Schmitt*, 413.
42. Bendersky, *Carl Schmitt*, 202.
43. Müller, *A Dangerous Mind*, 207.
44. Müller, *A Dangerous Mind*, 226.
45. H. Arendt, *The Origins of Totalitarianism* (New York: Harcourt, Brace, Jovanovich, 1973), 339.
46. J. W. Bendersky, 'Carl Schmitt at Nuremberg', *Telos* 72 (1987): 91–6, 91.
47. Bendersky, 'Carl Schmitt at Nuremberg', 91.
48. Bendersky, 'Carl Schmitt at Nuremberg', 98.
49. See Schmitt, *The Concept of the Political*, 54; C. Schmitt, *Theory of the Partisan: Intermediate Commentary on the Concept of the Political* (New York: Telos, 2007), 95.
50. Loewenstein, 'Observations on the Personality and Work of Professor Carl Schmitt' (1945). Karl Loewenstein Papers, Box 46, Folder 46, Amherst College Archives and Special Collections, Amherst, MA. cited in A. Sitze, 'Carl Schmitt: An Improper Name' (2014). https://infrapolitica.files.wordpress.com/2014/10/carl-schmitt-an-improper-name.pdf.
51. Loewenstein, 'Observations', 1.
52. Loewenstein, 'Observations', 1.
53. Mehring, *Carl Schmitt*, 416.
54. Schmitt, *Political Theology II*, 121.
55. Schmitt, *Political Theology*, 100.
56. Schmitt, *Political Theology*, 102.
57. Schmitt, *Political Theology*, 106.
58. Mehring, Carl *Schmitt*, 413.
59. Schmitt, *Political Theology*, 99.
60. Schmitt, *Political Theology*, 98.
61. Schmitt, *Political Theology II*.
62. Mehring, Carl *Schmitt*, 66.
63. G. L. Ulmen, 'Return of the Foe', *Telos* 72 (1987): 187–93.
64. H. Melville, *Benito Cereno* (Raleigh, NC: Freebook, 2008).
65. Mehring, *Carl Schmitt*, 412.

66. A. Fischer-Lescano and G. Teubner, *Regime-Kollisionen* (Frankfurt: Suhrkamp, 2006), 127; C. Joerges and N. Singh Galeigh, *Dark Legacies of Europe* (Oxford: Hart, 2003).
67. T. Beebee, 'Carl Schmitt's Myth of Benito Cereno', *Seminar: A Journal of Germanic Studies* 42 (2012): 114–34.
68. C. Schmitt, *The Nomos of the Earth in the International Law of the Jus Publicum Europaeum* (New York: Telos, 2006).
69. Beebee, 'Carl Schmitt's Myth of Benito Cereno', 122.
70. Beebee, 'Carl Schmitt's Myth of Benito Cereno', 127.
71. Schmitt, *The Nomos of the Earth*, 192.
72. Schmitt, *The Nomos of the Earth*, 235.
73. Schmitt, *The Nomos of the Earth*, 235.
74. Mehring, *Carl Schmitt*, 422.
75. Mehring, *Carl Schmitt*, 410.
76. Simpson, *Law, War and Crime: War Crimes Trials and the Reinvention of International Law* (Cambridge: Polity Press, 2007), 159.
77. Schmitt, *Writings on War*, 157; W. Schabas, *The International Criminal Court: A Commentary on the Rome Statute* (Oxford: Oxford University Press, 2010), 40.
78. F. Mégret, 'Practices of Stigmatization', *Law and Contemporary Problems* 76, no. 3 (2013): 287–313.
79. D. Heller-Roazen, *The Enemy of All: Piracy and the Law of Nations* (Cambridge, MA: Zone Books, 2011), 23.
80. Schmitt, *Writings on War*, 29.
81. Simpson, *Law, War and Crime*, 177.
82. E. H. Gould, *Among the Powers of the Earth: The American Revolution and the Making of a New World Empire* (Cambridge, MA: Harvard University Press, 2012), 55.
83. S. Nouwen and W. Werner, 'Doing Justice to the Political: The International Criminal Court in Uganda and Sudan', *The European Journal of International Law* 21 (2010): 941–96, 963.
84. Nouwen and Werner, 'Doing Justice to the Political', 963.
85. G. Agamben, *Opus Dei: An Archaeology of Duty* (Stanford CA: Stanford University Press, 2013), 84.
86. Agamben, *Opus Dei*, 84.
87. United Nations, *Charter of the International Military Tribunal – Annex to the Agreement for the Prosecution and Punishment of the Major War Criminals of the European Axis ('London Agreement')*, Article 6 (8 August 1945), subsequent trials on Control Council Law No. 10, *Punishment of Persons Guilty of War Crimes, Crimes Against Peace and Against Humanity*, 20 December 1945, Official Gazette of the Control Council for Germany, No. 3, 31 January 1946, pp. 50–5 emphasis added.
88. *The Justice Case, Case No. 3, United States v. Altstoetter et al.*, Opinion and Judgment and Sentence, Green Series, Vol. 3 at 954 (Mil. Trib. No. 31947-12-04) [ILDC]. www.worldcourts.com/ildc/eng/decisions/1947.12.04_United_States_v_Altstoetter.pdf#.
89. *The Justice Case, Case No. 3.*
90. *The Justice Case, Case No. 3.*

91. *The Justice Case, Case No. 3.*
92. Agamben, *Opus Dei*, 21.
93. Agamben, *Opus Dei*, 23.
94. Agamben, *Opus Dei*, 23.
95. Schmitt, *Political Theology*, 420.
96. Agamben, *Opus Dei*, xii.
97. Agamben, *Opus Dei*, xii.
98. Agamben, *Opus Dei*, 84.
99. I. Kant, *The Philosophy of Law: An Exposition of the Fundamental Principles of Jurisprudence as the Science of Right* (Edinburgh: T. & T. Clark, 1887), 204.
100. Kant, *The Philosophy of Law*, 194.
101. Kant, *The Philosophy of Law*, 201.
102. Kant, *The Philosophy of Law*, 202.
103. H. Arendt, *Eichmann in Jerusalem: A Report on the Banality of Evil* (Harmondsworth: Penguin, 2006), 136.
104. Arendt, *Eichmann in Jerusalem*, 137.
105. Arendt, *Eichmann in Jerusalem*, 137.
106. Arendt, *Eichmann in Jerusalem*, 137.
107. M. D. A. Freeman and D. Lloyd, *Lloyd's Introduction to Jurisprudence* (London: Sweet & Maxwell, 2001), 113.
108. I. Kant, *The Metaphysical Elements of Justice* (Indianapolis, IN: Bobbs-Merrill, 1965), 86.
109. Müller, *A Dangerous Mind*, 206.
110. T. Weigend, '"In General a Principle of Justice": The Debate on the "Crime Against Peace" in the Wake of the Nuremberg Judgment', *Journal of International Criminal Justice* 10, no. 1 (2012): 41–58, 50.
111. A. Gattini, 'Kelsen's Contribution to International Criminal Law'. *Journal of International Criminal Justice* 2, no. 3 (2004): 795–809, 796; Kelsen 1994, 81).
112. H. Kelsen, *Peace Through Law* (Chapel Hill, NC: University of North Carolina Press, 1994), 86.
113. Kelsen, *Peace Through Law*, 4.
114. I. Kant, *Perpetual Peace* (New York: Liberal Arts Press, 1957) *Perpetual Peace;* Kelsen, *Peace Through Law*; D. Zolo, 'Hans Kelsen: International Peace Through International Law', *European Journal of International Law* 9, no. 2 (1998): 306–24.
115. D. Zolo, *Victors' Justice: From Nuremberg to Baghdad* (London: Verso, 2009).
116. Zolo, 'Hans Kelsen', 319.
117. Freeman and Lloyd, *Lloyd's Introduction to Jurisprudence*, 305.
118. Burchard, 'The Nuremberg Trial'.
119. Müller, *A Dangerous Mind*, 255.
120. See K. J. Greenberg and J. L. Dratel, *The Torture Papers: The Road to Abu Ghraib* (New York: Cambridge University Press, 2005).

5

Saving Humanity from Hell: International Criminal Law and Permanent Crisis

The UN was not created to take mankind to heaven, but to save humanity from hell.

Dag Hammerskjöld (quoted in Weiss 2011, 2)

Between Utopia and Dystopia

Crises – a medical term that has made its way into the heart of law and theology[1] – abound in international criminal law. The ravages of World War II brought forth the International Military Tribunal at Nuremberg (IMT) and the International Military Tribunal for the Far East at Tokyo (IMTFE). The break-up of the former Yugoslavia necessitated the creation of the International Criminal Tribunal for the former Yugoslavia (ICTY). Civil war in Rwanda brought the International Criminal Tribunal for Rwanda (ICTR) in its wake. Suffice to say that each of these crises, among others, was exemplary in providing the basis for creating and extending (once novel and temporary but now commonplace and permanent) international criminal jurisdiction. Agamben notes that:

> The very word expresses two semantic roots: the medical one, referring to the course of an illness, and the theological one of the Last Judgement. 'Crisis' in ancient medicine meant a judgement, when the doctor noted at the decisive moment whether the sick person would survive or die. The present understanding of crisis, on the other hand, refers to an enduring state. So this uncertainty is extended into the future, indefinitely and an endless process of decision never concludes.[2]

Koselleck noted that although the legal, theological and medical meanings of crisis were distinct and separate they could be taken together:

> The legal, theological, and medical usage of 'crisis' thus contains discipline-bound, specific meanings. Taken together, however, they could – in different ways – be incorporated into modern social and political language. At all times the concept is applied to life-deciding alternatives meant to answer

questions about what is just or unjust, what contributes to salvation or damnation, what furthers health or brings death.[3]

To demonstrate how crisis grounds legal and political jurisdiction, it is necessary to link the UN Security Council's (UNSC) role in international criminal law to liberal democratic values such as the rule of law. In addition, it is required to show how those values have been extended into international criminal law through crisis. In times of crisis, the gravity of the situation is such that decisive action is called for and yet the correct solution does not suggest itself. In a crisis anything is possible and necessity is the only available justification. A paradigmatic instance of this was the end of World War II and the dilemma of how to deal with the war criminals from the Axis powers.

Broadly speaking, the IMT and IMTFE prosecutions exemplified the legalisation of politics, punishing as they did what previously was a political act outside the realm of law.[4] Gerry Simpson relates how Winston Churchill for the UK initially contemplated summary execution, where Josef Stalin of the Soviet Union favoured show trials with no possibility of acquittals.[5] Franklin Roosevelt for the United States, however, came to the view that the best way to deal with the situation was through fair trials affording due process guarantees. Antonio Cassese retells of this as in principle a mainstay of democracy.[6] Carl Schmitt refers to it as inaugurating a global legal order of liberal democratic international justice.[7] Indeed, as Victoria Sentas and Jessica Whyte note, the 'law remains a fundamental source of legitimation of a crisis prone system'.[8] In other words, the crisis of armed conflict enabled the extension of the liberal democratic idea of the rule of law into international affairs through international criminal law.

As a result of this triumph of the liberal democratic approach to crisis in international criminal law, it is this chapter's argument that crisis in international criminal law provides a negative grounding for legal and political jurisdiction where, because nothing is ruled out, all things are possible and anything necessary is permissible simply by not or no longer being forbidden.[9] The law meanwhile remains in force but, given the UNSC's unique law-making and law-derogating role, is of no real significance, except as a mechanism for generating legitimacy that founds legality.[10] Political power and its own justification are not only ultimately unbridled, but the exigencies of a given critical situation even negatively ground the legality of the decisions taken. Crisis, moreover, can only be temporally and geographically limited in a local context, but not in a global one. It will be argued below that only efficacy can provide legitimacy in crisis, and thus it positively founds both jurisdiction and legality. However, if it were only simply a matter of efficacious conduct, why is the law necessary? This chapter proposes that the law is nevertheless necessary because liberal democratic political power absolutely needs the glory of judicial acclamation for its own legitimacy as a matter of the rule of law. Political power exercised outside of or contrary to law, even if effective, is inglorious and thus lacks the necessary qualities to found the consensus that liberalism requires. Institutional legitimacy and efficacy, as well as relationships between necessity and contingency, are resolved through judicial affirmation as legal glorification of political actions that have no positive grounding other than in themselves. This is because crisis itself cannot be a positive ground, but can only be used as negative justification.

First, the argument is made that international criminal law as a discipline was historically both born of crisis and specifically designed to meet crisis. Ordinarily, crises as overwhelming emergent situations are antithetical to laws, which are the product of time and reflection. Examining international criminal law invites us to reflect on what happens when quick action is required wherever there is seemingly little time for reflection. Moreover, whenever rules are laid down in response to crisis, then such rules gradually become permanent and institutionalised responses to crisis. This leads to the second point: that in practice there is a discernible shift through which once exceptional mechanisms gradually become so common and familiar as to be rendered indistinguishable from normal ones. This is true regarding not just the ICTY, the ICTR and the International Criminal Court (ICC), but also in relation to the examples of the Special Court for Sierra Leone (SCSL), the Extraordinary Criminal Chambers for Cambodia (ECCC) and the Special Tribunal for Lebanon (STL).

Third, the role of the UNSC in justifying and developing international criminal justice is absolutely ambivalent in that the UNSC rhetorically and practically navigates to avoid both utopian promises and dystopian futures. This is because it is implicitly charged with arresting catastrophe in a chaotic world, with the potential for oscillating towards either utopia or dystopia. Indeed, a momentary perfect balance between utopia and dystopia becomes virtually indistinguishable from either of them when viewed through the constraining keyhole of crisis. By employing its primary power to declare official crises, the UNSC tends to focus more on immediate crises that seem to require an element of force or coercion as opposed to real, slow-motion, ongoing accompaniments to those crises, such as environmental degradation, trade injustices, war profiteering and the like. International criminal law helps to harness this oscillation without end in the name of crisis as if acts done in response to crisis have something other than their own effectiveness as justification.

International Criminal Law: A Discipline of and for Crisis

Crisis, as far as the UNSC and the international criminal law it generates and triggers are concerned, is permanent and institutionalised. This is because, during crises, UNSC referrals invoke Chapter VII of the UN Charter, which deals with both actual breaches of international peace and security and potential threats to them.[11] In the first few months of 2013, the UNSC had over a dozen particular crises to deal with all over the globe.[12] Even though a crisis is imagined as immediate, localised and temporary, from the UNSC's perspective there is generally one either actual or potential crisis somewhere on the planet. As we shall see below, entertaining the very idea of the end of conflict and the finality of crisis with the triumph of liberal democracy resonates with the theological notion of an eschatology or end of time.[13] For better or worse, the UNSC is institutionally charged with the primary responsibility to deal with crisis, and crises are permanent. Effectively, exceptional circumstances are normalised in reality while at the same time being rhetorically maintained as exceptional.

One permanent paradox of international criminal law, as a subset of international law, that is brought to the fore during crises is its legitimacy, which depends on the extent to which it is able to provide for justice while its effectiveness relies on credible means for its enforcement. As Kofi Annan put it in the context of the Second Gulf War regarding the use of force to gain compliance with international law from Saddam Hussein: 'You can do a lot with diplomacy, but with diplomacy backed up by force you can get a lot more done.'[14] In this sense, the international community has itself set up a system where force is produced to 'solve' problems.[15] International lawyers in their own way essentially minister to this mysterious conjunction of might and right in the institution of the UNSC. That is, we are emphatically not revolutionaries but essentially proselytise the view that the best possible order is coincident with the necessary order.[16]

Dag Hammarskjöld, quoted in the epigraph that opens this chapter, succinctly anchors the poles of debate examined here. The wording is expressed in an unmistakeably faux-religious idiom. It defers paradise in order to postpone perdition by counselling giving up on utopia in order to escape dystopia. Most importantly, its import is to maintain the purpose of the United Nations in the perpetual interim, which is based on actual activity rather than any future realisation of an abstract principle. It is pragmatic not messianic, materialist rather than idealist, and imagines time as cyclical rather than linear. Herbert Knust observes that glancing 'through the gallery of demonic partnerships throughout the ages shows that no rank of society, no station of life was immune against the devil'.[17] Indeed even holy men and Christ himself as narrated in Mathew 4 are not excluded from the temptation to a deal with the devil where the promises of heaven and the fears of hell are both eschewed in favour of earthly or secular powers and wealth. Related to these themes, as we shall see, Hilary Charlesworth notes:

> What if we were to change the type of questions we ask? We could begin from the opposite end and examine what international law has to offer to the person who wants to pollute the environment or violate human rights. I imagine this as an international lawyer's version of C.S. Lewis' *Screwtape Letters* in which cheery letters from the Devil mock the ease of corrupting humans.[18]

This passage evokes at the very least the historically ambivalent role of lawyers who have not only set about limiting the use of power but have concurrently facilitated, enabled, justified and maintained its use.[19] What would Mephistopheles make of international criminal law other than reading its foundational texts with an ironic inflection? Agamben accuses lawyers of complicit silence about the killing machine inherently tied to law that he refers to as the state of exception.[20] In their defence, some lawyers have not been silent but have raised their voice in court.[21] Bonnie Honig agrees: The state of exception should be 'seen as part (even if an extreme part) of the daily rule of law-generated struggle between judicial and administrative power'.[22]

Agamben, in turn, is accused of making a dangerous move away from understanding law in its context as an epistemic practice of practical reasoning to a kind of ontological or metaphysical presentation of law.[23]

All that notwithstanding, this chapter takes the methodological approach of looking for historical 'signatures' of concepts in Agamben's sense of the term in the practice of the UNSC. These 'signatures' will be taken as indicating where a latter-day concept refers back to that concept's presence in and persistent reference to a separate sphere of thought.[24] In the present instance, the fields sharing a history of ideas are politics, law and religion. Examples include the temporary loanwords to law from the religious lexicon, such as Hammarskjöld and Charlesworth's words above, and sharing words, such as guilt between law and religion, immunity between biology and law, and the notion of 'body' between law, politics, religion and biology. This chapter focuses on a religious signature regarding the very words and ideas used in and structuring crucial legal and political contexts. This signature has been identified and outlined as affecting not merely vocabulary, idiom and grammar, but most importantly also conceptual structure, the foundational efficacy of paradoxes and generally accepted understandings of time as duration. It is hoped that in the end this effort will open up possibilities to alternative ways of thinking about the fundamental conceptual structures of international criminal law as well as provide food for new thoughts, such as refocusing international law on issues of structural justice and 'an international law of everyday life' that needs a methodology to consider non-elite perspectives.[25] This exploration includes analysing international criminal justice interventions from the point of view of the people at the business end of international criminal law. Those on whose behalf such intervention purportedly takes place at times have radically different appreciations of the relevant historical arc and its legal and political ramifications.

Martti Koskenniemi states that historical narrative as a style of legal writing liberates the political imagination to move more freely in the world of alternative choices while illuminating its false necessities and false contingencies.[26] Although legal vocabulary can seem deceptively open-ended, legal practice is often quite predictable.[27] This gap between vocabulary and practice can be explained when global politics is brought into the equation. For instance, as Charlesworth observes,[28] the legality of the NATO intervention in the then Federal Republic of Yugoslavia (FRY) was unsuccessfully brought before the International Court of Justice by the FRY in April 1999.[29] Carla Del Ponte, the then ICTY Prosecutor, considered, but ultimately dismissed, prosecutions of NATO actors over the bombing.[30] Even so, Milosevic was indicted in May 1999 by the ICTY for war crimes, surrendered to that Tribunal by the Serbian government and died during the trial.[31] Antonio Cassese, a towering international criminal law expert, justified the intervention in terms that the international rule of law should be 'sacrificed on the altar of human compassion'.[32] In general, the discursive structure of international law is for making arguments and not for arriving at conclusions.[33] It is necessarily contingent because a legal pronouncement would not be certain unless and until it was competently and officially delivered. The point is that even though good legal arguments could be made for either side in both cases, the side that carried the day was the more politically powerful one.

International lawyers are preoccupied with great crises rather than the politics of everyday life.[34] Charlesworth's argument is that when international law rhetorically focuses on crises, it is static, unproductive and severely restricts what are considered 'fundamental' questions and inquiries.[35] Crises divert attention from structural issues of global justice. One aspect of this restricted approach is that the 'facts' with which international lawyers deal are typically outside their own experiences and the discipline does not encourage weighing up competing versions of events.[36] For instance, the perspective of the developing world is not as prominent as it could be. The greatest political stakes in this legal debate are whether a new generation of developing world scholars can combine legal professionalism with strategic awareness of the limits and possibilities of international law.[37] As Charlesworth notes, developing world approaches to international law rarely if ever provide alternatives to what they critique.[38] From such a perspective, the historically Christian Eurocentricism of international law is not so much a criticism as a trite observation. However, this very triteness conceals the ongoing sway and profound power of that unique legacy. Moreover, while not precluded in principle, introducing, say, Confucian or even African ideas is exceedingly rare in practice.[39] Such scholars, in any case, will have to reckon with a ready-made constricting idiom and structural bias in international institutions.[40]

As part of the idiomatic structure, numerous international law texts employ case studies of crises as a counterweight to the formalism of the study of rules.[41] The reliance on these case studies actually illustrates that UNSC action itself greatly influences the perception of what the law actually is.[42] Often in UNSC practice, internal legal coherence and consistency are pitted and subsequently lose against existential problems of peace and war.[43] A case in point is the requirement under Article 27(3) of UN Charter regarding a concurrent vote of permanent members, which is not really observed, as abstention is not counted as a veto.[44] Given this legally unclear state of affairs, judicial authority carries with it the weighty expressive function of law where a law can have effect even outside of its direct enforcement.[45] In international criminal law, the UNSC's creation of ad hoc international criminal tribunals, as well as its referrals to the ICC under Chapter VII of the UN Charter, are excellent examples of the use of crises. The courts and tribunals themselves have at best solely expressed and affirmed a negatively grounded jurisdiction only by finding as a matter of strict legality that nothing prohibits its exercise.[46] Yet these judicial pronouncements in effect only affirm the power of the political institution that created the court itself, and thus enable the court's initial acceptance of jurisdiction and subsequent provision of legality. This judicial affirmation approving a political action that founds jurisdiction is subsequently referred to as evidence of a legally and politically efficacious decision. The legal decision demonstrably acts as an acclamation that provides glorification of an already effected political action. That legal glory is therefore only a reflection of an existing political power, but that self-same power is considered not fully efficacious (because it is not yet legitimised) until it is glorified. Power thus refers to glory and glory reflects back the power. That is why the law matters to politics or, put another way, why power needs glory.[47] So how does this legal machine that utilises false contingency and false necessity to generate glory operate?

Getting To and From 'twas never thus' to 'twas ever thus'

A major flaw of utilising crisis as a model to understand international criminal law is the repetitive rediscovery of an issue as if for the first time. Therefore, analyses have little to no reference to past knowledge or present conventions.[48] That is, every set of circumstances constituting a crisis is taken to be unique – literally without precedent, even when followed subsequently by similar iterations of the same mechanism. This is especially true in international criminal law. Moreover, as can be seen from the proliferation of international criminal tribunals, these so-called exceptions frequently become the new rule.[49] The legal basis for establishing international tribunals and furnishing them with criminal jurisdiction is a case in point.

The legal basis for establishing the ICTY was written up only after the political decision to set it up had been made. In the UN Secretary-General's report that led to the establishment of the ICTY, he noted that treaty-based bodies were the normal way of setting up judicial bodies that would exercise international jurisdiction over individuals criminally responsible for violating international humanitarian law.[50] Such a method allowed not only for detailed and comprehensive discussion of issues regarding establishment, but also enabled the full exercise of sovereign will. However, the usual way of doing things would not do because of the considerable amount of time it would take to debate, draft, sign and ratify such an instrument and the fact that its coming into force would by no means be a given. Such was the urgency of the situation that it even precluded the UN General Assembly's participation. The exceptional procedure of a Chapter VII resolution setting up a tribunal was favoured for reasons of immediacy and efficiency, and justified in the particular circumstances of the former Yugoslavia. Indeed, as a reaction to the particularity of the situation, the relevant UNSC Resolution was so limited in scope and duration that it did not provide a general or permanent international criminal jurisdiction.[51] The treaty route was described as too cumbersome and uncertain for the circumstances at hand. The report noted that discussions at the General Assembly and within the ILC canvassing a permanent court that would have universal jurisdiction were already in the offing. A UNSC resolution under Chapter VII was thus expeditious to meet this particular set of events. It was therefore intended not to legislate new law but only to provide a new mechanism for the enforcement of established law: an unprecedented tribunal applying existing law. Despite the language repeatedly emphasising the particular nature of the Yugoslavian crisis, the report noted that setting up a tribunal was itself legally justifiable both by being consistent with previous UNSC practice and as an enforcement measure under Chapter VII. This would provide it with the extraordinary effect of being immediately effective and accompanied by a binding obligation over all states to do whatever was necessary to achieve its aims.

The legal basis for establishing the ICTR only took four paragraphs to outline, whereas it had taken thirteen in the case of the ICTY.[52] The case of

Rwanda followed a similar pattern to the former Yugoslavia in referencing exceptional circumstances particular to it. Even if the model of setting up the ICTR drew from the experience of, and closely followed, the ICTY in practice, it would appear from the relevant report of the UN Secretary-General (UNSG) as if the ICTY was not for that reason to be considered wholly adequate legal precedent. This was because Rwanda was still considered on its own particular merits, the ICTY notwithstanding. A significant difference was that Rwanda itself fully participated in the ICTR's establishment and so its sovereignty was not in question. Subsequent judicial decisions and state practice do appear to confirm in principle the legality of the establishment of such ad hoc tribunals by the UNSC.[53]

The ICC then came along and was established in a hybrid form, as can be seen in Article 13 of its Rome Statute.[54] The court may exercise jurisdiction if a State Party refers a situation to the Prosecutor, by the UNSC acting under Chapter VII of the UN Charter, or by the Prosecutor initiating an investigation of their own motion. It is therefore not only a treaty-based body following the recognised-as-normal form and process, but it also institutionalises the exceptional power first seen and developed with the ad hoc tribunals created by UNSC referrals under the UN Charter. This exceptional power has now been normalised in the Rome Statute and enshrined in treaty law. Furthermore, under Article 10, matters of jurisdiction, admissibility and applicable law do not affect existing law, nor do they create new law outside of the Statute. Effectively, that provision insulates the core portions of the Rome Statute from being invoked as authoritative on either customary or general international law.[55] This effectively means that both treaty and UNSC powers to create tribunals are concurrently inside and outside the Statute. They are, to borrow a phrase from Equity, like two streams in a river whose waters do not mix, as the cases of ad hoc tribunals set up after the ICC for Lebanon, Cambodia and Sierra Leone also attest. George Fletcher and David Ohlin consequently view the ICC as two courts, an independent criminal court enacted by parties to the Rome Statute and, in the case of referrals by the Security Council under Article 13(b) of the Statute, an organ for restoring collective peace and security transcending 'the classic goals of criminal law to adjudicate individual guilt'.[56] Therefore, depending 'on how a case is generated, then, the ICC can be either an independent criminal court, prosecuting international criminality for its own sake, or a UN body prosecuting criminals as an instrument to advance the Council's security objectives'.[57]

By the time setting up the Special Tribunal for Lebanon (STL) came round, a single paragraph sufficed to provide and explain its legal basis.[58] That legal basis is a treaty between the United Nations and Lebanon.[59] The STL is *sui generis* being neither a subsidiary organ of the United Nations, nor part of the Lebanese judiciary.[60] In defining the legal basis, the UN Secretary-General reviewed UN practice over the past thirteen years, which revealed three different types of founding instruments for international or internationally assisted tribunals. These bodies were established by Security Council resolution, national statute or by agreement between the United Nations and the country directly interested in the creation of the tribunal.[61]

Bruno Simma acknowledges that in so-called 'hard cases' or for our purposes, crisis situations political imperatives and morally based arguments dictate actions outside the law.[62] The UNSC Chapter VII power is inexhaustible. It uses crises as a state of exception in order to simultaneously suspend and fulfil the law.[63] Even when courts examine this power, it is only confirmed in the double negative (the UNSC does not have this power to found legal tribunals). The suppleness of crisis is such that not even Chapter VII exhausts its fecundity in creating precedents in fact that are not precedents in law. This extract from the UK House of Lords debating the resort to force in Iraq before the Second Gulf War makes the points discussed above clear. It is grounded on a false necessity for war, relies upon decisions to be taken in light of circumstances at the time (not previously laid-down rules), all options are left open (nothing is ruled out – meaning therefore force is ruled in) and the Kosovo campaign is cited for support but emphatically not as precedent:

> *Lord Bach*: What I have mentioned today are, I repeat, prudent preparations: first, to put up a credible threat of force against Saddam Hussein, but also in case war is necessary – which is something that is neither imminent nor inevitable. It would be the Government's preference that there should be a second resolution, if that is necessary, before any force was used. But I have to tell the noble Lord that any decision on further action by the Security Council will be taken in the light of the circumstances at the time and that all options are open.
>
> It is important to state that it is up the Security Council to uphold its authority and to take whatever action is necessary to ensure full compliance. Historical parallels can be dangerous, but it is perhaps worth noting that the Kosovo campaign was not one that was supported by the Security Council. I think that very few Members of this House would say that that was not a campaign that deserved to succeed or that it was not in the interests of humanity.[64]

The NATO bombing campaign in the FRY reinforced the idea that collective security and the international order, at the end of the day, are based on the threat of the use of force (Charlesworth 2002, 390). This flight from law makes violence seem, if not intuitive, then inevitable. International lawyers interpret intervention as in itself almost automatically active and productive, while non-intervention is inactive and negative.[65] The only possible courses of action in the face of a crisis are to act or not to act. In this way, international law steers clear of analysis of longer-term trends and structural problems. Robin Cook, the then British Foreign Secretary, compared the intervention in Kosovo to the fall of the Berlin Wall in 1989, marking the end of another crisis, the Cold War.[66] In his view, the Kosovo intervention appeared to violate international law because it began without taking the matter to the UNSC under Chapter VII of the United Nations Charter. However, the United Kingdom together with the United States argued that it was consistent with the humanitarian values of the Charter and that armed intervention in another state to protect human rights was acceptable in international law regardless of national sovereignty.[67] Here crisis enabled sovereignty, a key principle of international law to be trumped by humanitarian principles.

Opposed to this position, Simon Chesterman and Michael Byers point out that the NATO bombing was a regression by centuries to when military force was the default tool of powerful states and the less powerful sought protection in alliances rather than liberal democratic multilateral institutions or international law.[68] Similarly, the report of the Independent International Commission on Kosovo concluded that the NATO intervention breached international law because it was not authorised by the UN Security Council; still, it was morally and politically legitimate as a response to serious human rights violations.[69] These legal arguments did not carry the day in the face of NATO opposition. International relations scholars appear less exercised taking a position on the NATO campaign, perhaps because it is more easily interpreted in the paradigm of power politics than in the international lawyers' world of objective legal principles that are justified by reference to the rule of law.[70]

UNSC as a Force Arresting Catastrophe

The essential connection between the UNSC's power to regulate international violence and its ability to set up criminal tribunals was first judicially confirmed in the *Prosecutor v. Tadić* case in 1995.[71] Only then did it subsequently find its way into the Rome Statute. As mentioned earlier, Article 13 of the Rome Statute codifies three separate modes for exercising jurisdiction. A referral by the UNSC, however, is conceptually a very different proposition in that the power therein flows from UNSC action that was not explicitly provided for in the UN Charter. As explained above, it took judicial affirmation by the ICTY in the *Tadić* case to confirm it.[72] That court said that 'neither the text nor the spirit of the [United Nations] Charter conceives of the UNSC as *legibus solutus* (unbound by law)'. Yet the court essentially recognised a power of the UNSC that did not proceed from anything more than the acts of the UNSC itself. However, as the court pointed out, because that power was not limitless or subject to no review, it had to comply with the conditions of its exercise, which in this case were the restoration and maintenance of international peace and security. The inherent jurisdiction of the court to decide was described as inversely proportional to the textual discretion of the UNSC to act. In other words, the UNSC could act to give jurisdiction to the ICTY only insofar as doing so was not inconsistent with the Council's mandate. Further, the court clarified that the Charter conceived of the Council as having specific powers (not absolute fiat), which could not exceed those of the United Nations itself in its jurisdiction and its internal divisions of power.

The capacity of the UNSC to invoke Chapter VII powers to initiate or indeed stop an investigation by the ICC as enshrined in Article 15 of the Rome Statute thus historically originated from UNSC Resolution 808 of 1993 as affirmed by the ICTY. José Alvarez unfavourably compares the decision of the Appellate Chambers of the Special Tribunal for Lebanon (STL) in the case of *Ayyash and others*, to the ICTY's *Tadić* judgment. In the *Ayyash* case, as it was in the *Tadić* case, the defence fundamentally challenged the jurisdiction and legality of the Tribunal. It, however, met with different results at the appellate stage where that tribunal found that it did not have the power to engage in 'judicial review' over the UNSC.[73] Alvarez criticises this STL Appeal Chamber's finding as affirming that the UNSC is unbound by law.[74] The thing to note, however, is that regardless of the opposed finding, the effect of both *Tadić* and *Ayyash* is that the UNSC gets its way and the accused is still subject to trial.

It is interesting that when the ICTY needed to explain and justify the then novel idea that the UNSC could indeed create an international tribunal, it reached for the obscure phrase to state that the Security Council is a creature of law, not a lawless entity. Thanos Zartaloudis traces how the expression *'legibus solutus'* was transferred from imperial Rome to medieval ecclesiastical authorities and onward to the notion of 'the people' as a politically legitimising entity.[75] Kenneth Pennington, in turn, provides four different but related meanings for *legibus solutus*.[76] The first is the prince's authority to change, derogate or dispense from positive law. The second is the prince's immunity from prosecution. The third is the prince's authority to transgress or dispense from the normal rules governing the legal system. The fourth is the prince's power to transgress the rights of the subject.

This taxonomy seems to indicate that the ICTY in *Tadić* only referenced the third meaning regarding the transgression of or dispensation from the normal rules governing the legal system. The ICTY was therefore saying that the UNSC was not *legibus solutus* in the sense that it did not have the authority to transgress the system's normal legal rules, even though it left unsaid that the UNSC was *legibus solutus* in at least the first sense by not being explicitly excluded from setting up novel international criminal tribunals and therefore able to do so. The UN Charter, along with the Nuremberg trials, brought forth the international community as a legal concept that placed the leaders of all human communities under the rule of international law.[77] Therefore, in their wake, any authority should theoretically never be above the law in the sense of acting completely outside of and with no reference to the law. The point is that the UNSC is not absolved of legal obligations.[78] Setting up criminal tribunals is part of its power, even though that is in tension with its primarily police functions.[79] This is the only legally defensible position because a legal system is the weaving of legal rules to legally regulated institutions, leaving no power in the state or in society that is *de legibus solutus*.[80] That is, all powers are subject to the legal authority of other powers and nobody is supposed to be above or beyond the rules. How can the rules address imminent or actual crises or catastrophes when these by their nature seem to resist the application of ordinary rules or regimes of law? How do we extend the rule of law to cover crisis through international criminal law?

Hammarskjöld's crucial words quoted at the beginning of the chapter were not only expressed in a Christian idiom, but sit squarely within a framework with Christian antecedents. Secularisation is intrinsic to Christianity.[81] As the religion of secularisation, it is 'no longer, but still, religion'.[82] The Peace of Augsburg in 1555 inaugurated the modern European settlement between politics and religion that was reinforced and augmented by the Westphalian Peace of 1648.[83] It is easy to forget Westphalia's secularised religious power turning the earlier logic on its head. Instead of religious leaders choosing temporal rulers, temporal rulers chose the religion for their realms. The notion that now political rulers could choose the faith of their realms, rather than religious leaders choosing political leaders, *cuius regio, eius religio,* led to 'a Christian and Universal Peace'.[84] Modern politics was rendered possible because it acquired formerly religious power. Even while liberal politics disarticulates religious authority *de facto*, if not *de jure*, liberal peace is derivative of as well as parodying a transcendent sovereignty (Fletcher 2004, 59). Thus imperial theology feeds 'on the remnants of eschatological history and their abandoned meanings'.[85] Speaking with reference to these abandoned meanings, George Steiner states that when belief in neither Heaven nor Hell exists, Hell nevertheless proves easier to recreate, thus there is currently an extinct theology at work, whose death has produced its parody where 'the concentration and death camps of the twentieth century are Hell made immanent'.[86] This hell is directly resonant with Hammarskjöld's quote as well as with the atrocities that gave rise to international criminal law.

According to Agamben, there is more at stake here than meets the eye because every power that thinks of itself as destined to block or delay catastrophe may be considered a secularisation of the '*Katechon*' – a biblical idea of something restraining hell but in the process perpetually postponing heaven.[87] This is specifically from Thessalonians 2, 6–7 where Paul states in an eschatological context that Christians must not behave as if the apocalypse would happen tomorrow, since the revelation of the Antichrist is conditional upon the removal of something or someone that restrains him – that restraint being the *Katechon*. The *Katechon* therefore prevents the eschatological crisis of the end of the world, but by so doing also prevents the apocalypse where Christ reveals himself. Koselleck notes the crossover between the juridical and theological meanings of crisis regarding the Last Judgment and the expectation of the apocalypse.[88]

According to Paul Fletcher, imperial political theology utilises the metaphysics of crisis and, given its necessary temporality, its mood is unequivocally imperative.[89] Chapter VII resolutions are in the imperative mood, which is to say in the form of a commandment. To further understand the rhetoric used by the UNSC, Aristotle's classification can be relied on. He classified rhetoric in three ways: political, which looks to the future and is hortatory; law, which looks at the past in making judgments; and ceremony, which focuses on the present.[90] In a somewhat different manner, Giorgio Agamben traces two ontologies relevant to this discussion. The first is the assertion, which is in the indicative mood, and the second is the commandment, which is in the imperative mood. One refers to 'is', the other to 'be'. One belongs to science and philosophy, the other to politics, law, religion and magic.[91] The UNSC is definitely political in its rhetoric and in that regard brings into being legal jurisdiction merely by the power of pronunciation.

Martti Koskenniemi notes in passing the ambivalence of the *Katechon* while coincidentally identifying Carl Schmitt as the most acerbic critic of liberal universal humanitarianism.[92] Schmitt utilises this idea of what or who restrains to describe the contemporary as caught between the in-between times. Just as UNSC actions are.[93] Schmitt then recasts history as a long interim and not a long march towards some imagined goal.[94] For Agamben, the *Katechon* defers the end of days from becoming concrete.[95] This neutralises the very idea of salvation in history of any sort (including through international criminal law). In accordance with Agamben,[96] with specific application to international criminal law, Walter Benjamin's definition of guilt as an originally juridical concept that was transferred to the religious sphere supports Schmitt's thesis that the concept of guilt is 'not an essence but an operation'.[97] For Benjamin, law is a residue of demonic existence, while Schmitt asserts that the basis of guilt is not the freedom of the ethical human, but only the controlling force of a sovereign power that only slows the Antichrist.[98] For Schmitt, therefore, the notion of guilt, which is central to international criminal law, is linked to the *Katechon* and refers to an operation of law rather than an intrinsic objective quality. It is the result of an official act rather than the status of any real being.

A crisis allows us to factor out ambiguities and complex contexts.[99] For Paolo Virno, this ambivalence of the *Katechon* is accompanied by oscillation and makes up cultural apocalypses such as we see conjured up to justify actions undertaken in response to crisis.[100] Roberto Esposito expounds further on this ambivalence of the *Katechon* as the positive of a negative: the *Katechon* restrains evil by holding it within itself, confronts evil from within by hosting it, defers evil but does not eradicate it because eradicating evil would be to eliminate itself.[101] It delays the explosion of evil at the price of preventing the victory of good. The constitutive juridical principle of the *Katechon* opposes the absence of law by taking it up inside itself and giving it form, rule and norm.[102] It nurtures and is nurtured by iniquity, opposing by preserving and confronting by incorporating.[103] It fulfils the law not through obedient action but in the form of potential action.[104] The *Katechon* imposes the norm on both messianic and satanic anomie.[105] It can be any institution that guarantees order such as any state, or the Church or even be the point of intersection between politics and law and religion. It is expressible as a structural analogy and may even function as a religious legitimation of power. The sovereign state, which the UNSC imitates, now and then 'needs a sacred core around which to establish its legitimacy in a way that goes beyond its historical origin and prolongs its life over time'.[106] The UNSC reprises the *Katechon* function in that they are both made immortal by the infinite mortality of sacrificed subjects under their jurisdiction.[107] The UNSC plays the role of *Katechon* during crisis to restrain total breakdown, and crisis itself is actually or potentially (which is really the same thing) permanent.

Virno is of the view that because the *Katechon* impedes the coming of the Antichrist, yet this coming is a condition for the redemption promised by the Messiah, the *Katechon* also impedes the redemption.[108] Institutionally, the *Katechon* adapts itself best to the permanent state of exception in the boundary between legal and factual questions.[109] The ambivalence of the infinite regress by which questions of fact can always be seen in questions of law and vice versa is restrained (but not removed) by the *Katechon* (Virno 2008, 64). Virno notes the ambivalence of critical situations where loss offers the only possibility of redemption, where crisis offers no remedy apart for what the danger itself describes and prescribes.[110] Culturally, apocalypse is the ritualistic accompaniment of the state of exception where crisis implies the suspension of ordinary law.[111] This provides an environment where a normative proposition is simultaneously an instrument of control and a phenomenon to be controlled, the unit of measurement and the reality to be measured.[112] Virno further locates the *Katechon* in verbal language as 'the maximum source of danger' as well as 'the authentic arresting force'.[113] Language therefore has a dual structure especially in the context of constructing the apocalypse where the crisis is also a renewal for humanity.[114] Language brings forth the danger and is also the force that restrains it.[115]

What could be a more exemplary *Katechon* than the referee of the football match that took place between the SS and inmates during a break from work at Auschwitz as recounted by Primo Levi?[116] Presumably, despite the sheer horror of the camp, he was scrupulously fair in administering the game, and was equally ready to award free kicks for infringements to either side. Is the referee like Faust or like Mephistopheles? Agamben says that this moment of normalcy is the true horror of the camp and if we do not succeed in understanding and stopping the match then all hope is lost.[117] The match is never over but continues regardless of time and place.[118] Therefore, while seemingly neutral, ambivalent and ambiguous, the *Katechon* is on balance necessarily tolerant of evil and is therefore to be resisted.

Real Versus Official Crises

On the back of the preceding discussion we can make at least three provisional conclusions to help us drive to a final conclusion. First, international criminal law is both made in and made for crisis; second, it is designed to address brief moments in time that are in reality of perpetual continuation; and third, the UNSC has the central role in responding to crisis by ambivalently restraining catastrophe. Setting up or setting in motion the machinery of international criminal justice is one of the tools at its disposal. Essentially, the UNSC administers international order through, among other means, international criminal justice. International justice depends as much on matters of administration as on questions of law.[119] This administrative managerial approach is mostly about actor's interests so the formal aspects of legality, such as hard and fast rules, are viewed unfavourably as obstacles.[120] The task at hand for many lawyers, according to Koskenniemi, remains 'how to smooth the prince's path'.[121] This approach also conceals a normativity privileging values and actors occupying dominant positions in international institutions without any critical stance.[122] Liberal democracy in the form that is now global in its reach is and always will be in crisis because it constantly redirects its subject's gaze from the unsatisfactory present toward a future of unfulfilled possibilities.[123] This notion of management of crisis is therefore key, and the law is only a handmaiden to this. In Agamben's terms, we should focus more on the police and less on law, less on sovereignty and more on government.[124]

By focusing on how the response to crisis is governed and administered, we can see through the analysis above that it is only by the UNSC considering a particular situation as critical that it becomes officially so. Not as a matter of essence, but one of operation. This separates the subject of the action from the action itself. In international criminal law, crisis is not an essence but an operation. Likewise, and by extension, guilt is not an essence but an operation. The action is effective regardless of the morality of the actor or the factual basis of the situation.[125] That is why non-elite perspectives are routinely ignored and thereby are as good as non-existent. The efficacy of official UNSC actions under crisis is indifferent to its morality because morality is not what affects its actions. Only its official status as being primarily responsible for keeping the peace brings efficacy to its acts. Moral principles are consequently only reached for to provide rhetorical legitimation. It is this paradigm of official acts being effective notwithstanding reality that we need to interrogate to meaningfully distinguish 'real' from 'official' crises.

Notes

1. R. Koselleck. 'Crisis', trans. M. W. Richter, *Journal of the History of Ideas* 67 (2006): 358.
2. Agamben, cited in Koselleck, 'Crisis', 358.
3. Koselleck, 'Crisis', 358.
4. G. J. Simpson, *Law, War and Crime: War Crimes Trials and the Reinvention of International Law* (Cambridge: Polity Press, 2007), 97.
5. Simpson, *Law, War and Crime*, 112.
6. A. Cassese and P. Gaeta, *Cassese's International Criminal Law*, 3rd ed. (Oxford: Oxford University Press, 2013), 256.
7. C. Schmitt, *Writings on War*, trans. T. Nunan (Cambridge, Polity Press, 2011), 39.
8. V. Sentas and J. Whyte, 'Law, Crisis, Revolution: An Introduction', *Australian Feminist Law Journal* 31 (2009): 9.
9. *S.S. Lotus (France v Turkey)* (1927), Permanent Court of International Justice Publications, Series A, No. 9, at 18 (7 September).
10. G. Agamben, *Homo Sacer: Sovereign Power and Bare Life* (Stanford, CA: Stanford University Press, 1998), 36.
11. Article 39 of United Nations, Charter of the United Nations, 24 October 1945, 1 UNTS XVI.
12. Meetings conducted/Actions taken by the Security Council in 2013. www.un.org/Depts/dhl/resguide/scact2013.htm.
13. See critique of F. Fukuyama, *The End of History and the Last Man* (New York: The Free Press, 2006) in J. Gray, *Black Mass: Apocalyptic Religion and the Death of Utopia* (New York: Farrar Straus and Giroux (2007).
14. United Nations. UN Press Release SG/SM/6470 Transcript of Press Conference by Secretary-General Kofi Annan at United Nations Headquarters, 24 February 1998. www.un.org/News/Press/docs/1998/19980224.SGSM6470.html.

15. H. Charlesworth, 'International Law: A Discipline of Crisis', *The Modern Law Review* 65 (2002): 385.
16. R. Esposito, *Immunitas: The Protection and Negation of Life* (Cambridge: Polity Press, 2011), 77.
17. H. Knust, 'From Faust to Oppenheimer: The Scientist's Pact with the Devil', *Journal of European Studies*, 13 (49–50) (1983): 123.
18. Charlesworth, 'International Law', 392.
19. M. Koskenniemi, 'The Politics of International Law, 20 Years Later', *European Journal of International Law* 20, no. 1 (2009): 17.
20. G. Agamben, *State of Exception* (Chicago: Chicago University Press, 2005).
21. B. Schotel, 'Reviews: Defending Our Legal Practices: A Legal Critique of Giorgio Agamben's *State of Exception*' (2009) *Amsterdam Law Forum*. http://ojs.ubvu.vu.nl/alf/article/view/68/124.
22. B. Honig, *Emergency Politics: Paradox, Law, Democracy* (Princeton: Princeton University Press, 2009), 85.
23. Schotel, 'Reviews: Defending Our Legal Practices'.
24. G. Agamben, *The Signature of All Things: On Method* (New York: Zone Books, 2009), 40.
25. Charlesworth, 'International Law', 390.
26. Koskenniemi, 'The Politics of International Law', 18.
27. Koskenniemi, 'The Politics of International Law', 9.
28. Charlesworth, 'International Law', 390.
29. *Case Concerning the Legality of the Use of Force (Yugoslavia v United States et al.)* 1999 ICJ Rep.
30. *Final Report to the Prosecutor by the Committee established to Review the NATO Bombing Campaign Against the Federal Republic of Yugoslavia*, para 1, www.un.org/icty/pressreal/nato061300.htm.
31. See www.un.org/icty/indictment/english/2,<4-05-99milo.htm, cited in Charlesworth, 'International Law', 379.
32. A. Cassese, '*Ex Iniuria Ius Oritur*: Are We Moving Towards International Legitimation of Forcible Countermeasures in the World Community?', *European Journal of International Law* 10 (1999): 25.
33. M. Koskenniemi, *From Apology to Utopia: The Structure of International Legal Argument* (New York: Cambridge University Press, 2005), 67.
34. Charlesworth, 'International Law', 389.
35. Charlesworth, 'International Law', 377.
36. Charlesworth, 'International Law', 384.
37. Koskenniemi, 'The Politics of International Law', 9; S. Marks, 'False Contingency', *Current Legal Problems* 62, no. 1 (2009), 17.
38. H. Charlesworth, 'Current Trends in International Legal Theory. In *Public International Law: An Australian Perspective*, 2nd ed., edited by S. K. N. Blay, R. W. Piotrowicz and B. M. Tsamenyi (Melbourne: Oxford University Press, 2005), 407.
39. N. Muvangua and D. Cornell, *uBuntu and the Law: African Ideals and Post-Apartheid Jurisprudence* (New York: Fordham University Press, 2012); C. G. Weeramantry, *Universalising International Law* (Leiden: Martinus Nijhoff, 2004).
40. Koskenniemi, 'The Politics of International Law', 10.

41. R. Wedgwood, 'Unilateral Action in the UN System', *European Journal of International Law* 11, no. 2 (2000): 377.
42. Wedgwood, 'Unilateral Action in the UN System', 356.
43. Koskenniemi, 'The Politics of International Law', 8.
44. Wedgwood, 'Unilateral Action in the UN System', 354.
45. C. R. Sunstein, 'On the Expressive Function of Law', *University of Pennsylvania Law Review* 144, no. 5 (1996): 2021–53.
46. *Prosecutor v. Tadić*, Appeals Chamber, Decision on the Defence Motion for Interlocutory Appeal on Jurisdiction, ICTY, case No IT-94-1-AR72, of 2 October 1995.
47. G. Agamben, *The Sacrament of Language: An Archaeology of the Oath* (Stanford, CA: Stanford University Press, 2011), 195.
48. Charlesworth, 'International Law', 384.
49. Koskenniemi, 'The Politics of International Law', 10.
50. Paragraphs 18–30 of Report of the Secretary General pursuant to paragraph 2 of Security Council Resolution 808, 3 May 1993. www.icty.org/x/file/Legal%20Library/Statute/statute_re808_1993_en.pdf.
51. UNSC, UNSC Resolution 808/1993, www.icty.org/x/file/Legal%20Library/Statute/statute_808_1993_en.pdf 1993).
52. Paragraphs 6-9 S/1995/134, 13 February 1995, Report of the Secretary-General on International Tribunal (Rwanda), paragraphs 18–30, http://daccess-ods.un.org/access.nsf/Get?Open&DS=S/1995/134&Lang=E&Area=UNDOC. Report of the Secretary General pursuant to paragraph 2 of Security Council Resolution 808, 3 May 1993. www.icty.org/x/file/Legal%20Library/Statute/statute_re808_1993_en.pdf.
53. A. Cassese, *International Criminal Law*, 2nd ed. (Oxford: Oxford University Press, 2008), 327; A. Zahar and G. Sluiter, *International Criminal Law: A Critical Introduction* (New York: Oxford University Press, 2008), 9.
54. Opened for signature 17 July 1998, 2187 UNTS 3, art 83(2) (entered into force 1 July 2002).
55. W. Schabas, *The International Criminal Court: A Commentary on the Rome Statute* (Oxford: Oxford University Press, 2010), 267.
56. G. P. Fletcher and J. D. Ohlin, 'The ICC – Two Courts in One?', *Journal of International Criminal Justice* 4, no. 3 (2006): 427.
57. Fletcher and Ohlin, 'The ICC – Two Courts in One?', 427.
58. Report of the Secretary-General on the establishment of a special tribunal for Lebanon 15 November 2006, S/2006/893. http://daccess-dds-ny.un.org/doc/UNDOC/GEN/N06/617/97/PDF/N0661797.pdf?OpenElement.
59. Report of the Secretary-General S/2006/893.
60. Report of the Secretary-General S/2006/893.
61. Report of the Secretary-General pursuant to paragraph 6 of resolution 1644 (2005) 21 March 2006, S/2006/176. http://daccess-dds-ny.un.org/doc/UNDOC/GEN/N06/277/44/PDF/N0627744.pdf?OpenElement/.
62. B. Simma, 'NATO, the UN and the Use of Force: Legal Aspects', *European Journal of International Law* 10 (1999): 22.
63. Agamben, *State of Exception*, 106.
64. United Kingdom Parliament House of Lords Daily Hansard. www.publications.parliament.uk/pa/ld200203/ldhansrd/vo021218/text/21218-09.htm.

65. Charlesworth, 'International Law', 387.
66. Charlesworth, 'International Law', 379.
67. Charlesworth, 'International Law', 378.
68. S. Chesterman and M. Byers, 'Has US Power Destroyed the UN?' *London Review of Books*, 21 (1999), 9.
69. Independent International Commission on Kosovo (2000: 288–9), cited in Charlesworth, 'International Law', 380–1, along with a House of Commons Foreign Affairs Select Committee, reporting in May 2000, which reached a similar conclusion: see www.parliament.the-stationery-office.co.uk/pa/cm199900/cmselect/cmfaff/28/2802.htm.
70. Charlesworth, 'International Law', 381.
71. *Tadić*, paras 26–8.
72. *Tadić*, paras 26–8.
73. *Ayyash and others*, Decision on the Defence Appeals Against the Trial Chamber's 'Decision on the Defence Challenges to the Jurisdiction and Legality of the Tribunal', Case No STL-11-O1/PT/AC/AR90.1, Appeals Chamber, 24 October 2012.
74. J. E. Alvarez, '*Tadić* Revisited: The Ayyash Decisions of the Special Tribunal for Lebanon', *Journal of International Criminal Justice* 11, no. 2 (2013): 301.
75. T. Zartaloudis, *Giorgio Agamben: Power, Law and the Uses of Criticism* (New York: Routledge, 2010).
76. K. Pennington, *The Prince and the Law 1200–1600: Sovereignty and Rights in the Western Legal Tradition* (Berkeley, CA: University of California Press, 1993), 90–1.
77. C. Tomuschat, 'The Legacy of Nuremberg', *Journal of International Criminal Justice*, 4, no. 4 (2006): 830.
78. T. D. Gill, 'Legal and Some Political Limitations on the Power of the UN Security Council to Exercise Its Enforcement Powers Under Chapter VII of the Charter', *Netherlands Yearbook of International Law* 26 (1995): 48.
79. B. Simma et al., *The Charter of the United Nations. A Commentary*, 3rd ed. (Oxford: Oxford University Press, 2012), 1320.
80. G. O'Donnell, 'The Quality of Democracy: Why the Rule of Law Matters', *Journal of Democracy* 15, no. 4 (2004): 37.
81. Esposito, *Immunitas*, 60.
82. Esposito, *Immunitas*, 71.
83. P. Fletcher, 'The Political Theology of the Empire to Come', *Cambridge Review of International Affairs*, 17, no. 1 (2004): 59.
84. Wright, *The Role of International Law in the Elimination of War* (Manchester: Manchester University Press, 1961), 21.
85. J. Hell, 'Katechon: Carl Schmitt's Imperial Theology and the Ruins of the Future', *The Germanic Review: Literature, Culture, Theory* 84, no. 4 (2009): 311.
86. G. Steiner, *In Bluebeard's Castle: Some Notes Towards the Redefinition of Culture* (New Haven, CT: Yale University Press, 1971), 54.
87. Agamben, *State of Exception*, 10.
88. Koselleck, 'Crisis', 359–60.
89. Fletcher, 'The Political Theology of the Empire to Come', 59.
90. Aristotle, *The Rhetoric and the Poetics of Aristotle* (New York: Modern Library, 1984), 32.

91. G. Agamben, 'The Archaeology of Commandment', European Graduate School Video Lectures, 21 May, www.youtube.com/watch?v=T4MjMj4S4B810.

92. M. Koskenniemi, *The Gentle Civilizer of Nations: The Rise and Fall of International Law 1870–1960* (Cambridge: Cambridge University Press, 2007), 422–3.

93. C. Schmitt, *The Nomos of the Earth in the International Law of the Jus Publicum Europaeum* (New York: Telos, 2006), 59–60.

94. C. Schmitt, *Political Theology II: The Myth of Closure of Any Political Theology* (Cambridge: Polity Press, 2008).

95. G. Agamben, *The Kingdom and the Glory: For a Theological Genealogy of Economy and Government* (Stanford, CA: Stanford University Press, 2011), 7–8.

96. Agamben, *Homo Sacer*, 28.

97. W. Benjamin, *Reflections: Essays, Aphorisms, Autobiographical Writings* (San Diego, CA: Harcourt Brace Jovanovich, 1978).

98. Agamben, *Homo Sacer*, 28.

99. Charlesworth, 'International Law', 390.

100. P. Virno, *Multitude: Between Innovation and Negation* (Los Angeles: Semiotext(e), 2008), 52.

101. Esposito, *Immunitas*, 63.

102. Esposito, *Immunitas*, 63.

103. Esposito, *Immunitas*, 64.

104. Esposito, *Immunitas*, 65.

105. Esposito, *Immunitas*, 65.

106. Esposito, *Immunitas*, 68.

107. Esposito, *Immunitas*, 71.

108. Virno, *Multitude*, 60.

109. Virno, *Multitude*, 62.

110. Virno, *Multitude*, 52.

111. Virno, *Multitude*, 54.

112. Virno, *Multitude*, 55.

113. Virno, *Multitude*, 64.

114. Virno, *Multitude*, 64.

115. Virno, *Multitude*, 64.

116. P. Levi, *The Drowned and the Saved* (New York: Summit Books, 1988), 54–5.

117. G. Agamben, *Remnants of Auschwitz: The Witness and the Archive* (New York: Zone Books, 2000b), 26.

118. Agamben, *Remnants of Auschwitz*, 26.

119. Fletcher and Ohlin, 'The ICC – Two Courts in One?', 247.

120. Koskenniemi, 'The Politics of International Law', 15.

121. Koskenniemi, 'The Politics of International Law', 16.

122. Koskenniemi, 'The Politics of International Law', 16.

123. O'Donnell, 'The Perpetual Crises of Democracy'.

124. Agamben, *The Kingdom and the Glory*, 276.

125. G. Agamben, *Opus Dei: An Archaeology of Duty* (Stanford, CA: Stanford University Press, 2013), 40.

6

Artificial Islands, Artificial Highways and Pirates: An East African Perspective on the South China Sea Disputes

And tempests in contention roar
From land to sea, from sea to land;
And, raging, weave a chain of power,

– Goethe, *Faust*

World history is a history of land powers against sea powers.

Schmitt, *Land and Sea*

Introduction

Precisely what is at stake in the contemporary South China Sea? The content, effect and application of legal rules? The basis for those rules? The order within which those rules exist? Or order in another sense, that of an implied hierarchy with only room for the United States right at the very top? This chapter invokes Johann Wolfgang von Goethe's version of the Faust myth with an eye on, and in the context of, the South China Sea but from the removed if not quite neutral perspective of the East African Coast. Specifically, how would the struggle look to a Somali pirate? This follows the example of Niccolò Machiavelli's famous dedication of *The Prince* to the Magnificent Lorenzo di Piero de' Medici that one needs to be down in the plains to study mountains and in the mountains to study plains.

The chapter begins more conventionally, with an outline of the legal dispute at hand. This is in order to demonstrate that legal analysis is not quite up to the task of explaining the entirety of the dispute – particularly due to the historical as well as contemporary political context – and its global implications. Consequently, the chapter next reviews Carl Schmitt's (2015) *Land and Sea* to broaden the temporal and geographic scope through and beyond the law of the sea and the present-day South China Sea. That extends the analysis enough to highlight the contribution as well as inadequacies of the preceding approach to explaining the basis of the rules earlier invoked. It sets the stage to once more shift registers on to a traditionally non-legal text, Goethe's (2014) *Faust*, to use its explanatory power in explaining how and why a geopolitical order could be disputed in the South China Sea. Can Goethe's literary genius help us to begin to appreciate, understand and explain the vistas opened up by the disputed waters and land of the South China Sea? The chapter concludes that it can, and that both protagonists display Faustian characteristics. This is additional evidence, if any were needed, that the Faustian motif is a particularly German instantiation of a universal feature of the human condition. That is to say that we are all Faust and Faust is all of us.

Innocent Passage and Freedom of Navigation

On 22 December 2015, then US Secretary of Defense Ashton Carter sent a letter to Arizona Senator John McCain explaining a freedom of navigation operation (FONOP) conducted in the South China Sea fifty-six days earlier:

> On October 27, 2015, the U.S. Navy destroyer *USS Lassen* (DDG-82) conducted a FONOP in the South China Sea by transiting inside 12 nautical miles of five maritime features in the Spratly Islands – Subi Reef, Northeast Cay, Southwest Cay, South Reef, and Sandy Cay – which are claimed by China, Taiwan, Vietnam, and the Philippines. No claimants were notified prior to the transit, which is consistent with our normal processes and with international law.[1]

Through its Foreign Ministry spokesperson, Kang Lu, China in turn resolutely opposed 'any country using freedom of navigation and over flight as a pretext for harming China's national sovereignty and security interests'.[2] On the face of it, this is a dispute pitting freedom of navigation against territorial sovereignty over ocean areas, islands (the Paracels as well as the Spratlys), rocky outcrops, atolls, sandbanks and reefs, including the Scarborough Shoal.[3]

According to media reports, more than $5 trillion of world trade passes through the area annually.[4] China has backed its territorial claims through a combination of building artificial islands and conducting naval patrols, while the United States continues to oppose any restrictions on freedom of navigation and sovereignty claims using naval means.[5] In a speech in Australia, the Commander of US Pacific Fleet said China was building a 'great wall of sand' to create artificial land in disputed waters by pumping sand on to live coral reefs and paving them with concrete.[6]

The Philippines even launched and won an arbitral decision in China's absence with the Annex VII arbitration under UNCLOS on its territorial dispute with China over the islands.[7] The subsequent administration, however, signalled its preference for a negotiated resolution to the dispute.[8]

Liu Haiyang argues that this dispute between China and the Philippines is about either sovereignty over islands, which is not governed by the UNCLOS, or maritime delimitation, which China excluded through a 2006 declaration based on Article 298 of the Convention.[9]

Kenya, which has a maritime dispute of its own with its neighbour Somalia pending at the International Court of Justice (ICJ), is one of a handful of countries that essentially supports China's position:[10]

> The Government of the Republic of Kenya believes that any disputes over the South China Sea should be peacefully resolved through consultations and negotiations in accordance with bilateral agreements and the Declaration on the Conduct of Parties in the South China Sea.
>
> The Government of the Republic of Kenya respects China's statement of optional exception in light of Article 298 of the United Nations Convention on the Law of the Sea (UNCLOS).
>
> The international community should continue playing a constructive role in supporting the efforts made by the region to safeguard regional peace and stability.[11]

In the event, China is widely interpreted as not just metaphorically creating facts on the ground to frustrate rival claims, but rather literally 'creating the very ground itself'.[12] A Pentagon report stated that China had reclaimed 200 hectares (500 acres) in 2014 at five of its outposts in the Spratly Islands and another 610 hectares (1,500 acres) since then.[13] The report claims that the: 'ultimate purpose of the expansion projects remains unclear', but suggests the possibility that 'China is attempting to change facts on the ground by improving its defence infrastructure in the South China Sea'.[14]

It has to be said, however, that according to a US think-tank, Vietnam has added eight hectares (twenty-one acres) to its own land-reclamation projects in the same group of islands.[15] Additionally, there is an issue regarding the demand by China that foreign aircraft observe certain protocols for identification while in the area:

> Originating at the height of the Cold War, Air Defense Identification Zones (ADIZs), i.e. non-territorial airspace unilaterally designated by States for aircraft identification, had not encountered substantial protests until China's declaration of the East China Sea ADIZ in November 2013.[16]

While other countries accuse China of illegally taking measures to create artificial islands with facilities that could potentially be put to military use, China defends the legality of its work and the need to safeguard its sovereignty.[17] The Chinese Navy has even engaged in live-fire exercises in the South China Sea.[18]

Beijing's own legal formulation of the dispute was addressed to the Secretary-General of the United Nations as follows:

> China has indisputable sovereignty over the islands in the South China Sea and the adjacent waters, and enjoys sovereign rights and jurisdiction over the relevant waters as well as the seabed and subsoil thereof. China's sovereignty and related rights and jurisdiction in the South China Sea are supported by abundant historical and legal evidence.[19]

At least one commentator claims that China implicitly acknowledges that the artificial features do not support legal entitlement to any kind of territorial sea.[20] Instead, what the Chinese are attempting to do is 'make other actors treat the waters surrounding their features as though it were a territorial sea'.[21] In this way, consistent practice can become legally binding under customary international law, 'either through generally agreed norms of behaviour or a gradual solidification it into written law'.[22] It is therefore crucial for countries wishing to prevent the high seas around the Chinese features from becoming a territorial reality to halt the norm-creation process before it can gather steam.[23] This is at the very heart of the legal dispute.

A good starting point in beginning to resolve these issues is the United Nations Convention on the Law of the Sea (UNCLOS). It establishes and maintains 'the current marine legal order in the world'; it 'is commonly regarded as the constitution of oceans and has incorporated almost all previously existing conventional and customary rules and norms concerning the oceans'.[24] The United States is not a party. However, it accepts and acts in accordance with 'traditional uses of the oceans – such as navigation and overflight' as they are set out in the Convention as being reflective of customary international law.[25] Under Articles 2 and 3, UNCLOS provides that a country can only claim sovereignty over its land and up to twelve nautical miles of sea perpendicular to its coastline when used as a baseline.

This was the purpose of the FONOP 'sending the *USS Lassen* within 12 nautical miles of the Chinese build-up on Subi Reef' in order to seemingly challenge any claimed sovereignty.[26] On the other hand, Article 87 of UNCLOS provides for freedom of the high seas to all states, whether coastal or land-locked. The mere sailing within twelve nautical miles of the maritime features is not in itself sufficient to demonstrate that the waters are indeed on the high seas.[27] The reason for this is that UNCLOS Article 17 provides for the right of innocent passage through the territorial sea. Such sailing as has occurred could plausibly be read as innocent passage within territorial waters and therefore inadvertently bolster China's territorial claims.[28] In this matter, the law and the effect of the law are in dispute. At a minimum, the situation could be read as either innocent passage in territorial waters *or* freedom of navigation on the high seas.

Although China is a contracting party to UNCLOS, the United States is not, and the full extent to which UNCLOS either codifies or is reflective of customary international law to which the US will concur in each and every detail is unclear. According to the International Court of Justice (ICJ), for a rule to be established as customary, the corresponding practice need not be in absolutely rigorous conformity with the rule.[29] However, the conduct of states should in general be consistent with such rules, and state conduct inconsistent with a given rule should be treated as a breach of that rule, not the existence of a new rule.[30] A rule should be widespread and systematic, but not necessarily universal.[31] Furthermore the *Nicaragua (Merits) Case* stated that customary rules in the nature of *jus cogens* could not be varied by treaty.[32] Even where principles of customary international law are codified into treaties, they continue to exist side by side. The court relied on the *North Sea Continental Shelf Cases* to support the assertion that principles of customary international law can exist side by side with identical treaty law provisions. There is consequently no lack of legal ambiguity surrounding the South China Sea.[33]

This is probably why, on 30 January 2016, the US Navy conducted another FONOP in the South China Sea three months after the previous effort.[34] In it, American destroyer *USS Curtis Wilbur* sailed within twelve nautical miles of Triton Island in the Paracels. Unlike the *USS Lassen Case*, which approached an artificial island, built atop a reef that consequently did not enjoy a twelve-nautical mile territorial water zone, Triton island is an actual island, and therefore entitled to a twelve-nautical mile territorial water zone.[35] Both instances of transit, however, did not address the larger point of speculation that China seeks to establish new precedents by building entire islands anew and then claiming territorial sea and exclusive economic zones around them.[36] The *Wilbur* and *Lassen* operations were similar with respect to legal assertion contrary to claims by multiple states.[37] Here, the Chinese response was broadly similar, with Foreign Affairs spokesperson Chunying Hua stated that, 'the US warship violated Chinese law and entered China's territorial sea without authorization'.[38] Despite that strongly worded diplomatic statement, the *USS William P. Lawrence*, a guided missile destroyer, conducted a third FONOP on 10 May 2016, exercising the right of innocent passage – this time within twelve nautical miles of Fiery Cross Reef in the Spratly Islands.[39] A fourth FONOP was conducted by the *USS Decatur*, this time a guided missile destroyer near but not within the twelve-nautical mile limit of the Paracel Islands.[40] The thing to note is that none of these examples cited a single incident of navigation being hampered in the South China Sea. Perhaps the concern is to prevent potential disruptions of navigation.

The resort to using naval destroyers by parties to the dispute to assert rival legal claims has a basis that goes at least as far back as Hugo Grotius writing about the requirement of having effective control to adjoining waters by coastal states in order to be able to found territorial claims. This is especially as read with Cornelius van Bynkershoek's requirement that this legal control be restricted to the range of coastal weapons, which as at that time he was writing was three nautical miles.[41] There is a view, though, that the origin of this three-nautical mile limit could be based upon either the range of coastal cannon or that it followed long-standing Danish/Swedish practice – or perhaps both of them.[42] In any event, with inter-continental ballistic missile technology, this rule of thumb is no longer a viable statement of the applicable law, although it does begin to explain why military assets would be utilised in this manner as a sort of rough and ready, but nevertheless highly visible, legal instrument.

At present, this construction of new islands in the disputed South China Sea by the Chinese state has been compared to US President James Monroe's Monroe Doctrine of 1823.[43] The doctrine identified the Western hemisphere as America's backyard, and old European colonial powers were told to keep out.[44] Shirley V. Scott surveys the vast literature on the Monroe Doctrine and finds that, in relation to the South China Sea, China may very well seek to superimpose a novel legal regime in the region that subsumes the current one without necessarily replacing it.[45] In other words, rather than just a legal dispute here, there could be rival conceptions of the legal order regionally at the very least but with global ramifications. This is clearly *not* about the content, effect and application of legal rules.

China could well start with the point that there is no absolute freedom in today's oceans.[46] As a consequence, it could argue that its claim to the South China Sea Islands and the adjacent waters is supported both by historical facts as well as the rules of international law pertaining to the acquisition of territorial sovereignty, specifically discovery and naming.[47]

Furthermore, from the Chinese perspective, bitter memories of colonialism and national humiliation are never far from the surface:

> Basically speaking, China enjoyed peaceful and uninterrupted control over the South China Sea Islands and the surrounding waters until the 1930s when France seized the opportunity to occupy and 'annex' several islands in the South China Sea. This took place at a time when the Chinese government was preoccupied with internal conflicts and threatened by the

full-scale Japanese aggression and was therefore unable to effectively defend herself except for lodging the strongest possible protests to the French government time and again.[48]

There is, however, more to it than simply righting the wrongs of the past. It could be that this assertion of claims by China goes beyond its immediate territory to encompass the region at large.

In the past, Xi Jinping, the General Secretary of the Communist Party of China, has suggested that he is more committed to a long-term maritime strategy than his predecessors. According to Sukjoon Yoon, he is basically attempting 'to restore the Middle-Kingdom regional order through four thrusts':

1. establishing new high-profile organisations dealing with maritime policy and strategy
2. upgrading naval capabilities to counter the US pivot to Asia
3. reframing the issues away from prevailing international law and toward China's rights as derived from historical precedence, and
4. demonstrating China's ostensible goodwill through participation in international forums and multilateral exercises in the region.[49]

According to an observer, the real purpose underlying Xi Jinping's maritime power policy is the restoration of China's traditional maritime order as a true maritime power.[50] This is being pursued through an incremental strategy modelled upon 'the historical advances of Western colonial powers', while avoiding any serious reaction until the Chinese position is beyond challenge.[51] Furthermore, any nation attempting to obstruct Xi's salami-slicing tactics will quickly feel the consequences of China's displeasure.[52]

The legal use of military assets by both sides to the dispute does seem to broadly conform to the dichotomy Walter Benjamin identified between law creating and law destroying violence.[53] Francis Fukuyama places all this in an even broader geopolitical context than China's immediate backyard:

> In 2013, President Jinping Xi announced a massive initiative called 'One Belt, One Road,' which would transform the economic core of Eurasia. The One Belt component consists of rail links from western China through Central Asia and thence to Europe, the Middle East, and South Asia. The strangely named One Road component consists of ports and facilities to increase seaborne traffic from East Asia and connect these countries to the One Belt, giving them a way to move their goods overland, rather than across two oceans, as they currently do.[54]

Fukuyama neglects to mention that in Africa and Latin America, Carl Schmitt predated Fukuyama's observation above of a 'strangely named One Road' when he observed that, 'We speak, in relation to the sea, of sea lanes, although there are only traffic lines and no lanes as there are on land'.[55] Furthermore, these coordinates of a struggle between land and sea where law, economic prosperity and conceptions of legal order are at stake almost self-evidently invite analysis through Schmitt's *Land and Sea*.[56] Through its lens, we can see the United States, predominantly a sea power, vying with China, predominantly a land power, and recognise how this struggle both reflects and generates the underlying global legal order. In that framing, the United States champions the artificial highways of sea lanes for freedom of navigation while China builds up artificial islands in what was once sea to bolster its claims of territorial sovereignty.

How can this rivalry be resolved, if at all? Would a Chinese triumph, for instance, usher in a renewed age of a land-based global order? Is the current status quo of the free sea, or *mare liberum*, therefore rivalled by a shift towards returning to a state of exerting territorial dominion over the high seas, or *mare clausum*? Do we see a return to the seventeenth-century debate between Hugo Grotius and John Selden, except that instead of the Netherlands and England we have the United States and China? Is China attempting to make the South China Sea into a *mare nostrum* – essentially a private sea – as the Romans did with the Mediterranean Sea? Not quite.

There are statements from semi-official sources that, 'China cares about freedom of navigation in the South China Sea more than any other country. Disputes should be resolved by exercising restraint, not by speculation.'[57] Should this be taken at face value, then at least one area of mutual concern regarding piracy off the Somali coast in East Africa would demonstrate that the costs of mutual antagonism are outweighed by the benefits of cooperation.[58] As the second largest global economy, China has a significant stake in the current legal order and is in a unique vantage point to independently evaluate the costs as well as the benefits of cleaving to and supporting the current legal order right from its backyard. As it happens, piracy is another of Schmitt's concerns and ties in with his idea of *Nomos* as expanded upon below.

Carl Schmitt's *Land and Sea: A World-Historical Meditation*

Written in the final stages of World War II, *Land and Sea* manages to be a critique – masquerading as a propagation – of National Socialist propaganda.[59] In the first instance, Schmitt marvels at the seemingly pedestrian fact that the human being is a land dweller, and as a consequence, 'humans call the planet we live in "earth" although . . . it is known to be almost three-quarters water and a quarter earth by surface and indeed the largest pieces of earth float like islands'.[60]

Schmitt conceives of land and sea as 'elements', not 'as mere natural scientific quantities', but as being somehow open to human choice and empowerment.[61] The struggle is therefore not because of land and sea as such, but rather what humans make of them in intra-human relationships.[62] It is here that Schmitt discloses his core thesis that, 'World history is a history of land powers against sea powers'.[63] Schmitt credits Admiral Raoul Castex for the inspiration behind this statement.[64]

Schmitt recasts the struggle between the land and the sea by transposing it to the land creature Behemoth and the sea creature Leviathan, each drawn from the biblical Book of Job (a major plot device of Goethe's *Faust*). The biblical connection is further emphasised by Schmitt's view that from beginning to end, the Bible is about a struggle between land and sea.[65] Schmitt extends the metaphorical allusion to actual countries, with Behemoth referencing Germany, Russia and Italy, and Leviathan being shorthand for England and America. It has to be said that in a related work, *Dialogues on Power and Space*, Schmitt explicitly includes China as among land powers.[66] Mark Salter discusses the significance of this. Schmitt added a layer of complexity when he opposed a maritime West to a terrestrial East.[67] For Schmitt, the East encompassing the land powers of Russia and China stood for barbarism, while the Western sea powers stood for civilisation.[68] This symbolism is present even in current discussions of the South China Sea.[69]

Schmitt moves on to plot an arc from the coast onward to the ocean in the context of a historical progression from river culture to inland seas and on to oceanic culture.[70] He writes that, 'Mere navigation of the sea and a culture erected upon an advantageous coastal position is indeed something other than resituating a complete historical existence from the land to the sea as into another element.'[71] Schmitt then eulogises the whale and its hunters as providing a new spatial sensibility based on the sea through the ship-building that accompanied whale hunting.[72] For Schmitt, 'the technological achievement of moving from oars to sails makes possible the actual turning point in the history of the relation between land and sea'.[73]

Because Schmitt both cites and alludes to Goethe's *Faust* right from the start of his meditation on land and sea, its spectre hovers over the work. Indeed, *Dialogues on Power and Space* even ends with a quote from the beginning of *Faust* Part II: 'You, Earth, stood firm this night.'[74] Yet does Goethe's *Faust* help us begin to appreciate, understand and explain the South China Sea dispute? From the evidence above, both sides of the dispute evince some Faustian aspects. This should be no surprise given that, as Jane K. Brown writes, 'Faust has been seen as the paradigmatic text of modernity almost since its conception.'[75] Joan Hoff appositely observes that:

> The comparison to Faust is especially apt in terms of US foreign policy after the end of the Cold war. Faust, at the zenith of his happiness and potency, broke his pact with the devil by wishing that things would never change. Carrying the metaphor forward, it could be argued that the United Sates, at the height of its power upon winning the Cold War, made a similar mistake by trying to stop time and impose its hegemony indefinitely on the rest of the world. Philosophically, one could retreat to Oswald Spengler's much maligned theory about the decline of the West and see the United Sates as the ultimate example of his 'Faustian civilization' where the populace constantly strives for the unattainable and goes into protracted, inevitable, and tragic decline, knowing that is goals cannot be achieved but refusing to settle for less. In either metaphor, Faust's relationship to Mephistopheles is emblematic of the ways the United States has conducted its foreign policy from 1920 through 2007.[76]

But let us not forget that 'boundless ambition' is not a purely American monopoly. It is at the very least a striking coincidence that Faust's dying wish/final ambition is to turn water into land by means of draining a swamp. This is, of course, not all that different from turning water into land by building artificial islands. Both sides in the dispute therefore fit within a Faustian paradigm.

Pirates are yet another area of Schmitt's discussion and analysis. He uses them as a tool to demonstrate how a pirate developed from a means to conduct 'war at sea' to be transformed and recast so as to 'become a sad criminal'.[77] Pirates, at least to Schmitt's own satisfaction, are an integral part of installing Elizabethan England as heir to European maritime legacy.[78] Schmitt provides a colourful potted history of the infamous Pettigrews, a notorious sixteenth-century pirate clan, as if their example explains an entire epoch.[79] To be sure, Schmitt did discuss piracy elsewhere.[80]

A feature story in *The Guardian* newspaper on a prominent Somali pirate leader notes that neither Boyah, the individual in question, nor his companions referred to themselves as 'pirates' in the Somali language.[81] Instead – and this matters for our present purposes – they referred to themselves as 'saviours of the sea', which was often translated to 'coastguard' in English:

> Boyah joked that he was the 'chief of the coastguard', a title he invoked with pride. To him, his actions had been in protection of his sea, the native waters he had known his whole life; his hijackings, a legitimate form of taxation levied in absentia on behalf of a defunct government that he represented in spirit, if not in law.[82]

Boyah's tale was not just a personal story, but emblematic of Somalia as a whole since the collapse of its central government:

> His story was typical of many coastal dwellers who had turned to piracy since the onset of the civil war almost 20 years ago. In 1994, he still worked as an artisanal lobster diver in Eyl – 'one of the best', he said. Since then, the lobster population off the coast of Eyl has been devastated by foreign fishing fleets – mostly Chinese, Taiwanese and Korean ships, Boyah said.[83]

They initially began with fishing vessels and then moved on:

> From 1995 to 1997, Boyah and others captured three foreign fishing vessels, keeping the catch and ransoming the crew. By 1997, the foreign fishing fleets had become more challenging prey, entering into protection contracts with local warlords that made armed guards and anti-aircraft guns regular fixtures on the decks of their ships. So, like all successful hunters, Boyah and his men adapted to their changing environment, and began going after commercial shipping vessels.[84]

Interestingly enough, they even self-consciously cleave to the distinction between land and sea:

> Boyah's moral compass seemed to be divided between sea and shore; he warned me, half-jokingly, not to run into him in a boat, but, despite my earlier misgivings, assured me that he was quite harmless on land.[85]

Furthermore, given his expressed approval of the view that piracy was a 'pre-scientific stage of conducting war at sea', Schmitt would probably have had an element of sympathy for Somali pirates.[86] Goethe also put in the mouth of Mephistopheles the lines:

> War, trade, and piracy, allow
> As three in one, no separation.[87]

Indeed, at least some of the Somali pirates see themselves as 'coast guards' of a failed state.[88] The legal history of piracy illuminates how free trade and liberal values based upon sea power universalised issues of law and right at the expense of the land power based *jus publicum Europaeum* that had had Germany at its geopolitical centre.[89] It would not be lost on the Somali pirate that the key legal reference points for the so-called scramble for Africa were precisely freedom of trade, freedom of navigation and the rules for the occupation of the African coast.[90] None of these would be lost on Schmitt either, of course: he rightly emphasises their significant influence upon the subsequent development of international law.[91]

For Schmitt, piracy was politicised by sea powers as an interim concept between war and peace at the expense of 'continental international law'.[92] The international community thus needed pirates as agents and objects of imperial ambition.[93] According to Schmitt, it is at precisely this point that 'the specifically European order dissolved into a spaceless universalism, and no new order took its place'.[94] In this regard, Schmitt said 'a global universalism lacking any spatial sense' prevailed.[95] For Schmitt, as for Mephistopheles, the globalisation of trade is analogous to piracy.[96]

Doctrinally speaking, piracy belongs simultaneously to the law of the sea and international criminal law. Piracy is located where the protection of international trade bisects the suppression of criminality on the aterritorial space of the high seas. It also, by necessary implication, invokes the protection by states of their monopoly on the legitimate use of force.[97] Huang justifies universal jurisdiction over piracy by making three points. First, it fills the jurisdictional gap on the high seas where the jurisdiction of any state is easily evaded. As a consequence, international law extends an invitation to all states to exercise jurisdiction and in that way prevent the impunity of pirates. Second, universal jurisdiction over piracy is desirable because freedom and safety of navigation upon the high seas is an interest held in common by all states. Third, universal jurisdiction over piracy allows the states with appropriate naval and other capabilities to act in the place of those that lack the same capabilities.

As leading members of the international community, the United States, China, the European Union and Australia all have a common interest in Somali piracy – some of them, indeed, would seem to bear some small proportion of responsibility for the conditions that led to piracy in Somalia as well as its instability. This should demonstrate that keeping to the law bears fewer costs for the key protagonists than not keeping to it, or even trying to fundamentally overturn the legal order. Put another way, the basis for the rules applicable is not under challenge.

Schmitt proceeds to expand on what a spatial revolution is when 'even the structure of the concept of space itself is altered'.[98] In what can only be described as a critical section, Schmitt next describes what was for him the initial planetary spatial evolution.[99] He says:

> Now a new world emerges, in the bravest sense of the term, and the collective consciousness, first of the western and central European peoples, and then, finally, the whole of human collective consciousness is transformed from the ground up. This is the first authentic spatial revolution in the full, earth- and world- encompassing sense of the term.[100]

It is now clear that, for 'the first time in its history, the human held the whole terrestrial orb like a ball in its hand'.[101]

Schmitt here shows his indebtedness to Oswald Spengler's notion of Faustian civilisation[102] if the following passage is relevant:

> That which is called the rational superiority of the European, that which has been termed the European spirit and 'Occidental rationalism' now advances irresistibly. It develops in the western and central European peoples. Destroys the medieval forms of human community, builds new states, fleets, and armies, invents new machines, subjugates the non-European peoples, and places them before the dilemma of either adopting European civilization or of descending to the status of a mere colonial people.[103]

He goes on to provide three examples from world history – Alexander the Great, the Roman Empire in the first century CE and the crusades to make his point that spatial transformation is at the same time a cultural transformation.[104]

Schmitt then moves on to the momentous occasion of the European land-appropriation of the new world.[105] This provides the opportunity to make a statement that later informed the entirety of his *Nomos of the Earth* that: 'Every fundamental order is spatial order. One speaks of the constitution of a country or piece of earth as of its fundamental order, its *Nomos*.'[106] It is no coincidence, of course, that the US pivot to Asia aimed at containing China echoes Halford John Mackinder's 'Geographical Pivot of History'.[107] Schmitt acknowledges his debt to Mackinder in *Nomos of the Earth*.[108] Clearly *Nomos of the Earth* belongs alongside *Land and Sea*. Lauren Benton notes the limitations of Carl Schmitt's approach to global law as a bracketing of violence in the Eurocentric sphere at the expense of the colonies and other areas external to the European empires.[109] For her, despite its temptations, Schmitt's theory is at variance with the historical account and tends to oversimplify imperial sovereignty.[110] Schmitt relates how 'the battle for the land appropriation of the new earth became a battle between the Reformation and the Counter-Reformation, between the World Catholicism of the Spanish and the World Protestantism of the Huguenots, the Dutch and the English'.[111] This battling between land appropriators continued in the context of the war of religion. Schmitt does not mention it, but the myth of Faust is itself traceable to this specific struggle.[112] However, 'The religious fronts and the theological battle parlance of this period also carry in their core the opposition between elementary forces that effected a re-positioning of world-historical existence from solid land to the sea.'[113]

British or English sea appropriation and the separation of land and sea constituted a definitive world historical moment for Schmitt: 'The firm land belongs to a dozen sovereign states, the sea belongs to no one or to all or finally only to one: England.'[114] Apparently, 'Here you can see that the great Leviathan has power even over the spirits and minds of humans. This is what is most astounding about its dominion.'[115] England was as a result at the centre of the transformation of the essence of the island:

> We name the image that we make of our planet simply our image of the earth, and we forget that there can also be a sea-image of it. We speak in relation to the sea, of sea lanes although there are only traffic lines and no lanes as there are on land . . . Conversely, for a perspective oriented only by the sea, the fixed land is a mere coast, a beach with a 'hinterland'.[116]

England became like a ship, or better a fish:

> The ship could lift anchor and lay anchor in another part of the earth. The great fish, the Leviathan, could set itself in motion and seek out other oceans . . . Then presently the Leviathan transformed itself from a great fish into a machine . . . Then, whether fish or machine, the Leviathan in any case, became ever stronger and more powerful and its empire appeared to have no end.[117]

These ideas are built upon the dichotomy of *Land and Sea*, the battle between Leviathan and Behemoth. However, Schmitt draws upon the possibility of a third element – air – and the effect that this has upon the international dynamics. The invention of aeroplanes and the discovery of radio waves added a new element, air.[118] 'To both the mythic beasts, Leviathan and Behemoth, a third would be added, a great bird or perhaps it would be fire that is the additional, genuinely new element of human activity.'[119] This dichotomy is one that can be seen even within Greek mythology, where there is a clear parallel between Leviathan and Behemoth with Scylla and Charybdis. Not only that, but this introduction of an interruption into the dichotomy – through air or fire – can be captured perfectly through the function of the Prometheus legend. The fact that this battle between dichotomies exists, and continues to be an archetype for how we describe the human condition, is essential to understanding the structure of societies. Schmitt moves on to the influential subject of American Admiral Alfred Thayer Mahan's greater island.[120] 'For him what is decisive is that the Anglo-Saxon dominion over the seas of the world must be upheld, and that can only happen on an "insular" basis through a union of both Anglo-American powers.'[121] This heralds a 'new stage of planetary spatial evolution brought on by new technology'.[122]

This consideration of air would go some way to explaining why nuclear-tipped intercontinental ballistic technology combining both air and fire elements could then supersede both land and sea in terms of founding a genuinely new *Nomos* for the Earth. In his analysis, Schmitt reaches two conclusions. The first is the rather Heideggerian observation that, 'The world is not in space, rather space is in the world';[123] the second is that the 'sea is no longer an element as it was in the time of the whale hunters and corsairs'.[124] He rather tellingly concludes with lines from German poet Friedrich Hölderlin:

> Here, too, there are Gods and Gods hold sway,
> Great is their mass.[125]

By this, Schmitt clearly expresses the idea of installing a human in the place of God – the apotheosis of the human – that is at the heart of the myth of Faust. Playing God becomes the relentless pursuit of ultimately unattainable goals, the saving grace of which is supposed to be the consequent enlargement of human achievement. Elsewhere, and subsequent to this, Schmitt seemed to indicate the explicitly non-Faustian view that human morality itself placed limitations on human endeavour.[126] This acceptance of morality as a limit on human endeavour would at the very least by this point rule Schmitt out as either a Faustian or Mephistophelean character.

Competing Visions of the World? A Global Rules-based Order

Now the chapter has placed the South China Sea disputes in a geopolitical context by using Schmitt's poetic vision of the struggle between land and sea, we can turn to his shrewd deployment of the idea of *Nomos* to answer whether China is challenging the contemporary *Nomos* or rules-based order. Throughout Schmitt's work, he highlights the development of his *Nomos*, the ordering of territory, law, regulation or norms, and the concrete form in which a political, economic and social order becomes apparent.[127] Reading Schmitt, we can now identify the current global legal order as being a sea-based *Nomos*, and it is by looking at the *Nomos* surrounding the South China Sea that we will be able to observe that the order within which the legal rules exist is also demonstrably not under threat as such from China, except insofar as it is being waged by the United States and its allies, as set out below.

The Deputy Chair of the Australian Joint Parliamentary Committee on Treaties (JSCOT) spoke of his committee's support for the 'international rule of law'.[128] Americans tend more transparently to call it the 'liberal international order'.[129] This turn of phrase echoes the so-called 'rules-based international order' used by both the Australian Foreign Minister and the Australian

Shadow Defence spokesperson demonstrating its bipartisan acceptance. The very idea of an international rule of law, or international rules-based order, or rules-based global order, or liberal international order – however it is expressed – could only be a customary international law rule or, perhaps better, a principle.

In the words of the Australian Foreign Minister:

> [We] agree on the importance of a rules-based international order, respect for international law, ensuring freedom of navigation and overflight. As a country that does not have a territorial claim in the South China Sea, Australia nevertheless has a very deep interest because about two-thirds of our trade transits the South China Sea, so regional peace and stability is very important to Australia.[130]

The Shadow Defence spokesperson stated:

> We believe that Australia and other like-minded countries should act to support the international rules-based order in the South China Sea.[131]

Chatham House, an important think-tank based in the United Kingdom, has a quite striking view on this:

> The international order established by the victorious allies after the Second World War has been remarkably enduring. The framework of liberal political and economic rules, embodied in a network of international organizations and regulations, and shaped and enforced by the most powerful nations, both fixed the problems that had caused the war and proved resilient enough to guide the world into an entirely new era. They provoke violent and understandable resistance from those who see themselves as champions of their own established order, based on different rules.[132]

The Lowy Institute, an important Australian think-tank, notes:

> The over-arching principle that Australian leaders of all political stripes have used to describe Australia's Asia-Pacific policy is maintaining a 'rules-based order'. Kevin Rudd, Julia Gillard and Julie Bishop (under two prime ministers) have all employed this turn of phrase. In Prime Minister Malcolm Turnbull's recent address in Washington, he reminded his audience that 'the US-anchored rules-based order has delivered the greatest run of peace and prosperity this planet has ever known'. Its preservation is therefore 'a consistent and absolutely central objective'.[133]

From Japan's Prime Minister, we get the view that:

> Maintaining the seas of all humankind as a 'global commons' accomplished through the rule of law is an interest shared in common by the entire international community . . . I sincerely hope that Marine Day will serve as an opportunity for the Japanese people to become fond of and familiar with the sea and appreciate the benefits we receive from the sea, as well as to think deeply about the future of Japan through the medium of the sea.[134]

Even a published Australian Defence White Paper engages in an extensive discussion of what it prefers to term 'a rules-based global order' as having the following characteristics:

1. A rules-based global order means a shared commitment by all countries to conduct their activities in accordance with agreed rules which evolve over time, such as international law and regional security arrangements.[135]
2. Competition between countries and major powers trying to promote their interests outside of the established rules-based global order have implications for free and open trade and can lead to uncertainty and tension, raising the risk of military confrontation.[136]
3. Australia's security and prosperity rely on a stable, rules-based global order which supports the peaceful resolution of disputes, facilitates free and open trade and enables unfettered access to the global commons to support economic development.[137]
4. Underpinning the rules-based global order is a broad architecture of international governance which has developed since the end of World War II. This governance framework, including the United Nations, international laws and conventions and regional security architectures, has helped support Australia's security and economic interests for seventy years.[138]
5. The framework of the rules-based global order is under increasing pressure and has shown signs of fragility. The balance of military and economic power between countries is changing and newly powerful countries want greater influence and to challenge some of the rules in the global architecture established some seventy years ago.[139]
6. While it is natural for newly powerful countries to seek greater influence, they also have a responsibility to act in a way that constructively contributes to global stability, security and prosperity. However, some countries and non-state actors have sought to challenge the rules that govern actions in the global commons of the high seas, cyberspace and space in unhelpful ways, leading to uncertainty and tension.[140]

For some, the term 'rules-based' (occurring fifty-six times in the 2016 Defence White Paper) is short-form for 'Australia prefers the status quo', 'is an expression of fear and uncertainty, given that the status quo is being challenged', 'and perpetual American primacy cannot be guaranteed'.[141] This American primacy is what the FONOPs and the accompanying political policy seek to protect. Only the United States and its allies invoke it at every turn as their stake in the dispute. Consequently, in that light Schmitt's work in part can be seen as a more or less accurate prognostication of the subject of the political speeches as well as the content of the Defence White Paper. What the United States is apprehensive about is the hierarchy implied in the global legal order with only room for one right at the very top.

Conclusion

The land and sea binary is illuminating, but real life is not at all black and white. The American Monroe Doctrine, for instance, was based on land while the New Silk Route has a crucial maritime component. We therefore cannot give fixed and definite meaning to all the implications of contemporary applications of *Land and Sea*. Schmitt himself is far too enigmatic to be pigeonholed in this way. On a somewhat autobiographical note, in naming his residential cottage San Casciano, Schmitt compared his exile with that earlier endured by Machiavelli. Each of them in different ways, after initial resistance, hastily pledged allegiance to a regime that was subsequently overthrown. This comparison could not be more apt, as Isaiah Berlin (1980) could probably testify. Among Berlin's interesting observations are that, 'There is something surprising about the sheer number of interpretations of Machiavelli's political opinions.'[142] The same could easily be said of Schmitt and his three-year membership of the National Socialist Party.

Berlin also adds that, 'But the commonest view of him [Machiavelli], at least as a political thinker, is still that of . . . a man inspired by the Devil to lead good men to their doom' (Berlin 1980, 394). Indeed, 'His name adds a new ingredient to the more ancient figure of Old Nick. For the Jesuits he is "the devil's partner in crime"'.[143] Schmitt himself was described as 'a strong spirit of a satanic kind'.[144] More crucially for our purposes, he has also been described as 'an author of Faustian temperament'.[145] The enduring irony was that they were both indisputably highly talented men who had to live the latter part of their lives in disgrace because of their association with failed regimes, which they had supported albeit briefly and with some reluctance. This is the lens through which their work is refracted to us, making it virtually impossible finally to definitively assign a fixed meaning of their work that will stand the test of time.

This form of analysis is consequently useful, but only up to a point. The danger of applying the land–sea binary too strictly and in a fashion divorced from the reality is especially to be avoided. Both, after all, are grounded upon the Earth, as Schmitt notes.[146] The work consequently needs to be updated and supplemented by contemporary developments. Its underlying principles, however, remain as relevant as they ever were. What are the lessons to be drawn from looking at the dispute through a Schmittian lens for a Somali pirate figure like Boyah? At the very least, Boyah could reflect on the protagonists as being 'a little more than kin', yet 'less than kind' – which is to say that although they are distant and different, they are also occurrences of an identical phenomenon: ambitious grasping for power, seeking to justify itself by the fruits of that grasping. To return to the opening research question, is China challenging the rules? Not really. Is it challenging the basis of the rules? Not even that. How about the hierarchical order? Perhaps at some time in the future. However, by definition, protecting a specific hierarchical order cannot be the basis of a universal law. It is not that China is challenging the rules-based order as such, but that the rules-based order is what is at stake in challenging China.

Notes

1. A. Carter, 'SECDEF Carter Letter to McCain on South China Sea Freedom of Navigation Operation', *UNSI News,* 5 January 2016, https://news.usni.org/2016/01/05/document-secdef-carter-letter-to-mccain-on-south-china-sea-freedom-of-navigation-operation.
2. A. Greene and B. Birtles, 'South China Sea: Audio Reveals RAAF Plane Issuing Warning to Chinese Navy During "Freedom of Navigation" Flight', *ABC News,* 15 December 2015. www.abc.net.au/news/2015-12-15/audio-captures-raaf-challenging-chinese-navy-in-south-china-sea/7030076.
3. *BBC News,* 'Q&A: South China Sea Dispute', 12 July 2016, www.bbc.com/news/world-asia-pacific-137483492016.
4. A. Panda, 'Everything You Wanted to Know About the *USS Lassen* FONOP in the South China Sea', *The Diplomat,* 6 January, www.thediplomat.com/2016/01/everything-you-wanted-to-know-about-the-uss-lassens-fonop-in-the-south-china-sea.
5. Panda, 'Everything You Wanted to Know'.
6. Associated Press, 'US Navy: Beijing Creating a "Great Wall of Sand" in South China Sea', *The Guardian,* 31 March 2015, www.theguardian.com/world/2015/mar/31/china-great-wall-sand-spratlys-us-navy.
7. The Permanent Court of Arbitration (PCA) in the Matter of the South China Sea Arbitration (The Republic of the Philippines v. the People's Republic of China) PCA Case No 2013-19, https://pca-cpa.org/wp-content/uploads/sites/175/2016/07/PH-CN-20160712-Award.pdf; see also Lowy Institute for International Policy, 'South China Sea: Conflicting Claims and Tensions', 20 May 2016, www.lowyinstitute.org/issues/south-china-sea.

8. Joint Statement of China and the Philippines, http://news.xinhuanet.com/english/2016-10/21/c_135771789.htm.
9. L. Haiyang, 'The Lawfare Over South China Sea: Exceptional Rules vs. General Rules', *Opinio Juris*, 14 July 2016, http://opiniojuris.org/2016/07/14/the-lawfare-over-south-china-sea-exceptional-rules-vs-general-rules.
10. *Maritime Delimitation in the Indian Ocean (Somalia v. Kenya)*, www.icj-cij.org/docket/index.php?p1=3&p2=3&code=SK&case=161&k=00.
11. 'Government of the Republic of Kenya's Statement on the South China Sea', www.mfa.go.ke/?p=604; see also 'Government of the Republic of Kenya statement on South China Sea', *China Daily*, 9 June 2016, www.chinadaily.com.cn/world/2016-06/09/content_25659530.htm.
12. J. Marcus, 'US–China Tensions Rise Over Beijing's "Great Wall of Sand"'. *BBC News*, 29 May 2015, www.bbc.com/news/world-asia-32913899.
13. *BBC News*, 'China "Expanding Island Building" in South China Sea', 8 May 2015, www.bbc.com/news/world-asia-china-32666046.
14. *BBC News*, 'China "Expanding Island Building"'.
15. *BBC News*, 'China "Expanding Island Building"'.
16. S. Jinyuan, 'The East China Sea Air Defense Identification Zone and International Law', *Chinese Journal of International Law* 14 (2015): 271.
17. Jinyuan, 'The East China Sea Air Defense Identification Zone', 271.
18. B. Blanchard, 'China Navy Carries Out More Drills in Disputed South China Sea', Reuters, 13 December 2015, www.reuters.com/article/us-southchina-sea-china-idUSKBN0TW01D20151213#4lceWmQbXGhM3QvL.97.
19. B. Ki-moon, 'Oceans and Law of the Sea', 14 April 2011, www.un.org/depts/los/clcs_new/submissions_files/mysvnm33_09/chn_2011_re_phl_e.pdf.
20. T. Choi, 'Why the US Navy's First South China Sea FONOP Wasn't a FONOP'. *The Diplomat*, 4 November 2015, www.thediplomat.com/2015/11/why-the-us-navys-first-south-china-sea-fonop-wasnt-a-fonop.
21. Choi, 'Why the US Navy's First South China Sea FONOP'.
22. Choi, 'Why the US Navy's First South China Sea FONOP'.
23. Choi, 'Why the US Navy's First South China Sea FONOP'.
24. Z. Keyuan, 'Disrupting or Maintaining the Marine Legal Order in East Asia?' *Chinese Journal of International Law* 1 (2002): 449.
25. R. Reagan, 'President Ronald Reagan's Statement on United States Participation in the Third United Nations Conference on the Law of the Sea', US Navy Judge Advocate General's Corps, 10 March 1992, www.jag.navy.mil/organization/documents/Reagan%20Ocean%20Policy%20Statement.pdf.
26. Choi, 'Why the US Navy's First South China Sea FONOP'.
27. Choi, 'Why the US Navy's First South China Sea FONOP'.
28. Choi, 'Why the US Navy's First South China Sea FONOP'.
29. *Military and Parliamentary Activities in and Against Nicaragua (Nicaragua v. United States of America)* (Merits) (1986) ICJ Rep 14 at 62.
30. *Military and Parliamentary Activities in and Against Nicaragua*.
31. *North Sea Continental Shelf Cases (Germany v. Denmark and the Netherlands)* Judgment (1969), ICJ Rep 1, at 42–7.
32. *Nicaragua v. United States of America*.
33. Panda, 'Everything You Wanted to Know'.

34. N. Bisley, 'We Should Think Carefully About an Australian FONOP in the South China Sea', *The Lowy Interpreter,* 4 February 2016, www.lowyinstitute. org/the-interpreter/we-should-think-carefully-about-australian-fonop-south-china-sea.

35. D. Cheng, 'US Conducts Freedom of Navigation Operation in South China Sea', *The Daily Signal,* 3 February 2016, http://dailysignal.com/2016/02/03/us-conducts-freedom-of-navigation-operation-in-south-china-sea.

36. Cheng, 'US Conducts Freedom of Navigation Operation'.

37. M. Rapp-Hooper, 'Confronting China in the South China Sea', *Foreign Affairs,* 8 February 2016, www.foreignaffairs.com/articles/china/2016-02-08/confronting-china-south-china-sea.

38. S. LaGrone, 'China Upset Over "Unprofessional" US South China Sea Freedom of Navigation Operation', *UNSI News,* 31 January 2016, www.news.usni.org/2016/01/31/china-upset-over-unprofessional-u-s-south-china-sea-freedom-of-navigation-operation.

39. E. Graham, 'US Navy Carries Out Third FONOP in South China Sea', *The Interpreter,* 10 May 2016, www.lowyinterpreter.org/post/2016/05/10/US-Navy-carries-out-third-FONOP-in-South-China-Sea.aspx?utm_source=Lowy+Interpreter&utm_campaign=da05f2f7bd-RSS_EMAIL_CAMPAIGN&utm_medium=email&utm_term=0_eed7d14b56-da05f2f7bd-59370029.

40. *ABC News,* 'South China Sea: US Warship Challenges Beijing's Territorial Claims with Freedom of Navigation Exercise', 22 October 2016, www.abc.net.au/news/2016-10-22/us-warship-challenges-chinas-claims-in-south-china-sea/7956826.

41. L. Oppenheim and R. Roxburgh, *International Law: A Treatise* (Clark, NJ: Lawbook Exchange, 2005), 335.

42. H. Kent, 'The Historical Origins of the Three Mile Limit', *American Journal of International Law* 48 (1954): 537.

43. R. Wingfield-Hayes, 'China's Island Factory', *BBC News,* 9 September 2014, www.bbc.co.uk/news/resources/idt-1446c419-fc55-4a07-9527-a6199f5dc0e2.

44. Wingfield-Hayes, 'China's Island Factory'.

45. S. V. Scott, 'China's Nine-Dash Line, International Law, and the Monroe Doctrine Analogy', *China Information,* 30, no. 3 (2016): 310.

46. H. Zhang, 'Is it Safeguarding the Freedom of Navigation or Maritime Hegemony of the United States? Comments on Raul (Pete) Pedrozo's Article on Military Activities in the EEZ', *Chinese Journal of International Law* 9 (2010): 31–47.

47. J. Shen, 'China's Sovereignty Over the South China Sea Islands: A Historical Perspective', *Chinese Journal of International Law* 1, no. 1 (2002): 101.

48. Shen, 'China's Sovereignty Over the South China Sea Islands', 99.

49. S. Yoon, 'Xi Jinping's "True Maritime Power" and ESCS Issues', *Chinese Journal of International Law* 13, no. 4 (2014): 887.

50. Yoon, 'Xi Jinping's "True Maritime Power"', 887.

51. Yoon, 'Xi Jinping's "True Maritime Power"', 887.

52. Yoon, 'Xi Jinping's "True Maritime Power"', 887.

53. W. Benjamin, *Reflections: Essays, Aphorisms, Autobiographical Writings* (San Diego, CA: Harcourt Brace Jovanovich, 1978), 281.

54. F. Fukuyama, 'One Belt, One Road: Exporting the Chinese Model to Eurasia', *Project Syndicate*, 12 January 2016, www.project-syndicate.org/commentary/china-one-belt-one-road-strategy-by-francis-fukuyama-2016-01#s7b-gUL8SCvH50lMf.99.
55. Keyuan, 'Disrupting or Maintaining the Marine Legal Order', 449.
56. C. Schmitt, *Land and Sea: A World-Historical Mediation* (New York: Telos, 2015).
57. A. Jun, 'China's Island Construction Facilitates Navigation Freedom', *Global Times,* 17 September, www.globaltimes.cn/content/942948.shtml.
58. A. Erickson and J. Mikolay, 'Welcome China to the Fight Against Pirates', *Proceedings Magazine*, 153, no. 3 (2009): 34–41; *BBC News*, 'China's Anti-Piracy Role Off Somalia Expands', 29 January 2010, http://news.bbc.co.uk/2/hi/asia-pacific/8486502.stm.
59. Schmitt, *Land and Sea*, lxix.
60. Schmitt, *Land and Sea*, 6.
61. Schmitt, *Land and Sea*, 10–11.
62. Schmitt, *Land and Sea*, 132.
63. Schmitt, *Land and Sea*, 11.
64. Schmitt, *Land and Sea*, 11.
65. Schmitt, *Land and Sea*, 66.
66. C. Schmitt, *Dialogues on Power and Space* (Cambridge: Polity Press, 2014), 54.
67. M. Salter, 'Law, Power and International Politics with Special Reference to East Asia: Carl Schmitt's Grossraum Analysis', *Chinese Journal of International Law* 11, no. 3 (2012), 393.
68. Schmitt, *Land and Sea*, 61.
69. *The Economist*, 'Full Steam: If Long-standing Tensions ease in the South China Sea, China will Ensure They Rise Elsewhere', 20 August 2016, www.economist.com/news/asia/21705373-if-long-standing-tensions-ease-south-china-sea-chinawill-ensure-they-rise-elsewhere-full.
70. Schmitt, *Land and Sea*, 20–1.
71. Schmitt, *Land and Sea*, 21–2.
72. Schmitt, *Land and Sea*, 25.
73. Schmitt, *Land and Sea*, 31.
74. Schmitt, *Dialogues on Power and Space*, 82.
75. J. K. Brown, *The Cambridge Companion to Goethe* (Cambridge: Cambridge University Press, 2006), 84.
76. J. Hoff, *A Faustian Foreign Policy from Woodrow Wilson to George W. Bush: Dreams of Perfectibility* (Cambridge: Cambridge University Press, 2007), 308.
77. Hoff, *A Faustian Foreign Policy*, 36.
78. Hoff, *A Faustian Foreign Policy*, 39.
79. Hoff, *A Faustian Foreign Policy*, 41–4.
80. Schmitt, *The Nomos of the Earth in the International Law of the Jus Publicum Europaeum* (New York: Telos, 2006); C. Schmitt, 'The Concept of Piracy', *Humanity* 2 (2011): 27–9; C. Schmitt, *Writings on War*, trans. T. Nunan (Cambridge: Polity Press, 2011).
81. J. Bahadur, 'Somali Pirates: "We're Not Murderers … We Just Attack Ships"', *The Guardian*, 25 May 2011, www.theguardian.com/world/2011/may/24/a-pioneer-of-somali-piracy.

82. Bahadur, 'Somali Pirates'.
83. Bahadur, 'Somali Pirates'.
84. Bahadur, 'Somali Pirates'.
85. Bahadur, 'Somali Pirates'.
86. Schmitt, *Land and Sea*, 36–7.
87. Goethe, *Faust Volumes 1 and 2: Goethe's Collected Works* (Princeton, NJ: Princeton University Press).
88. D. Axe, '10 Things You Didn't Know About Somali Pirates', *The Wall Street Journal*, 27 April 2009, www.wsj.com/articles/SB124060718735454125.
89. Schmitt, *Land and Sea*, 127.
90. AJIL 1909; M. Craven, 'Between Law and History: The Berlin Conference of 1884–1885 and the Logic of Free Trade', *London Review of International Law* 3, no. 1 (2015): 31–59.
91. Schmitt, *The Nomos of the Earth*, 216.
92. Schmitt, 'The Concept of Piracy', 29.
93. G. J. Simpson, *Law, War and Crime: War Crimes Trials and the Reinvention of International Law* (Cambridge: Polity Press, 2007), 177.
94. Schmitt, *Land and Sea*, 192.
95. Schmitt, *Land and Sea*, 235.
96. T. Beebee, 'Carl Schmitt's Myth of Benito Cereno', *Seminar: A Journal of Germanic Studies* 42 (2012): 114–34.
97. Y. Huang, 'Universal Jurisdiction Over Piracy and East Asian Practice', *Chinese Journal of International Law* 11 (2012): 625.
98. Huang, 'Universal Jurisdiction Over Piracy', 49.
99. Huang, 'Universal Jurisdiction Over Piracy', 49.
100. Huang, 'Universal Jurisdiction Over Piracy', 55.
101. Huang, 'Universal Jurisdiction Over Piracy', 55.
102. Schmitt, *Land and Sea*, 55.
103. Schmitt, *Land and Sea*, 59.
104. Schmitt, *Land and Sea*, 49–54.
105. Schmitt, *Land and Sea*, 59.
106. Schmitt, *Land and Sea*, 59.
107. H. J. Mackinder, 'The Geographical Pivot of History', *The Geographical Journal*, 23, no. 4 (1904): 421–37.
108. Schmitt, *The Nomos of the Earth*, 37.
109. L. Benton, *A Search for Sovereignty: Law and Geography in European Empires, 1400–1900* (Cambridge: Cambridge University Press, 2010): 281.
110. Benton, *A Search for Sovereignty*, 282.
111. Schmitt, *Land and Sea*, 66.
112. Hawkes 2016, 31.
113. Schmitt, *Land and Sea*, 72.
114. Schmitt, *Land and Sea*, 72; see also M. Salter, *Carl Schmitt: Law as Politics, Ideology and Strategic Myth* (London: Routledge-Cavendish, 2012).
115. Schmitt, *Land and Sea*, 76.
116. Schmitt, *Land and Sea*, 79.
117. Schmitt, *Land and Sea*, 83–6.
118. Schmitt, *Land and Sea*, 90.
119. Schmitt, *Land and Sea*, 91.

120. Schmitt, *Land and Sea*, 86.
121. Schmitt, *Land and Sea*, 87.
122. Schmitt, *Land and Sea*, 89.
123. Schmitt, *Land and Sea*, 92.
124. Schmitt, *Land and Sea*, 93.
125. Schmitt, *Land and Sea*, 93.
126. Schmitt, *Land and Sea*, 64.
127. Schmitt, *The Nomos of the Earth*, 70–8.
128. K. Thompson, 'In Our Best Interest: Treaty Scrutiny in a Connected World: Session 1', in *Proceedings of the Joint Standing Committee on Treaties: 20th Anniversary Seminar* (2016), www.aph.gov.au/Parliamentary_Business/Committees/Joint/Treaties/ 20th_Anniversary?
129. A. Connelly, 'The Problem with American Assumptions About Australia', *The Lowy Interpreter,* 17 May 2016, www.lowyinterpreter.org/post/2016/05/17/The-problem-with-American-assumptions-about-Australia.aspx?utm_source=Lowy+Interpreter&utm_campaign=a23bcf2aaf-RSS_EMAIL_CAMPAIGN&utm_medium=email&utm_term=0_eed7d14b56-a23bcf2aaf-59370029.
130. Department of Defence, 'Australia–Indonesia 2+2: Joint Press Conference by Australian Foreign Minister Bishop and Australian Minister for Defence Payne', 21 December 2015, www.minister.defence.gov.au/2015/12/21/minister-for-defence-transcript-joint-press-conference-by-australian-foreign-minister-bishop-and-australian-minister-for-defence-payne-australia-indonesia-22.
131. S. Conroy, 'Turnbull Government Adrift on Ambiguous South China Sea Rhetoric', *The Interpreter*, 24 February 2016, www.lowyinterpreter.org/author/Stephen%20Conroy.aspx.
132. Chatham House, 'Challenges to the Rules-Based International Order' (2015), www.chathamhouse.org/sites/default/files/London%20Conference%202015%20-%20Background%20Papers.pdf.
133. M. Jorgensen, 'East Timor: Concession is the Price for a Rules Based Order', *The Interpreter*, 15 February 2016, www.lowyinterpreter.org/post/2016/02/15/East-Timor-Concession-is-the-price-for-a-rules-based-order.aspx.
134. S. Abe, 'Message from Prime Minister Shinzo Abe on the occasion of "Marine May"', http://japan.kantei.go.jp/96_abe/statement/201407/20140718uminohi.html.
135. Department of Defence, *2016 Defence White Paper* (2016), www.defence.gov.au/whitepaper/Docs/2016-Defence-White-Paper.pdf.
136. Department of Defence, *2016 Defence White Paper*, 32.
137. Department of Defence, *2016 Defence White Paper*, 44.
138. Department of Defence, *2016 Defence White Paper*, 45.
139. Department of Defence, *2016 Defence White Paper*, 45.
140. Department of Defence, *2016 Defence White Paper*, 45–6.
141. C. Rovere, 'Defence White Paper 2016: Eight Strategic Observations', *The Interpreter,* 29 February 2016, www.lowyinterpreter.org/post/2016/02/29/Defence-White-Paper-2016-Eight-strategic-observations.aspx?utm_source=Lowy+Interpreter&utm_campaign=69e96e8a4f-RSS_EMAIL_CAMPAIGN&utm_medium=email&utm_term=0_eed7d14b56-69e96e8a4f-59370029.

142. I. Berlin, 'The Originality of Machiavelli in Berlin', in *Against the Current: Essays in the History of Ideas*, edited by H. Hardy, 25–79 (New York: Viking, 1980).
143. Berlin, 'The Originality of Machiavelli in Berlin', 25.
144. Mehring, *Carl Schmitt: A Biography* (Cambridge: Polity Press, 2014), 445.
145. G. Sartori, 'The Essence of the Political in Carl Schmitt', *Journal of Theoretical Politics* 1, no. 1 (1989): 64.
146. Schmitt, *The Nomos of the Earth*.

7

Follow your Leader – I Prefer Not to: Models for Non-violent Resistance in Giorgio Agamben Via Herman Melville

Agamben and Slavery

This chapter engages with the work of Giorgio Agamben and American literary figure Herman Melville to conclude that the most effective antidote to political violence is not better violence, but better politics. It does this through the admittedly risky and controversial argument that the figure of the slave within the philosophical schematics of Agamben's work counter-intuitively paves the way to an authentic freedom that is not underwritten by violence. The chapter begins by demonstrating and outlining aspects of Agamben's engagement with slavery. It then turns to Melville's work to discuss the various alternatives to violent politics that Agamben could proffer as models of emancipatory politics. The model of Bartleby that Agamben sources from Melville is then used to show how to escape the strictures of the office (per Agamben's take on that notion) with specific reference to the office of master in the master–slave dialectic.

The Use of Bodies, opens with an extended discussion of slavery.[1] Prior to this, an apparent omission often cited with regard to Agamben was his supposed neglect of slavery in favour of an obscure figure of Roman law, the 'sacred man', or *homo sacer*.[2] Antonio Negri expresses this as 'resistance is interpreted by Agamben as passivity rather than as rebellion, represented by Bartleby rather than Malcolm X, by *homo sacer* rather than the slave or the proletariat'.[3] Those pointed criticisms by Negri and others concerning Agamben's valorisation of passivity over resistance, exemplification of Bartleby rather than Malcolm X and preferring the *homo sacer* to the slave or the proletarian are the impetus and starting point for this chapter's argument. The discussion of slavery in *The Use of Bodies* might very well be a response to the criticism. However, whether it was included to amend a supposed omission or merely to amplify or render explicit something that was already present in the work is less clear. This chapter favours the latter view.

For Agamben, modern humans appear to be virtually sacralised or reduced to *homine sacri* in that all human life as a bare biological fact is banned or excluded from political calculation, yet it is the basis for those calculations.[4] However, is the relative obscurity of slavery in Agamben's project an actual lack? On the face of it, the critique admittedly appeared sound – perhaps even necessary – when it was made. In the volume *Homo Sacer* that begins the multi-book project of the same name, Agamben cites Aristotle's *Politics* regarding the *oikos* or homestead as being excluded from the *polis* or city as the space of politics, but does not see fit to mention Aristotle's views on the naturalness of slavery expressed in the same source and at the same place.[5] Further, in Roman Law, of which he writes ostensibly, the primary distinction was the division between slaves and free men.[6] As Magnus Fiskesjö very pithily puts it, 'In ancient Rome – the source of Agamben's *homo sacer* – slaves were everywhere'.[7] Further, Agamben recalls the Magna Carta as being the first instance in which bare life was inscribed in the law but takes no note of the fact that the *homo liber*, or free man, upon which its freedom is based was defined negatively with regard to slavery.[8]

Additionally, Thomas Hobbes arises in Agamben principally in support of the thesis that bare life, or *nuda vita*, is the foundation upon which the political society of the state is founded. This is the bare life, which by its exclusion from political life founds political life, bringing the violence of the state of nature to an end. However, the fact that the social contract itself is without valuable consideration, and consequently a bare agreement, or *nuda pacta*, is not mentioned. Can we also look at this agreement without valuable consideration as the bare contract that through its exclusion founds political society? Although Agamben insists this is the wrong way to approach Hobbes, what if we nonetheless did so? How would this affect the way we look at Agamben's work?[9]

Positing either bare life or bare contract still generates a law-shaped void, a yearning for law prior to the instatement of law. By this void, whatever its provenance, the mere fact of living presence in a territory where a sovereign claims authority is sufficient to construct general acquiescence to that sovereign's will. This presence gives purchase to the law with every member of the political community's assumed consent as well as that of every visitor to that territory. Consequently, Agamben could plausibly substitute bare contract for bare life and still make his main point of a disenfranchising moment at the simultaneous emergence of law, the state and the sovereign. To restate these general observations, all three of which are mainstays of Agamben's political thought, in Ancient Greece slavery was considered natural; in Roman law, birth or capture in war sufficed to make one a slave; while in Hobbes, the war in the state of nature was the basis for slavery. Clearly slaves – just like *homine sacri* – were excluded from the Greek *polis*, outside of Roman civil law and not party to the Hobbesian social contract.

Having said all that, it is not all that simple to diagnose slavery as lacking in Agamben's project even if you put aside *The Use of Bodies*. Indeed Agamben references slavery and cognate terms such as 'slave', 'enslaved' and so on in at least twelve of his pieces, a substantial portion of which even predate the critique of his work for neglecting the figure of the slave.[10] Furthermore, in *The Use of Bodies*, Agamben clearly describes the special status of slaves who were both excluded and included in humanity in the sense that a free man implies a slave as a necessary condition of its possibility.[11] The slave is in between an artificial instrument and a living body.[12] Consequently, slavery does not appear to be that much of a blind spot for Agamben. One way to constructively approach this question of slavery is to take Agamben seriously and compare Bartleby the scribe, who Agamben proffers as the figure to emulate, versus Babo, a slave figure from a shared source: Herman Melville. As James Martel expresses it, Agamben uses Bartleby's signature phrase 'I prefer not to' to distinguish between immanent forms of power and potentialities of power to do and not to do.[13] The utility of that formulation of Bartleby is that it carves out a position beyond the prescribed binary of either doing or not doing.[14]

Having now established that Agamben did treat slavery previously, and in any event has definitely done so now, the next section will consider Negri's implied criticism that Agamben could and should have identified a slave figure from his various sources, both legal and literary, upon which to found his emancipatory project in order to answer what value Agamben gains and provides in singling out Bartleby as an exemplary figure.[15] In this way, as the argument unfolds it brings into dialogue the guiding principles as expressed in the signature phrases of the key (and eponymous) characters of Herman Melville's so-called three Bs: Bartleby, Benito Cereno and Billy Budd.[16]

Bartleby or Babo? Definitely not Billy Budd

Although Melville's three Bs as seen in the previous section are Bartleby, Benito Cereno and Billy Budd, it is a fourth B that invokes slavery: Babo the African slave leader of a mutiny. Although Babo's story is told through Amasa Delano, an American ship captain, as a plot device, the tale is named after Benito Cereno, a Spaniard and Babo's hostage. Melville could easily have titled it 'Babo' instead of 'Benito Cereno' but did not do so.

Bartleby from *Bartleby* is the figure on which Agamben relies as a model of political resistance. Agamben has referenced *Bartleby the Scrivener*.[17] The action takes place in a law firm on Wall Street. Initially, Bartleby's work as a clerk copying out documents is of the highest quality, the envy of his co-workers Nippers and Turkey and the pride of his lawyer boss. Later, however, when asked to do the routine work of verifying the accuracy of his copy, Bartleby utters the phrase 'I prefer not to' to his employer (the narrator of the story). That phrase gradually becomes his standard response to any task that he is assigned. This response is poised between the acquiescence of yes and the disobedience of no; it is neither defiance nor subservience but instead is studiously non-committal. His is neither a rebellion nor a straight-up refusal to do work, but merely the expression of a stubborn preference not to do the work. He remains unmoved by either threats or bribes. This is baffling to his boss, who would prefer Bartleby either did the work as asked or, alternatively, refused outright which would then provide grounds for an immediate dismissal. So uncomfortable does the lawyer (we are not told his name) become with Bartleby's persistent non-cooperative stubbornness that, rather than evict him from the office that has now become Bartleby's home, he himself moves out of the premises and abandons Bartleby to his fate. The narrator, however, cannot help but check on Bartleby and, upon learning of his subsequent imprisonment, tries to ensure that he is still kept fed while incarcerated. Bartleby, however, has other ideas and 'prefers not to eat', starving to death as a consequence.

For Robin West, *Bartleby* explores how positive law in liberal societies ensures compliance via a two-pronged strategy: brute force accompanied by influencing conscious compliance, thus ensuring both efficacy and legitimacy.[18] Thus Agamben proffers Bartleby's signature phrase, 'I prefer not to', as a way of paralysing the apparatuses of power without breaking the law in western liberal societies.

Benito Cereno is a character in another of Melville's short stories published in *The Piazza Tales* – the same collection in which *Bartleby* was published. Carl Schmitt, a common reference point of Agamben's, was not the only German intellectual immediately after World War II to see parallels between the stories and their situation under Nazi Germany.[19] Indeed, Schmitt often compared himself to Benito Cereno in the context of Nazi Germany with regard to defending himself against the Allies for international crimes.[20] Needless to say, Agamben is well aware of that fact.[21]

Moreover, a certain justification for a methodological approach surmising that Agamben is familiar with *Benito Cereno* is that Agamben himself does precisely this in relation to Schmitt being a reader of the Journal *Archiv* when Agamben says:

> Now, not only did Schmitt publish numerous essays and articles (including the first version of *The Concept of the Political*) in the *Archiv* between 1924 and 1927, but a careful examination of the footnotes and bibliographies of his writings shows that from 1915 on Schmitt was a regular reader of the journal (he cites, among others, the issues immediately preceding and

following the one containing Benjamin's essay). As an avid reader of and contributor to the *Archiv*, Schmitt could not easily have missed a text like 'Critique of Violence,' which, as we will see, touched upon issues that were essential for him.[22]

Additionally, prior to Agamben's example, Susan Buck-Morss argued that Georg Wilhelm Friedrich Hegel's master–slave dialectic (of which more below) was conceived in contemplation of the Haitian Revolution as reported in the Journal *Minerva,* of which she states that, 'another regular reader of *Minerva*, as we know from his published letters, was the philosopher Georg Wilhelm Friedrich Hegel'.[23] Further:

> We are left with only two alternatives. Either Hegel was the blindest of all the blind philosophers of freedom in Enlightenment Europe, surpassing Locke and Rousseau by far in his ability to block out reality right in front of his nose (the print right in front of his nose at the break-fast table); or Hegel knew – knew about real slaves revolting successfully against real masters, and he elaborated his dialectic of lordship and bondage deliberately within this contemporary context.[24]

It is consequently not unreasonable to surmise that Agamben had ample opportunity to consider Babo's plight, and it is inconceivable that a careful thinker of Agamben's calibre would not have done so.

Benito Cereno was the captain of a slave ship taken over by slaves, whose leader Babo forced him to act as the master while they feigned the condition of slaves in order to get provisions from Amasa Delano, an American ship captain who came to their aid.[25] The slaves for a time successfully staged a masquerade, a grim carnival that took advantage of Delano's racist attitudes and his natural affinity for Africans in servile roles, to hoodwink him under Babo the mutiny mastermind's harsh and cruel leadership. So much so that Babo could not only hold a cut-throat razor to Benito Cereno's neck and go ahead to draw blood but still convince Delano that he remained a loyal manservant ministering to his master as a barber. Babo – supremely self-aware – rules through delicately posed irony, terror, violence and cunning, exempli-fied by him displaying the body of Alexandro Aranda, his erstwhile owner, on the prow of the ship (later covered in tarpaulin but never far from the con-sciousness of his captives) under the hastily scrawled prescription 'follow your leader'. Benito Cereno as master-yet-captive-of-slaves has been interpreted in Germany as a symbol for the Germans or German generals under Hitler, Delano as symbolising a naive America and in at least one other instance (in addition to Schmitt), Babo as symbolising Hitler and later as embodying abstract evil.[26]

Now, with these in mind, we can return to the question structuring the present inquiry: to whom do we look as a model for political emancipation among the literary figures? Should we choose Bartleby standing in as a cipher for bare life/*homo sacer* through his signature phrase 'I prefer not to'? Or do we look to Babo as a political militant who is referent to the institution of slavery through bare contract through his signature phrase of 'follow your leader'?

As a preliminary step, we can contrast both of these with the respectful attitude towards law even unto death as portrayed in the shape of Billy Budd, yet another of Melville's characters, in a short story also with the same name. Melville's *Benito Cereno* and *Billy Budd* were translated into German in 1938.[27] For our purposes, Billy Budd's signature phrase is contained in his last words 'God bless Captain Vere!' They preceded his execution under Captain Vere's orders. This invocation of God's blessing was despite the execution being patently unjust even to those that presided over the verdict. The German reception of *Billy Budd* saw it as a political allegory, with Billy Budd initially seen as a sacrificial lamb quite willingly, and for the sake of salvation of the whole, going along with his sacrifice and later more critically as the sacrifice of innocents for the sake of social order in a manner in keeping with the letter of the law.[28] Agamben, of course, would emphatically reject the active acquiescence to the law as portrayed by Billy Budd and modelled on the exemplary law-abiding citizen. This is why the question arising is emphatically not the alliterative 'Bartleby or Babo or Billy Budd?' because Billy Budd as a solution to liberal democracy's deliberate coupling of brute force and conscious compliance is simply out of the question for Agamben. Billy Budd is thus only in play due to his exclusion from consideration. Bartleby's studied passivity and Babo's emancipatory violence, on the other hand, point to two different ways of approaching law's complicities with violence.

In some ways, Babo is a literal and literary embodiment of the slave element of Hegel's master–slave dialectic and is irony personified. He is simultaneously self-aware while also being aware of his master's inner psyche in a way that is not reciprocated. He has, with ample justification, even been referred to as 'the genius of the story'.[29] Through atrocious violence, solely a means to emancipation, Babo is the sovereign of the political space of a slave ship under revolt in the name of freedom, wanting nothing but to be returned to the homeland from whence they were abducted. Melville has Babo make his captives look at the skeleton of his former master and asks them whether the whiteness of his bones shows the skeleton of a white man. Babo believed that there would be no freedom while his master was still alive and therefore puts him to death. This murder does not reckon with succession law, which would in principle ensure Babo as property would either devolve onto his master's heirs or failing that, the state; nor did it reckon with the operation of the criminal law, which in the end tries, convicts, hangs and orders the public displaying of his head mounted on a spike. It needs emphasising that the law is actually necessary for that slavery to take place:

> The state of slavery is of such a nature, that it is incapable of being introduced on any reasons, moral or political; but only positive law, which preserves its force long after the reasons, occasion, and time itself from whence it was created, is erased from memory: it's so odious, that nothing can be suffered to support it, but positive law.[30]

As a matter of historical record, even legal emancipation and the criminalisation of slavery in fact guaranteed financial compensation for erstwhile slave owners.[31] Recall that the Faustian pact includes an element of mutual voluntary enslavement.[32]

Importantly for this chapter's argument, upon his capture Babo adopted Bartleby's attitude of withdrawal from social intercourse and mutely followed his fate wherever it led. Bartleby, who 'prefers not to', carves out a position of pure potentiality for himself: not quite defying the law but not cooperating either, merely acting in a place beyond the law's reach. He perplexes and haunts all those who try in vain to bind him to its strictures. It is precisely here that Babo himself ends up after all the violent struggle. At least one insight may be gleaned at this point, which is that regardless of whether you deploy violence fighting for or against the system, you are still within the system's parameters – either fighting to retain your place or fighting to gain or perhaps regain a place. The oppressive system itself is not in question, and is indeed the only element whose survival is guaranteed by the very terms of the violent exchange.

Consequently, violent struggle merely affirms the system and demonstrably does not weaken it in any way whatsoever. Indeed, it does precisely the opposite. Preferring not to participate is instead the genuine position of rejecting the system as such. Thus, to follow Agamben's lead is to unmask the apparent politics of the city as really being part of the apparatus of the camp. Both Billy Budd and Babo, in trying to preserve their lives in the face of the law, manifestly fail in directly opposed ways. Instead, they only succeed in taking responsibility for a system over which they have no actual power, being under constrained moral agency. Charles Mitchell observes that Melville investigated 'the moral psychology of the legalistic mind which supports the use of legal forms for the protection of evil' in three places, *Bartleby the Scrivener*, *Benito Cereno* and, for Mitchell, 'most penetratingly' in *Billy Budd*.[33] Resorting to violence is essentially a Faustian pact by way of conceiving of violence as inherently evil, but nevertheless capable of achieving good.

In Goethe's *Faust*, Faust asks Mephistopheles: 'Who are you then?' and is answered perhaps truthfully but not completely honestly: 'Part of that force which would do ever evil, and does ever good.'[34] This is ultimately an illusory hope. As Walter Benjamin points out, the difference between a strike as divine violence and a riot as law-making or law-preserving violence leaves the question of violence itself untouched and unquestioned.[35] The prevailing test is only violence as a means to an end, and therefore in this way violence is only to be evaluated strictly as a means – a so-called necessary evil whose evil is undisputed but necessity is impossible to prove or disprove.

Resort to violence is thus a Faustian pact, whose central feature is the quintessential legal instrument, a contract – the deal with the devil. Contracts are not observant of the public law–private law divide. Not only are they central to private relationships and commerce, but also the greatest contract of them all is the social contract, which is by definition outside of private relations. Pat Robertson, a well-known Christian television evangelist, expresses the view that he is unafraid to broadcast to the world even though it sides with slave owners against revolting slaves and invokes the wrath of God on the slaves for violently overthrowing their masters:

> The Haitians were under the heel of the French. And they got together and swore a pact to the devil. They said, 'We will serve you if you will get us free from the French.' The devil said, 'OK, it's a deal.' You know, the Haitians revolted and got themselves free. But ever since, they have been cursed by one thing after the other.[36]

All that needs to be said here is that the Haitian revolutionaries themselves did not believe they were worshipping the devil, which is what matters in this context; indeed, they expressed the opposite view to Robertson's. In the book that follows Buck-Morss's article above, she cites Baron de Vastey's words: 'Our Haitian painters depict the Deity and angels black, while they represent the devil as white.'[37] Quite appositely, too, the pact between Faust and Mephistopheles was one of mutual slavery here and then hereafter, respectively.

Only Bartleby therefore paralyses the mutual violence of the master–slave dialectic. Slavery is not merely an office; it is also a condition that is outside the social contract.[38] Babo demonstrates that, given sufficient violence, even someone in the condition of a slave can 'operate' the office of master but that does not free them from slavery. The emancipatory potential of a carnivalesque reversal of roles, while superficially attractive, is transient and therefore limited. The high point of moral, physical and intellectual courage when faced with the camp is to prefer not to cooperate. Taking up arms, like cooperating fully, is one of the system's own predefined roles. Consequently, violence does not work to achieve freedom while the law seems completely ambivalent at best, but complicit at worst. The master seems to be free until we look at Cereno, himself imprisoned in his mastery. The power of the tale in part lies in the racially inflected naiveté of narrator Amasa Delano, who is taken in right until the final moment by Babo's elaborate masquerade. Delano's confidence in his easy superiority over both the African slaves and Spanish slavers and crew makes him attribute agency to Cereno and not to Babo.[39] Morgan sees a similar sort of logic in Joseph Conrad's *Heart of Darkness*: 'Thus, the blackness and savagery initially associated with the African jungle and its people is eventually reversed with the progressive revelation of the unsavoury European lust after the white tusks of ivory.'[40]

Babo, with a certain element of both irony and false modesty, bats away Delano's praise of him in the presence of Aranda with the statement that 'what he has done was but duty'.[41] This is a disarmingly simple statement, yet it subtly yields at least three meanings. The first is the basic one speaking of his duty as a slave to serve his master; the second is his duty as a human being to revolt from slavery. These two meanings are simultaneously addressed to the two recipients present with opposed meanings. The third meaning is more allusive, and makes the first two meanings possible; it is that him playing the part of a slave is only possible by dint of the office of master. Recall that officiousness means taking on anything as a duty. Edward Gibbon provides such an instance: 'Constantius had a right to disclaim the officiousness of his ministers, who had acted without any specific orders from the throne.'[42] This is a deliberately exaggerated case, but still demonstrates the link between office and duty. A command is only effective as long as there is someone left to obey, as Agamben reminds us.[43] Babo skilfully reverses this to be as long as there is someone left to obey it, a command is effective. This is with or without the will of the master. In fact, the master may even be dead! In Agamben's work, we get the example of 'We have no king but Caesar', which is shown to be how the mob forces Pilate's hand despite his expressed reluctance to crucify Christ.[44] George Orwell's *Shooting an Elephant* also cannily demonstrates the mutual embrace of the colonial encounter, where the ruled can effectively control the rulers while relying on the established institutions even against the will of the rulers. In that tale, Orwell – ostensibly as the Eton-educated colonial policeman with his rifle at his side – is browbeaten by his putative colonial subjects to shoot and kill an elephant despite his own personal misgivings. The natives use his office as policeman to overcome any personal squeamishness he may have. This externally prescribed logic is internalised by both the coloniser and colonised and, as a consequence, none of them is free of it. What, then, is this office which encompasses masters as well as slaves by holding them both in its deadly embrace and thrall?

The Absolute Ambiguity of Law and the 'Office'

The office in the sense of a socially constructed role that is fundamentally separate from its immediate holder has, as we have seen above, a fascinatingly enabling as well as constricting role. In *Opus Dei*, Agamben looks at the fundamental indifference of moral qualities to the efficacy of official acts.[45] The religious paradigm of *Opus Dei* provides the secular West with the term 'office', which

> is more efficacious than the law because it cannot be transgressed, only counterfeited. It is more real than being because it consists only in the operation by means of which it is realized. It is more effective than any ordinary human action because it acts *ex opere operato*, independently of the qualities of the subject who officiates it.[46]

Such diverse concepts as Kelsen's pure theory of law, Kantian ethics, the political militant and the ministerial functionary are modelled by 'acts of office' – that is, duties.[47] Agamben introduces the crucial distinction between an act in its effective reality and an action insofar as an agent carries it out.[48] This distinction goes back to affirming the validity of baptisms conferred by an unworthy priest. Agamben traces the doctrine to the theory of the action of the devil within the providential economy.[49] In it, the devil serves God and God approves his work, but not the way he has worked.

Agamben continues to trace the genealogy of office and the insertion of ethics into duty in the West to find that:

> *Officium* is neither a juridical or moral obligation nor a pure and simple natural necessity: it is the behavior that is expected among persons who are bound by a relation that is socially codified, but the compulsory nature of which is sufficiently vague and indeterminate that it can be connected – even if in a derisory way – even to behavior that common sense considered self-evidently offensive to decency . . . *Officium* is what causes an individual to comport themselves consistently: 'as a prostitute if one is a prostitute, as a rascal if one is a rascal, but also as a consul if one is a consul and, later, as a bishop if one is a bishop.[50]

For Agamben, it is clear that while obligation derives from an action, *officium* derives from a condition or a status. The Romans distinguished between an absolute material necessity and juridical obligation (of human or divine law). The distinction seems to coincide with what, according to Kelsen, opposes the material necessity and juridical necessity. To illustrate this, Agamben retells of how Seneca the Elder related the unconsciously illuminating gaffe of the orator Quintus Haterius, stating that unchastity is a crime for the freeborn, a necessity for the slave and a duty for a freedman.[51] This taxonomy, ranging from the slave to the freeborn, mediated by the freedman, is clearly founded on slavery and demonstrates that slaves are not autonomous individuals with any kind of free will or separate legal personality. Aquinas notes that 'even a slave can voluntarily do his duty by his master, and so he makes a virtue of necessity'.[52]

Slavery as metaphor roots its antithetical opposite, freedom.[53] In fact, the institution itself was intensifying and expanding as the power of the West encompassed the entire globe.[54] The material conditions were in complete contradiction to the intellectual climate. Thomas Hobbes's *Leviathan* is pivotal for Susan Buck-Morss because in it slavery is portrayed as a consequence of the war of all against all in the state of nature, hence belonging to 'the natural disposition of man'.[55] Hobbes considered the 'elemental struggle between two enemies' to be 'the natural condition which made slavery necessary as a social institution'.[56] By the eighteenth century, slavery had become the root metaphor of Western political philosophy, connoting everything that was evil about power relations.[57] Enlightenment thinkers considered freedom, its conceptual antithesis, as the highest and universal political value, rendering destitute the master–slave dialectic.

Agamben introduces three terms relevant to the discussion: inoperativity, destitution and use. Regarding inoperativity, he says, 'Only a power that is made inoperative and deposed is completely neutralized.'[58] Further, 'It is this operativity of the law that the messianic faith neutralizes and renders inoperative, without thereby abolishing the law.'[59] With regard to destitution, Agamben states that in order to resist something framed in the terms has-to-be (as the inherently violent institution of slavery was), we can counter it using as-not: 'The "as not" is a destitution without refusal. To live in the form of the as-not means to deactivate every juridical and social property, without establishing a new identity.' Agamben recommends the 'use' of a form of life to bring about this destitution. 'Use' names here the deposing potentiality in the Christian form of life, which destitutes 'the figure of this world'.

This is how then the abject and problematic figure of the slave has become the kernel of the solution at the end of the *Homo Sacer* project:

> the symmetry between the slave and the machine thus goes beyond the analogy between two figures of 'the living instrument': it concerns the ultimate achievement of anthropogenesis, the becoming fully human of the living human being . . . In this sense, slavery is to ancient humanity what technology is to modern humanity: both as bare life, watch over the threshold that allows access to the truly human condition (and both have shown themselves to be inadequate to the task, the modern way revealing itself in the end to be no less dehumanizing than the ancient).[60]

The importance of the slave to contemporary times for Agamben can hardly be overstated because the slave sits at the intersection of two sets of axes: the human–animal axis as well as the human–instrument or organic–inorganic axis:

> The slave is, on the one hand a human animal (or an animal human) and, on the other hand and to the same extent, a living instrument (or an instrument-human). That is to say, the slave constitutes in the history of anthropogenesis a double threshold, in which animal life crosses over to the human just as the living (the human) crosses over into the inorganic (into the instrument) and vice versa.[61]

Agamben ascribes specific responsibility to the law in initially conjuring up this figure of the slave as well as conjuring it away when it was no longer 'useful':

> The invention of slavery as a juridical institution allowed the capture of living beings and of the use of the body into productive systems, temporarily blocking the development of the technological instrument: its abolition in modernity freed up the possibility of technology, that is, of the living instrument.[62]

There is at least one real-life instance of the use of bodies being deployed to paralyse the violent force-of-law modelled on and mimicking the master–slave dialectic. This where the passengers in a Kenyan bus refused to distinguish themselves as either Christians or Muslims when confronted by Islamic militants drawn from the Al Shabab group.[63] What usually happened in cases such as these was that as soon as the Christians were separated from the Muslims, the Christians would be put to death and the Muslims spared and released to go on their way. The heroic actions of the Muslims saved their Christian compatriots, but at great risk to their own lives. They literally used their bodies to shield the Christians and by sharing items of clothing like veils, caps and scarves rendered themselves indistinguishable and thus not subject to the violence that mimics the force of law. It is an example for the rest of us. Al Shabab used political violence to self-consciously emulate the violence of the master–slave dialectic. The bus passengers, starting with the Muslims, indicated their preference not to divide themselves as ordered. This action of the Muslim travellers deprived the Islamic militants of the political basis for their violent actions and in that way paralysed the militants' political calculations, which had no purchase on their intended subjects. Both Christians and Muslims had to work together indistinguishably because the Christians could still have rejected the help of their Muslim travel companions and identified themselves as Christians, dying the deaths of martyrs. That self-sacrifice would have been sufficient for the militants' logic to proceed as they had anticipated.

Conclusion

This chapter began by demonstrating that Agamben did turn his mind to slavery, even prior to his *Homo Sacer* project, as well as by its end. The chapter then compared the opposed strategies of non-cooperation with political violence as distinguished from violent resistance, as expressed in signature phrases from Melville's characters to show not only that that the slave-figure is the shadow image of the free human in liberal democratic thought, but counter-intuitively, the abject figure of the slave gestured a way out of the politically sanctified violence of the master–slave dialectic. This is because violence is a wholly inappropriate basis for resistance to violence if the aim of resistance is to target violence. Because the ambiguity of law's relationship to violence – which enables the effectiveness of office – can be undone by preferring not to further participate in violent politics, it is now possible to conclude that the most effective antidote to political violence is not better violence, but rather better politics.

Robert Cover engages with both *Billy Budd* and *Benito Cereno* in *Justice Accused*, situating reading both through the prism of law's complicit role in the oppressive legal institution of slavery.[64] As a clear instance of a decision-maker's will being irrelevant to their decision, Cover quotes Captain Vere's words: 'however pitilessly that law may operate in any instances, we nevertheless adhere to it and administer it'.[65] Cover goes on to make the ingenious proposition that Captain Vere had a real-life model in Melville's father-in-law, Chief Justice Lemuel Shaw, who was privately opposed to slavery but yet applied the harsh laws against fugitive slaves unflinchingly despite the personal agony it caused him.[66] Cover also likened Billy Budd to a slave in their mutual mute subjection to the law's strictures. Cover also notes the theological aspect of Billy Budd, including 'the clash of elemental good and elemental evil' embodied in the characters.[67] Furthermore Cover highlights that a slaveholder could readily see that the law in certain instances recognised 'that in the natural order of things – even though not in the legal order – his slave had a right to kill him'.[68]

Notes

1. G. Agamben, *The Use of Bodies* (Stanford, CA: Stanford University Press, 2016), 23.
2. S. Bignall and M. G. Svirsky, 'Introduction: Agamben and Colonialism', in *Agamben and Colonialism*, edited by S. Bignall and M. G. Svirsky, 1–14 (Edinburgh: Edinburgh University Press, 2012), 1.
3. A. Negri, 'Giorgio Agamben: The Discreet Taste of the Dialectic', in *Sovereignty and Life*, edited by M. Calarco and S. De Caroli, 165–70 (Stanford, CA: Stanford University Press, 2007), 123.

4. G. Agamben, *Homo Sacer: Sovereign Power and Bare Life* (Stanford, CA: Stanford University Press, 1998), 111.
5. Agamben, *Homo Sacer*, 2.
6. W. Buckland, *The Roman Law of Slavery: The Condition of the Slave in Private Law from Augustus to Justinian* (New York: Cambridge University Press, 2010), 1.
7. M. Fiskesjö, 'Outlaws, Barbarians, Slaves: Critical Reflections on Agamben's *Homo Sacer*', *HAU: Journal of Ethnographic Theory* 2, no. 1 (2012): 166.
8. Agamben, *Homo Sacer*, 125.
9. Agamben, *Homo Sacer*, 106.
10. G. Agamben, *Language and Death: The Place of Negativity* (Minneapolis: University of Minnesota Press, 1991), 46–7, 49, 58, 73, 139; G. Agamben, *Infancy and History: The Destruction of Experience* (New York: Verso, 1993), 28; G. Agamben, *Stanzas: Word and Phantasm in Western Culture* (Minneapolis: University of Minnesota Press, 1993), xviii, 421; Agamben, *Homo Sacer*, 95; G. Agamben, *Remnants of Auschwitz: The Witness and the Archive* (New York: Zone Books, 2000), 108–9; G. Agamben, *The Open: Man and Animal* (Stanford, CA: Stanford University Press, 2004), 12, 37; G. Agamben, *State of Exception* (Chicago: Chicago University Press, 2005), 21, 71; G. Agamben, *The Kingdom and the Glory: For a Theological Genealogy of Economy and Government* (Stanford, CA: Stanford University Press, 2011), 17, 24, 31, 82, 86, 287; G. Agamben, *The Sacrament of Language: An Archaeology of the Oath* (Stanford, CA: Stanford University Press, 2011), 26, 60; G. Agamben, *The Church and the Kingdom* (London: Seagull Books, 2012), 13; G. Agamben, *Opus Dei: An Archaeology of Duty* (Stanford, CA: Stanford University Press, 2013), 72, 73, 102.
11. Agamben, *The Use of Bodies*, 20.
12. Agamben, *The Use of Bodies*, 23.
13. J. R. Martel, 'Book Review: *Decolonizing Democracy: Power in a Solid State*', *Law, Culture and the Humanities* 13, no. 2 (2017): 309.
14. M. J. Shapiro, 'The Micropolitics of Justice: Language, Sense and Space, *Law, Culture and the Humanities* 8, no. 3 (2012): 466–84.
15. A. Negri, 'Giorgio Agamben'.
16. D. McCall, *The Silence of Bartleby* (Ithaca, NY: Cornell University Press, 1989), 140.
17. See G. Agamben, *Potentialities: Collected Essays in Philosophy* (Stanford, CA: Stanford University Press, 1999); G. Agamben, 'Bartleby', in *The Coming Community* (Minneapolis: University of Minnesota Press), 35–8; G. Agamben, *Idea of Prose* (Albany, NY: State University of New York Press, 1995), 65; Agamben, *Homo Sacer*, 48; G. Agamben, *Means Without End: Notes on Politics* (Minneapolis: University of Minnesota Press, 2000), 23.
18. R. West, 'Invisible Victims: A Comparison of Melville's *Bartleby the Scrivener* and Glaspell's *A Jury of Her Peers*', *Cardozo Studies in Law and Literature* 8 (1995): 219.
19. L. R. Phelps, 'The Reaction to Benito Cereno and Billy Budd in German', *Symposium: A Quarterly Journal in Modern Literatures* 13, no. 2 (1959): 295.
20. R. Mehring, *Carl Schmitt: A Biography* (Cambridge: Polity Press, 2014), 412.
21. G. Agamben, *Stasis: Civil War as a Political Paradigm (Homo Sacer II, 2)* (Edinburgh: Edinburgh University Press, 2015b), vi.
22. Agamben, *Pilate and Jesus* (Stanford, CA: Stanford University Pres 2005), 52–3.

23. S. Buck-Morss, 'Hegel and Haiti', *Critical Inquiry* 26, no. 4 (2000): 842.
24. Buck-Morss, 'Hegel and Haiti', 844.
25. H. Melville, *Benito Cereno* (Raleigh, NC: Freebook, 2008).
26. L. R. Phelps, 'The Reaction to Benito Cereno and Billy Budd in German', *Symposium: A Quarterly Journal in Modern Literatures* 13, no. 2 (1959): 297.
27. Phelps, 'The Reaction to Benito Cereno', 295.
28. Phelps, 'The Reaction to Benito Cereno', 297.
29. F. Busch, 'Melville's Mail', *The Iowa Review* 16, no. 2 (1986): 159.
30. *Somerset v Stewart* (1772) 98 ER at 510.
31. N. Draper, *The Price of Emancipation: Slave-Ownership, Compensation and British Society at the End of Slavery* (Cambridge: Cambridge University Press, 2010), 8.
32. J. Goethe, *Faust Volumes 1 and 2: Goethe's Collected Works* (Princeton, NJ: Princeton University Press, 2014), lines 1656–9.
33. C. Mitchell, 'Melville and the Spurious Truth of Legalism', *The Centennial Review*, 12, no. 1 (1968): 110.
34. J. Goethe, *Faust: A Tragedy: Interpretive Notes, Contexts, Modern Criticism*, 2nd ed. (New York: W.W. Norton, 2001), 36.
35. W. Benjamin, *Reflections: Essays, Aphorisms, Autobiographical Writings* (San Diego, CA: Harcourt Brace Jovanovich, 1978), 277.
36. P. Robertson, 'Pat Robertson Says Haiti Paying for "Pact to the Devil"' (2010), http://edition.cnn.com/2010/US/01/13/haiti.pat.robertson/index.html.
37. S. Buck-Morss, *Hegel, Haiti and Universal History* (Pittsburgh, PA: University of Pittsburgh Press, 2009), 143.
38. The first article of the Slavery Convention of 1926 defines 'slavery' as 'the status or condition of a person over whom any or all of the powers attaching to the right of ownership are exercised'.
39. L. Balfour, 'What Babo Saw: Benito Cereno and "The World We Live In"', in A. Frank (ed.), *A Political Companion to Herman Melville* (Lexington, KY: University Press of Kentucky, 2013), 260.
40. E. Morgan, *The Aesthetics of International Law* (Toronto: University of Toronto Press, 2020), 30.
41. H. Melville, 'Benito Cereno', in *Melville's Short Novels: Authoritative Texts, Contexts, Criticism*, edited by D. McCall (New York: W.W. Norton, 2001), 329.
42. E. Gibbon, *The History of the Decline and Fall of the Roman Empire* (Harmondsworth: Penguin, 1996), 152.
43. G. Agamben, 'The Archaeology of Commandment', European Graduate School Video Lectures, 21 May 2011, www.youtube.com/watch?v=T4MjMj4S4B8.
44. Agamben, *Pilate and Jesus*.
45. Agamben, *Opus Dei*.
46. Agamben, *Opus Dei*, xii.
47. Agamben, *Opus Dei*, xii.
48. Agamben, *Opus Dei*, 21.
49. Agamben, *Opus Dei*, 47.
50. Agamben, *Opus Dei*, 72.
51. Agamben, *Opus Dei*, 72.
52. St T. Aquinas, *Summa Theologica* (New York: Benzinger Bros, 2013), 1524.
53. Buck-Morss, 'Hegel and Haiti'.
54. Buck-Morss, 'Hegel and Haiti'.

55. Buck-Morss, 'Hegel and Haiti', 826.
56. D. B. Davis, *The Problem of Slavery in Western Culture* (Ithaca, NY: Cornell University Press, 1966), 120.
57. Buck-Morss, 'Hegel and Haiti'.
58. G. Agamben, 'What is a Destituent Power?', trans. S. Wakefield, *Environment and Planning D: Society and Space* 32, no. 1 (2014): 71.
59. Agamben, 'What is a Destituent Power?', 71.
60. Agamben, *The Use of Bodies*, 78.
61. Agamben, *The Use of Bodies*, 78.
62. Agamben, *The Use of Bodies*, 79.
63. Charlton, 'Christians Escape Kenyan Terrorist Massacre After Muslim Passengers on Board Bus Say "Shoot Us All or Not at All"', *Daily Mail*, 21 December 2015, www.dailymail.co.uk/news/article-3369735/The-militants-threatened-shoot-Muslim-passengers-board-bus-defy-terrorists-demands-separate-Christians-deadly-terror-attack.html; *Guardian Africa*, 'Muslims Hailed for Protecting Christians During Terror Attack on Kenyan Bus'. *The Guardian*, 22 December 2015, www.theguardian.com/world/2015/dec/22/kenya-al-shabaab-attack-muslims-protect-christians-mandera.
64. R. M. Cover, *Justice Accused: Antislavery and the Judicial Process* (New Haven, CT: Yale University Press, 1975), 1–7, 108, 110.
65. Cover, *Justice Accused*, 3.
66. Cover, *Justice Accused*, 4–5.
67. Cover, *Justice Accused*, 5.
68. Cover, *Justice Accused*, 111.

8

The President's Two Bodies: A Study in Applied Political Theology

The medieval distinction between the official and the personal bodies of the state sovereign played out before the International Criminal Court in fairly dramatic action. This scenario involved the President of the Republic of Kenya willingly submitting to the jurisdiction of the International Criminal Court, but only in his personal capacity and not as president. Essentially this argument is based on the medieval doctrine of the 'King's two bodies'. The distinction of describing two bodies united in one in its origins sits at the crossroads of legal theory and political theology. As such, it draws from a rich heritage of these traditions that are of necessity developed through reconciling practical imperatives with theoretical niceties. Seeing the ancient doctrine of the King's two bodies manifested in a contemporary context thus provides the opportunity to observe a longstanding (if dormant and obscure) legal theory applied to a novel factual situation. It demonstrates that this legal fiction remains stubbornly useful and effective in navigating between political imperatives and legal strictures. Moreover, that unusual irruption of an arcane legal and political practice into a modern-day international courtroom shows that the practice still bears the unmistakeable signature of its mystical foundation.

On 8 October 2014, Uhuru Kenyatta the President of the Republic of Kenya became the first sitting Head of State in history to appear voluntarily in response to a summons before any international criminal court or tribunal. Or not. This chapter examines whether, and if so how far, his claims of attending in a personal capacity were sustainable as well as what its implications would be for sovereigns elsewhere. The charges against Kenyatta stem from the post-electoral violence that swept Kenya between the years 2007 to 2008 following the national elections. An International Criminal Court (ICC) Pre-Trial Chamber found that 'crimes against humanity had been committed on Kenyan territory'.[1] The basis for the case in part relies on the fact that Kenya signed the Rome Statute for the International Criminal Court (the Rome Statute) on 11 August 1999, then deposited its instrument of ratification on

15 March 2005 and passed it into domestic law by legislation giving effect to the Statute through the International Crimes Act.[2] That Act of Parliament makes provision for the punishment of genocide, crimes against humanity and war crimes, as well as to both enjoin and to enable Kenya's co-operation with the ICC. Consequently, Kenyatta had found himself in a legal and political double bind outlined below. The ICC case against him – which was the first and to date the only one initiated by the ICC Prosecutor acting on his own volition as opposed to a United Nations Security Council (UNSC) or State referral – was floundering for a lack of evidence. The prosecutor had continuously cited lack of cooperation from the Kenyan authorities as a key issue and was backed in this by the court.[3] The ICC Office of the Prosecutor (OTP) even stated on the record that the evidence available was insufficient to prove the charges.[4]

Ordinarily such a state of affairs regarding insufficient evidence would lead to a withdrawal of the charges or perhaps in the alternative, to even permanently stay the charges as an abuse of the criminal process. But these were no ordinary circumstances from the prosecution's perspective because they viewed the accused (through the State he headed) as being responsible for their lack of evidence by not providing it to them.[5] Consequently, the prosecution requested a *sine die* or perpetual adjournment until the cooperation sought was fulfilled.[6] The court for its part found Kenyatta's physical presence to be necessary at the hearing of that application given its serious subject matter.[7] This notwithstanding that – as only the dissenting judge pointed out – audio and video link technology was both available and had even been previously utilised by the court.[8]

Earlier moreover, the African Union (AU) in response to high-level Kenyan diplomatic lobbying passed a resolution that affirmed personal, which is to say procedural and not official, immunity from prosecution before the ICC for Heads of State and government as long as they remained such.[9] It therefore called for the trial of President Uhuru Kenyatta to be suspended until the completion of his term of office.[10] As a stratagem for evading the horns of the dilemma made out of these competing imperatives of the ICC summons and the AU resolution, Kenyatta claimed that he only appeared in his private capacity and not as president (Menya 2014). Indeed the Deputy President William Ruto (likewise facing a similar case before the same court and subject to the identical resolution) was sworn in as acting president, and the Kenyan State's functionaries resorted to elaborate lengths of public political choreography to treat him as such and emphasise the diminished status of Kenyatta.[11]

By asserting that he was attending only in his personal capacity it would appear that Kenyatta sought to fulfil the letter of the AU resolution if not quite be faithful to its spirit of defiance. He himself put it that he took this 'extraordinary and unprecedented step' in order 'to protect the sovereignty of the Kenyan republic'. Adding: 'to all those who are concerned that my personal attendance of the Status Conference compromises the sovereignty of our people, or sets a precedent for the attendance of presidents before the court – be reassured, this is not the case'.[12] By Kenyatta's reckoning, this unprecedented factual situation did not set a legal precedent for sovereigns appearing before the ICC. How far, if at all, is this correct?

Of course, the idea of a distinction between private citizen Kenyatta and Head of State Kenyatta is not exactly a Kenyan innovation. It goes back at least four centuries to *Calvin's Case*.[13] That famous English decision would be the relevant historical, logical and legal starting point under Kenyan law.[14] The relevant extract of the applicable Judicature Act contains the English Common Law reception clause which states that the jurisdiction of all Kenyan courts shall be exercised in conformity with (in order of descending priority) the Constitution, all written laws and 'so far as those written laws do not extend or apply, the substance of the common law, the doctrines of equity and the statutes of general application in force in England on the 12th August, 1897, and the procedure and practice observed in courts of justice in England at that date'.[15]

In *Calvin's Case,* the court found that there were distinct and separate political and personal capacities united in the King – a natural body and a political body.[16] As a result his 'Dignity never dies' but is passed on seamlessly to the next mortal body that is crowned sovereign.[17] This dignity is of juridical origin and enables the perpetuity of political power by emancipating the immortal sovereign persona from its mortal bearer.[18] As a legal and political doctrine it is completely ambiguous in that even as it distinguishes the office and the person of the sovereign it simultaneously extinguishes any notion of their separate existence.[19] No less an authority than Frederick Maitland considered this legal fiction to be illogical nonsense.[20] That has, however, neither hindered its durability nor diminished its utility. In keeping with the doctrine, the ICC Trial Chamber emphasised at the outset of the hearing that Kenyatta was before it not in his official capacity but only as an accused.[21] Schmitt first popularised the term 'political theology'.[22] In common terminology with, but without direct reference to Schmitt, Ernst Kantorowicz referred to this doctrine of the King's two bodies (modelled upon the mystical body of Christ whose divine person doubles his physical body) as an issue from the marriage of law and religion – political theology.[23] Elsewhere he has used it as synonymous with another Schmittian term *arcana imperii* or mysteries of state.[24] Political arcana are secret modes of the exercise of political power, ordinarily either hidden or obscured, or at any rate veiled from full public view.[25] What is interesting legally speaking, however, is the origin, outlines and provenance of this arcane political practice as it was evidenced in the appearance of Kenyatta before the ICC. Of all political theorists writing today perhaps Giorgio Agamben's work is most equal to the task of identifying, cataloguing and critiquing the fairly recent and intensifying global phenomena of sovereign Heads of State being treated as international criminals.[26] Furthermore, he has devoted part of his study to the phenomenon of the King's two bodies.[27] In 1991, Agamben stated that since World War I we have witnessed at least one positive development in the gradual intensification of sovereign police power:

> What the heads of state, who rushed to criminalize the enemy with such zeal, have not yet realized is that this criminalization can at any moment be turned against them. *There is no head of state on Earth today who, in this sense, is not virtually a criminal.* Today, those who should happen to wear the sad redingote of sovereignty know that they may be treated as criminals one day by their colleagues.[28]

In the event, Kenyatta's appearance was literally just that. He merely appeared but spoke not a word except through counsel. The ritualistic aspects of these proceedings as pageantry were therefore impossible to miss. That is to say, apart from political theatre, his physical presence did not seem otherwise necessary. Moreover his appearance, precedential or not, is as Agamben notes above, a template in fact if not law relevant and applicable to all other heads of state and government. The court's ruling in the end ordered the prosecutor to either prosecute the case or withdraw the charges.[29] The Chief Prosecutor complied by withdrawing the charges without prejudice to filing them later should new evidence come to light in the interim.[30] As it stands, however, the ICC in facing down the AU won the contest of wills regarding the appearance of a private citizen's body that is united with the public office of president. That legal victory can be expressed as a double negative: Heads of State and Government cannot not appear before the ICC. Phrased like that it covers the global category of sovereigns, not just Uhuru Kenyatta (despite his protestations) in Kenya, or even in Africa but the world at large. We need no reminding however that even King Pyrrhus won the Pyrrhic War but only at a prohibitive cost. Likewise the ICC in securing a sitting president's attendance and subsequently withdrawing his prosecution may have won a decidedly pyrrhic victory. That is, until we see the next sovereign in its dock.

Notes

1. International Criminal Court. 2010. 'Kenya: Situation in the Republic of Kenya', www.icc-cpi.int/kenya.
2. International Crimes Act 2008 (Laws of Kenya) A 16/08.

3. See *Prosecutor v Kenyatta* (Decision on Prosecution's applications for a finding of non-compliance pursuant to Article 87(7) and for an adjournment of the provisional trial date), International Criminal Court, Trial Chamber V(B), Case No ICC-01/09-02/11-908, 31 March 2014. www.icc-cpi.int/iccdocs/doc/doc1755190.pdf.

4. *Prosecutor v Kenyatta* (Prosecution notice regarding the provisional trial date), International Criminal Court, Trial Chamber V(B), Case No ICC-01/09-02/11, 5 September 2014, www.icc-cpi.int/iccdocs/doc/doc1826503.pdf.

5. *Prosecutor v Kenyatta* [3].

6. *Prosecutor v Kenyatta* [3].

7. *Prosecutor v Kenyatta* (Decision on Defence request for excusal from attendance at, or for adjournment of, the status conference scheduled for 8 October 2014), International Criminal Court, Trial Chamber V(B), Case No ICC-01/09-02/11, 30 September 2014 [20].

8. *Prosecutor v Kenyatta* (Partially Dissenting Opinion of Judge Kuniko Ozaki), International Criminal Court, Trial Chamber V(B), Case No ICC-01/09-02/11, 30 September 2014 [4]–[5]. www.icc-cpi.int/iccdocs/doc/doc1842119.pdf.

9. Extraordinary Session of the Assembly of the African Union of 12 October 2013 on Decision on Africa's Relationship with the International Criminal Court (ICC) (2013) AU/Dec.1-2 (October 2013), 1, art. 10(ii). www.iccnow.org/documents/Ext_Assembly_AU_Dec_Decl_12Oct2013.pdf.

10. Extraordinary Session of the Assembly of the African Union of 12 October 2013.

11. M. Pflanz, 'Uhuru Kenyatta's ICC Prosecution Close to Collapse as Lawyers Demand acquittal'. *The Telegraph*, 8 October 2014, www.telegraph.co.uk/news/worldnews/africaandindianocean/kenya/11149256/Uhuru-Kenyattas-ICC-prosecution-close-to-collapse-as-lawyers-demand-acquittal.html.

12. W. Menya, 'Fresh Push to Save Uhuru, Ruto from ICC', *Daily Nation*, 14 June 2014, www.nation.co.ke/news/politics/Fresh-push-to-save-Uhuru-and-Ruto-from-ICC/-/1064/2348938/-/k6ecsoz.

13. Calvin's Case (1608) 7 Co. Rep. 1a; 77 E.R. 377, 389.

14. Judicature Act 2012.

15. Judicature Act 2012.

16. Calvin's Case.

17. E. Kantorowicz, *The King's Two Bodies* (Princeton, NJ: Princeton University Press, 1957), 387.

18. G. Agamben, *Means Without End: Notes on Politics* (Minneapolis: University of Minnesota Press, 2000), 66.

19. M. P. Rogin, 'The King's Two Bodies: Abraham Lincoln, Richard Nixon & Presidential Self-Sacrifice', *The Massachusetts Review* 20, no. 3 (1979): 553.

20. F. Maitland, *English Law and the Renaissance* (Cambridge: Cambridge University Press, 1901), 134.

21. *Prosecutor v Kenyatta* (Prosecution notice regarding the provisional trial date), International Criminal Court, Trial Chamber V (B), Case No ICC-01/09-02/11, Status Conference Transcript Courtroom 1, [4] lines 4–5, <www.icc-cpi.int/iccdocs/doc/doc1846715.pdf > (last accessed 26 February 2018).

22. C. Schmitt, *Political Theology: Four Chapters on the Concept of Sovereignty*, trans. G. Schwab, 4th ed. (Chicago: University of Chicago Press, 1985).

23. E. Kantorowicz, *The King's Two Bodies* (Princeton, NJ: Princeton University Press, 1997), 59.
24. Kantorowicz, *The King's Two Bodies*, 65; C. Schmitt, *Dialogues on Power and Space* (Cambridge: Polity Press, 2014).
25. P. S. Donaldson, *Machiavelli and Mystery of State* (Cambridge: Cambridge University Press, 1988).
26. Agamben, *Means Without End*.
27. G. Agamben, *Homo Sacer: Sovereign Power and Bare Life* (Stanford, CA: Stanford University Press 1998).
28. Kantorowicz, *The King's Two Bodies*.
29. *The Prosecutor v Uhuru Muigai Kenyatta* (Situation in the Republic of Kenya) (Public Court Records, Trial Chamber V(b) Decision: 03/12/2014 Phase: Trial Decision on Prosecution's application for a further adjournment ICC-01/09-02/11-981, 9 December 2014).
30. *The Prosecutor v Uhuru Muigai Kenyatta* (Situation in the Republic of Kenya) (Public Court Records, Office of the Prosecutor Notice: 05/12/2014 Phase: Trial Notice of withdrawal of the charges against Uhuru Muigai Kenyatta ICC-01/09-02/11-983, 5 December 2014).

9

People, Politics and Populism in International Criminal Law

We the peoples of the United Nations
Preamble to the Charter of the United Nations

My first draft was quite good, I thought. I'd based it on the UN Charter itself. The Foreign Office sent me over a copy, with a note attached explaining that the preamble to the Charter was known as the Unconditional Surrender of the English Language.
The Complete Yes Prime Minister, p. 459

If what humans speak is a language, and if there is not only one language but many, then the plurality of languages corresponds to the plurality of people and political communities.
Giorgio Agamben, *What is Philosophy?*, p. 6

Introduction

According to the former President of the International Criminal Court (ICC), Judge Silvia Fernández de Gurmendi, populism – along with bigotry and xenophobia – has the potential to undermine 'international criminal justice and more broadly a rules-based order'.[1] John Dugard concurs, stating, 'At present the rule based international order is under threat from forces of nationalism and populism.'[2] In his speech, Dugard identifies the UN Human Rights Council and the ICC as two principal targets of these nationalist and populist forces. At least one witness in *The Prosecutor v. William Samoei Ruto and Joshua Arap Sang* identified 'a certain degree of anti-Kikuyu populism' in the run-up to the 2017 elections in Kenya.[3] Kagwanja examined how 'the resurgence of populism and ethnonationalism in the broader context of diffusion of 'informal' violence and widening inequality . . . sowed the seeds for the post-election violence'.[4] He notes that:

> Populism in Kenya has a long history in the struggle against colonialism and one-party tyranny . . . Like their global contemporaries, Kenyan populists

drew a sharp divide between 'the people' and 'the elite' and rhetorically appealed to change in the political order while invoking the idea of democracy as, above all, an expression of the people's will.[5]

Cas Mudde and Cristóbal Rovira Kaltwasser define populism as

> a thin-centred ideology that considers society to be ultimately separated into two homogeneous and antagonistic camps, 'the pure people' versus 'the corrupt elite,' and which argues that politics should be an expression of the *volonté générale* (general will) of the people.[6]

Mudde and Kaltwassser examine North America, South America, Eastern Europe and Western Europe, but they omit Africa from their analysis and do not address the question of violence in the context of populism. This chapter uses the work of Giorgio Agamben to analyse the banned Kenyan ethnic organisation the Mungiki as a case study, in order to argue that the Mungiki are populist purveyors of political violence above all else. Agamben is useful with regard to his work on the 'oath', the idea of a 'people', among others, which is of unique explanatory power with regard to the Mungiki case study. The Mungiki pose a significant populist challenge to international criminal law (ICL), given the failure to successfully repress and prosecute the phenomenon of the Mungiki despite the considerable time, effort and resources deployed to do so.

On 23 September 2011, during Francis Muthaura's pre-trial hearing for crimes against humanity before the ICC, his legal counsel, Karim Khan, said:

> Your Honours, another essential plank of this Prosecution's case is what can only be described as an unholy alliance, a deal with the devil, between the government and [sic] Kenya and a criminal, a lamentable, an invidious criminal group called the Mungiki.[7]

Describing the Mungiki as criminal was far from unusual; however, assimilating them to the devil was more so. Why did counsel Khan reach for the religious and literary metaphor of a 'deal with the devil' to express himself in the context of a trial? In one sense, Khan was in good company; however, even Special Rapporteur on Extrajudicial, Summary or Arbitrary Executions Philip Alston had described them as a criminal organisation that began as a cultural-religious movement and even provided basic services including sanitation and security to the poor in slum areas.[8] Furthermore, Mungiki members were both perpetrators and victims of serious crimes, including murder, both by the police and at the hands of vigilante groups – one of which, Alston notes, went by the moniker of 'The Hague'.[9] Alston's report on 'Extrajudicial, Summary or Arbitrary Executions' on his Mission to Kenya formed part of the court record in the Kenyan situation before the ICC.

The Mungiki have been accused of engaging in cyclical political violence in Kenyan elections, 'either as an intimidatory force (or political militia) operating prior to elections, or as perpetrators of retaliatory attacks (as in the 2007 post-election violence)'.[10] The campaign debate in the lead up to the post-electoral violence 'took a populist turn that paved the way for the ethnic violence after the elections', in which both sides were complicit.[11]

However, it is not the undeniable fact that the Mungiki engage in routine criminal activity that is the subject of this chapter, nor that it participated in both licit and illicit activities, nor even that its members were simultaneously perpetrators and victims of international crimes. Instead, what guides the present inquiry is that etymologically, the word 'Mungiki', in the language of the Kikuyu tribe, from which they principally draw their membership, is translatable to mean 'people' as a properly undifferentiated mass.[12] Grace Nyatuga Wamue has noted its close proximity in meaning to 'crowds' as well as 'masses' and that it 'reflects a belief that people are entitled to a particular place of their own in the ontological order. The term therefore means 'fishing the crowd from all corners of Kenya'. *Mungiki* also refers to a 'religio-political movement composed mainly of large masses of Gikuyu origin and other non-Gikuyu (Pokots, Luos and Maasais)'.[13] Jacob Rasmussen concurs with Wamue's view that, 'In Kikuyu, *Mungiki* means "multitude" or "masses"; the name powerfully communicates the movement's ambition of reaching out not only beyond the Kikuyu tribe, but also potentially beyond Kenya and Africa.'[14]

This aggressive mobilisation of the Kikuyu simultaneously as ethnos and demos against the spectre of both internal and external enemies with the Mungiki cast in the role of saviour through purificatory violence is what this chapter understands as populism in the Kenyan context. Here the Mungiki (in common with populists the world over) toy, in Agamben's terminology, with membership of a group (being present) versus inclusion in a group (being merely represented).[15] The stated aim of the Mungiki since their origins in the 1980s has been both to revive indigenous Gikuyu culture and religion and to liberate the Kenyan masses from political oppression and economic exploitation.[16] As Rasmussen notes, 'The movement's founders, and its adherents more generally, claim a specific heritage from the Mau Mau, Kenya's freedom fighters of the 1950s.'[17] Mungiki glide, navigate and oscillate between them as a Kikuyu-linked *ethnos*, which is to say they are a population group sharing a common descent and cultural tradition as well as a *demos*, which by contrast is people organised as a polity – usually by some form of democratic practice.

This last aspect is what renders the Mungiki a fit and proper subject of inquiry as a strain of African populism in a peculiarly Kenyan international criminal law context. As Sinja Graf ably demonstrates, 'the concept of crimes against humanity . . . in the Rome Statute of the International Criminal

Court criminalizes forms of direct, physical violence and thus excludes institutional and structural versions of violence from the range of practices that offend humanity'.[18]

This blind spot excluding institutional and structural forms of violence as identified by Graf is what this chapter tries to remedy, particularly by focusing on cultural and bodily violence perpetrated on women via the practice variously described as female circumcision/clitoridectomy/female genital mutilation/*Irûa* in the Kikuyu language (incorporating both female and male circumcision). This chapter will use the descriptive term 'female circumcision', combining as it does a communal practice incorporating both physical and ritualistic aspects that the medicalised 'clitoridectomy', condemnatory 'female genital mutilation' and approbatory *Irûa* do not adequately capture. This is done to demonstrate how an understanding of the central role of the practice is essential to link the key Mungiki characteristics (like the historical Mau Mau movement from which they trace their genealogy) of an anti-Western ideology that projects itself as an emancipatory force that is fixated on land and engages in political violence as a means to that end. Furthermore, Mutuma Ruteere makes the compelling argument that, 'rather than being one organization, Mungiki has become a discourse, invoked by different groups whether in authority or other criminal gangs to achieve particular ends'.[19]

The next section looks at how the term 'people' is treated in international criminal law and how the Mungiki as a phenomenon are not something with which the apparatus of international law was designed to deal. A theoretical and conceptual framework is then developed, based on the work of Giorgio Agamben, as a way to come to grips with this phenomenon of the Mungiki that is at once criminal, cultural, religious, economic, political, violent and founded on the subjugation of women's bodies and their simultaneous sidelining as active political subjects. That analysis is accomplished through categories derived from Aristotle's *Politics* by Giorgio Agamben, including *oikos* or home, *polis* or city, *stasis* or civil war, and finally amnesty. The third part looks at why the ICC grappled unsuccessfully with this unique and challenging strain of populism. The fourth section teases out why and how counsel Khan above would have reached for the devil as an apt metaphor to describe such practitioners and purveyors as well as victims of political violence as the Mungiki, in that way resisting his client being cast as an Africanised Faust. The conclusion summarises and explains what the inquiry has addressed, uncovered and suggests going forward.

People in the United Nations Charter and International Criminal Law

Why would a multi-faceted movement that, among other things, engages in political violence name itself as literally 'the people' or 'the masses', if not to politicise itself and in that way somehow legitimate itself as other than criminal? This section seeks to demonstrate that, by equating themselves with that elusive concept of 'the people', the Mungiki quite self-consciously seek to politically justify their use of violence as a legitimate emancipatory tool. To start with what the umbrella term 'people' covers in the context of the Mungiki, Rasmussen notes that:

> Since its inception Mungiki has been classified in a variety of ways: as a new religious and neo-traditionalist movement or occult sect, as a social movement or political party, and as a criminal gang or political militia. Though the importance of several of these labels has been overemphasised in the past, each contains some truth, a fact which indicates the movement's multilayered and multifaceted character. Its relatively large membership base, its extensive regional coverage (its members are drawn from both remote rural areas and densely populated urban neighbourhoods), and the many facets of the movement combine to make Mungiki a highly heterogeneous organisation.[20]

We can begin to make more sense of the Mungiki's high degree of heterogeneity by more closely analysing the term 'people', first in the context of international law and subsequently by engaging with Giorgio Agamben's philological work on the term. At the outset, the customary international law definition of a 'state' includes the key criteria of *population* (as well as territory, government and capacity to enter into relations with other states) but makes no explicit mention of 'people' as such.[21] This is perfectly congruent with the UN Charter's preamble, which opens with the phrase 'We the Peoples of the United Nations' with the term 'peoples' again used to reference 'the populations of the member States'.[22] It should be noted that this is not the uniform meaning of 'peoples' – not even in the Charter itself with, for example, 'peoples' bearing an ethnic connotation in Article 1(2) immediately following the Preamble.[23] Furthermore, out of a total of only twelve references to 'peoples', two are in the Preamble, another two make explicit reference to self-determination and the eight others are in the two chapters to do with the 'Declaration Regarding Non-Self-Governing Territories' and the now defunct 'International Trusteeship System'. That defunct Trusteeship System, moreover, has the only mention of 'people' in the entire Charter. Suffice to say the simultaneous overlap and distinction between population and people locates a population as an apolitical construct that is politically amenable to be constituted within a state while 'people' is politically instituted in and of itself, whether inside or outside the state. There is therefore scant scope for recognition of the Mungiki in public international law as currently constituted because the 'people' that would be recognisable would be the Kikuyu people and not the Mungiki as such, who would at best be a political movement dominated by, without being exclusively of, the Kikuyu as a vehicle for populist politics.

International criminal law, on the other hand, references 'people' at various points including the International Military Tribunal for the Major War Criminals of the European Axis (IMT) and the Nuremberg Charter, which only twice talks of 'civilian population' in the context of victims of war crimes and crimes against humanity but otherwise has nothing to say explicitly on people as such. Likewise, the International Military Tribunal for the Far East (IMTFE) Tokyo Trial Charter is silent on 'people' but does reference 'civilian population' once, in relation to crimes against humanity. This is the approach followed by the International Criminal Tribunal for the former Yugoslavia (ICTY), as well as the International Criminal Tribunal for Rwanda (ICTR) statutes, with their sole reference to 'civilian population', and also only in relation to crimes against humanity. The ICTR does, however, include a reference to 'civilised peoples', which the ICTY lacks. Furthermore, the ICTR's case law in *Akayesu* contributed the notion of 'any stable and permanent group' as being protected under the Genocide Convention.[24] The Rome Statute for the ICC is broader than all the preceding examples. Its Preamble opens with a reference to 'all peoples' and goes on to refer to 'population' twelve times with regard to both war crimes and crimes against humanity. However, because individual criminal responsibility and not group responsibility is the rule, there is limited scope for international criminal law to deal directly with a phenomenon like the Mungiki beyond the 'group of persons acting with a common purpose' meaning.[25] It is not just the UN Charter, or international criminal law, that has difficulty in finding purchase on the term 'people', but also political theory and practice.

In his essay, 'What is a People?', Giorgio Agamben begins by highlighting and demonstrating how the term 'people' in numerous examples also indicates 'the poor, the underprivileged, and the excluded'.[26] That is, it has the effect of connoting both the politically active subject as well as those that are excluded as anything other than abject, passive subjects. He goes on to claim, though, that this ambiguity is no accident but rather 'reflects an ambiguity inherent in the nature and function of the concept of *people* in Western politics'. This would make 'people' an 'oscillation between two opposite poles', not a unitary subject.[27] This also maps it into Agamben's most famous conceptual pair, *zoë* or 'naked life', represented in people and *bios* or political existence representing people.[28]

In contrast to the UN Charter, the international criminal law examples do not make reference to 'people' in the sense of a politically active population that is recognised as such, but rather as an abject population always and invariably in need of protection, and in no way directly present except as a void to be filled by humanitarian action. This is why populism here references a crisis of political representation where a schism is detected or claimed between the people and their rulers, where people are always spoken of but excluded because they are already spoken for. In the next section, this chapter will argue that populism pushes a form of illiberal democracy where human rights and the rule of law are sacrificed for political expediency in the name of the people, but really in the service of populism. Nothing illustrates this better than the position of women with regard to the Mungiki movement, as we shall see.

Female Circumcision and the Politics of Patriarchy

This section develops and builds on Graf's insight above[29] that there are certain constitutive elements of structural violence (in this specific instance symbolic as well as physical violence against women) that are rendered invisible in the ICC's practice. To start with, Beth Maina Ahlberg and Kezia Muthoni Njoroge note that the Mungiki are a predominantly young and predominantly male association.[30] Furthermore, there are no female leaders prominent anywhere in its ranks. Notwithstanding (or perhaps as a result of) that, the subjectification and subjugation of women are, as we shall see a key plank in Mungiki strategies: 'They have, for example, attacked women deemed improperly dressed for wearing trousers which in turn has led to public outcry against them.'[31] As Ahlberg and Njoroge note, 'one of its philosophies is to reinstate female genital cutting which has declined, as a result of which, *Mungiki* argues, society's good values have also declined'.[32] Neither consistency nor coherence of doctrine are the Mungiki's strong suit, as seen for instance in the fact that during the organisation's rampages, 'Men rather than women were hunted down and forcibly circumcised or had the penis cut or mutilated, sustaining long-lasting, and debilitating injuries.'[33] The Mungiki, through symbolic and physical violence – essentially in the name of protecting women – subsume women into men. The group then follows that up by progressively blurring the lines between Kikuyus, Kenyans and Africans generally.

Wamue notes that although the Mungiki are almost entirely a Kikuyu phenomenon, the movement has the ambition to embrace the Kenyan tribes through a shared African heritage involving 'a return to issues like female genital mutilation, sacrifices, oaths, and such outdated customs'.[34] Agamben situates the oath 'at the intersection of law and politics'[35] and notes its 'essential function' in the political constitution.[36] Moreover, Agamben obliquely references circumcision always and only in relation to belonging to a specific community.[37] This is the significance then of female circumcisions to Mungiki's populism or quasi-populism.

Wamue states that '*Mungiki* followers insist that their sect does not advocate the physical act of circumcision per se, but the moral grounding that is associated with the traditional rite'.[38] Mungiki further 'assert that less than 10 percent of *Mungiki* women are circumcised and that no one is insisting that they undergo circumcision'.[39] Jacob Rasmussen also states that 'Mungiki no longer advocate clitoridectomy' after noting that at the beginning that the Mungiki were of the view that 'many Kenyans operated with a fundamentally colonial mindset and needed to have their minds freed through a return to traditional religious and cultural values, including female circumcision'.[40] Nevertheless, the practice does persist, with Wairimu Ngaruiya Njambi self-reporting that:

> While the cultural significance of female circumcision has been waning in the past few decades, due mainly to church pressures, its cultural importance was still strong enough during my youth that I saw it as a necessity. It may seem ironic, given the tales of 'flight from torture' told in the media, but my parents refused to allow me to be circumcised, as it was against Catholic teachings. I had to threaten to run away from home and drop out of school before my parents relented and allowed me to be circumcised. The procedure was performed with a medical scalpel in a local clinic run by a woman who was a trained nurse in the western sense, and also a relative of an important Gikuyu female medical healer and powerful leader of the early 20th century, Wairimu Wa Kinene. During the operation, the hood of the clitoris was cut through its apex which caused the hood to split open and the clitoris to become more completely exposed. Such exposure has been associated with sexual enhancement. However, any generalization here might be unwise as it is likely that women's experience of *irua* [circumcision] varies, perhaps significantly.[41]

As already indicated in the literature surveyed above, the aim of the Mungiki since the 1980s has been to leverage religion for political and economic gain, not only 'to revive indigenous Kikuyu culture and religion, but also to liberate the Kenyan masses from political oppression and economic exploitation'.[42] With this background, we can now focus on the main objective of the Mungiki, which is allegedly to unite and mobilise the Kenyan masses to fight against the yoke of mental slavery to 'foreign cultures and agents of those cultures among the Kikuyu'.[43] It should be noted in the first instance that, 'Despite their Kikuyu heritage, the Kenyatta family are thus among the main offenders in what Mungiki perceive as 'historical injustices' to the Mau Mau and their kin.'[44] In other words (just like the Mau Mau before them), the Mungiki are very much an intra-Kikuyu phenomenon approximating a class conflict akin to civil war between the descendants of the Kikuyu peasantry and the

Kikuyu aristocracy.[45] This civil war nourishes the Mungiki's populism, in that it can claim to be fighting internal (fellow Kikuyu) and external (potentially anyone and everyone else) enemies of the Kikuyu simultaneously. Indeed, the vast majority of Mungiki victims are Kikuyus, a fact that was unacknowledged in the ICC proceedings, given its specific focus on Mungiki's violence against other groupings and tribes. Having said that, this intra-Kikuyu civil war is significant in understanding the context of the Mungiki's operations.

The theses advanced by Agamben in *Stasis: Civil War as a Political Paradigm* are first that civil war is the threshold between politicisation and de-politicisation (at least in the West), and second that the constitutive element of the state is the absence of a people.[46] Agamben goes on to note that 'a theory of civil war is completely lacking today', where 'hand in hand with the advance of global civil war' academic analysis is geared 'toward the conditions under which an international intervention becomes possible'.[47] His lament is that this 'seems incompatible with the serious investigation of a phenomenon that is at least as old as Western democracy'.[48] His work, however, does not purport to fill this gap on its own; rather, it restricts itself to examining *stasis* (treated as synonymous with civil war) in Ancient Greece and in Thomas Hobbes's work as representing 'two faces . . . of a single political paradigm', being 'the necessity of civil war' simultaneously with 'the necessity of its exclusion' – both of which mutually 'maintain a secret solidarity' that Agamben 'seek[s] to grasp'.[49]

The notion of *stasis* 'constitutes a zone of indifference between the unpolitical space of the family and the political space of the city'.[50] For Agamben, 'in Greek politics civil war functions as a threshold of politicisation and depoliticisation, through which the house is exceeded in the city and the city is depoliticised in the family'.[51] Agamben cites Greek law, under Solon the Athenian lawmaker, as punishing 'the citizen who had not fought for either one of the two sides in a civil war with the loss of civil rights'. Therefore, 'not taking part in civil war amounts to being expelled from the *polis* and confined to the *oikos*'.[52] Per Agamben, according to Aristotle:

> the invention of amnesty . . . with respect to civil war is thus the comportment most appropriate to politics. From the juridical point of view, *stasis* thus seems to be defined by two prohibitions, which perfectly cohere with one another: on the one hand, not participating in it is politically culpable; on the other, forgetting it once it has finished is a political duty.[53]

Rather provocatively, this is

> just the opposite, that is to say, of what civil war seems to be for the moderns: namely, something that one must seek to render impossible at every cost, yet that must always be remembered through trials and legal prosecutions.[54]

It is fully evident that in contrast to amnesty, repressing the Mungiki 'only makes its followers more determined and violent' (Wamue 2001, 453–67). Indeed, Agamben concludes the analysis by saying that '*stasis*, which can no longer be situated in the threshold between the oikos and the polis, becomes the paradigm of every conflict and re-emerges as terror'.[55]

Although he perhaps deems it too obvious to mention, Agamben's starting point of the centrality of civil war to Hobbes's state of nature is strengthened by the historical fact that *Leviathan* was conceived in and responded to the context of the English Civil War.[56] For Agamben, the mortal god Leviathan 'does not dwell within the city, but outside it'.[57] Further, the city is devoid of its inhabitants.[58] The iconic image thus discloses that 'political representation is only an optical representation (but no less effective on account of this)'.[59] Indeed 'at the very instant that the people chooses the sovereign it dissolves into a confused multitude'.[60] Consequently, 'the state of nature is the city from the perspective of civil war'.[61] Previously, in dialogue with Walter Benjamin and Carl Schmitt, Agamben has described this oscillation as between 'constituent power and constituted power'.[62] To put it more emphatically, 'the state of nature is a mythological projection into the past of the civil war; conversely, civil war is a projection of the state of nature into the city – it is what appears when one considers the city from the perspective of the state of nature'.[63] Furthermore, 'political theology appears in Hobbes in a decidedly eschatological perspective'.[64] For Agamben, 'it is certain that the political philosophy of modernity will not be able to emerge out of its contradictions except by becoming aware of its theological roots'.[65]

Agamben's work does delve deeply into theological concepts, but the focus is more on their strategic deployment rather than their systematic development over time.[66] As such, it is always political theology in the Schmittian sense. In the context of the law's complicity with violence generally, this is a political theodicy very much in the vein of his treatments of the Faustian pact, which is located at the intersection of philosophy, law and religion. The Mungiki as purveyors of political violence fall squarely within this formulation as we shall see. As Agamben's analysis has made it possible to see, violence is included in the juridical order as either sanctioned in the sense of permitted or sanctioned in the sense of not permitted.[67] This perfect ambiguity and dual valence of 'sanction' in law is key to the riddle of law's reliance upon and repressing of violence.

The Faustian Pact, Political Violence and Law

The Mungiki's rise in influence and popularity in part depended on 'the inability of the Government to demonstrate its monopoly over violence for the common good'.[68] Given their use of violent means, the Mungiki pose a conscious, clear, direct and deliberate threat to the Kenyan state's Weberian claim to 'the monopoly on the legitimate use of physical violence' within the Kenyan territory.[69] Writing in the period following Germany's defeat in World War I (and while resisting the notion of a collective 'war guilt'), Max Weber set out his task in *Politics as a Vocation* as an attempt to sociologically define a political association and stated that, 'in the final analysis, the modern state can be defined only sociologically by the specific *means* that are peculiar to it, as to every political association: namely, physical violence'.[70] Furthermore he went on to add that:

> If there existed only societies in which violence was unknown as a means, *then* the concept of the 'state' would disappear; *in that event* what would have emerged is what, in this specific meaning of the word, we might call 'anarchy'.[71]

Weber did add the proviso that, 'Violence, is of course, not the normal or the only means available to the state . . . But it is the means specific to the state.'[72] Derrida summarised this as:

> At its most fundamental level, European law tends to prohibit individual violence and to condemn it not because it poses a threat to this or that law but because it threatens the juridical order itself . . . Law has an interest in a monopoly of violence to protect neither justice nor legality but law as such.[73]

Weber's rightly famous passage defining the state deserves contextual quotation to demonstrate the stakes of Mungiki's political violence in its challenge to the Kenyan state apparatus:

> In the past the use of physical violence by widely differing organisations – starting with the clan – was completely normal. Nowadays, in contrast, we must say that the state is the form of human community that (successfully) lays claim to *the monopoly of the legitimate use of physical violence* within a particular territory – and this idea of 'territory' is an essential defining feature. For what is specific to the present is that all other organisations or individuals can assert the right to use physical violence only insofar as the *state* permits them to do. The state is regarded as the sole source of the 'right' to use violence. Hence, 'politics' for us means to strive for a share of power or to influence the distribution of power, whether between states or between the groups of people contained within a state.[74]

Less well known and less quoted is that in the same place Weber said: 'Anyone who wishes to engage in politics at all . . . is entering into relations with satanic powers that lurk in every act of violence.'[75] For removal of doubt,

Weber even goes on to quote the same passage of Goethe's *Faust* in *Politics as a Vocation* as well as *Science as a Vocation*: 'Reflect, the Devil is old, so become old if you would understand him.'[76] Given the irresistible logic that political science as a discipline would have to be located at the centre of the *Politics as a Vocation/Science as a Vocation* axis, the value of the Faustian pact as an explanatory framework for international criminal law's relationship with violence becomes increasingly clear. Namely, the analysis of that Mephistophelean pact analogy demonstrates that it is based on excusing otherwise evil acts by arguing that that evil will nevertheless promote good – which is to say that the socio-legal legitimation of violence links good to evil in purportedly productive ways. Giorgio Agamben speculates on a behind the scenes and covert engagement between Walter Benjamin and Carl Schmitt concerning a battle of these prominent intellectuals over the void that is the state of exception where nothing is forbidden and the law is neutralized[77] – which is to say where the force that usually accompanies law is freed up of the law's strictures. Furthermore, that decoupling of force from law is legitimated and justified in the name of emergency measures that are then progressively normalised.

Writing in the wake of Weber, Walter Benjamin, in his *Critique of Violence in Reflections*, sets out his own purpose as explicating the relationships between violence and law and justice:

> The task of a critique of violence can be summarized as that of expounding its relation to law and justice. For a cause, however effective, becomes violent, in the precise sense of the word, only when it bears on moral issues. The sphere of these issues is defined by the concepts of law and justice. With regard to the first of these, it is clear that the most elementary relationship within any legal system is that of ends to means, and, further, that violence can first be sought only in the realm of means, not of ends.[78]

Benjamin's own view of Weber's monopoly of violence as the specified means available to the state is instructive with regard to the political challenge directed to the Kenyan legal order (which view coheres perfectly with Derrida's, as noted above, because it was indeed the basis upon which Derrida relied):

> the law's interest in a monopoly of violence vis-à-vis individuals is not explained by the intention of preserving legal ends but, rather, by that of preserving the law itself; that violence, when not in the hands of the law, threatens it not by the ends that it may pursue but by it mere existence outside the law.[79]

Schmitt, also writing in the wake of Weber's secularisation thesis, famously said it was sociologically necessary to consider that, 'All significant concepts of the modern theory of the state are secularized theological concepts.'[80] According to him, this was 'because of their historical development' (he provides the example of a theological 'omnipotent God' reasserted as the political 'omnipotent lawgiver').[81] Schmitt makes no mention of the Faustian pact here, but the same logic would follow as we shall see when we return to 'the deal with the devil' that was referenced with regard to the Mungiki.

The precise contours of 'the deal with the devil to which counsel Khan referred were that Uhuru Kenyatta mediated between his political party, the Party of National Unity (PNU), and the Mungiki to organise retaliatory attacks against the rival political party, the Orange Democratic Movement (ODM), in order to consolidate PNU's hold on power.[82] In return, the allegation was that Kenyatta, in concert with others, 'provided funding, transportation, accommodation, uniforms, weapons and logistical support to the Mungiki and pro-PNU youth to carry out coordinated attacks in specific locations'. Additionally, they guaranteed safe passage with the knowing connivance of the police to not intervene both before and after attacks.[83] Essentially, therefore, the pact was for the Mungiki to provide political violence in exchange for funding, support and facilitation. Put simply, the Mungiki marketised their capacity for actual and symbolic political violence and were recompensed in return.

Rasmussen notes that:

> One of Mungiki's central political demands has been for a generational transfer of power, a demand rooted in the Kikuyu tradition, *itwika*, according to which an older generation hands over power to a younger generation in a 30–40-year cycle.[84]

This demand has led to a Machiavellian struggle between the state and the movement in a game of bluff, double bluff and even triple bluff that Rasmussen ably conveys and summarises as 'while Mungiki officially declared its support for Kenyatta and Moi [in the 2002 elections], in reality it supported the opposition candidate, Mwai Kibaki'.[85]

To start with the bluff, it began with then President Daniel Arap Moi anointing Uhuru Kenyatta as his successor (and in that way having him as the sole viable Kikuyu candidate – a plan that was scuttled by prominent Luo leader Raila Odinga supporting Mwai Kibaki, a Kikuyu who ultimately and unexpectedly won) in order to manipulate the large and recalcitrant Kikuyu voting bloc into aligning with this line of succession and power transfer:

> For Mungiki, Uhuru Kenyatta (son of Kenya's first President after independence, Jomo Kenyatta) was a bad choice. He was widely known as 'a spender', a businessman with little political experience and, more

controversially, he represented the Kenyatta family, who in Mungiki's eyes had betrayed their ancestors, the Mau Mau, at independence. It seems clear that Moi was trying to sell an ethnic Kikuyu leader to Mungiki in return for the votes of young Kikuyu that the movement could guarantee. But Mungiki's leader, Maina Njenga, had political ambitions of his own and wanted to run for parliament. The problem, as Muigai presents it, was that both Uhuru Kenyatta and Maina Njenga wanted the votes of the Kikuyu youth, but that Njenga (unlike Uhuru) had a massive organised following in the traditionally Kikuyu-dominated regions of the country.[86]

The double bluff arose because the Mungiki saw clearly through Moi's scheme and its motivations, and as a consequence took steps to neutralise these machinations:

> Mungiki suspected that Moi was playing a double game whereby he would gain the support of Mungiki's Kikuyu supporters for the election while simultaneously creating tension between Uhuru and Mungiki that would later allow Uhuru to denounce the movement.[87]

Mungiki's response was the triple bluff, which may be summarised as:

> The movement's hidden strategy was to declare its public support for Uhuru Kenyatta, thus denying him the votes of ordinary Kikuyu voters alarmed by Mungiki's violent reputation, while secretly directing its own members to vote for the opposition just one week before the elections.[88]

As seen below:

> Mungiki decided to cooperate with Moi and publicly support Uhuru Kenyatta. On one occasion, the movement organised a large fundraising event, attended by 10,000 people, in support of Uhuru. On another, Mungiki held a large prayer meeting in a field belonging to Uhuru (although Mungiki made it appear as though the proceedings had Uhuru's blessing, the event took place without his knowledge). The idea was to discredit Uhuru by making strategic use of Mungiki's own bad reputation; by associating him with the movement and with the political violence it had come to represent, Mungiki sought to scare off Uhuru's potential voters. The motivation for this strategy was to secure the election of the presidential candidate that the Mungiki leadership actually wanted: Mwai Kibaki. It also offered the opportunity for Mungiki to get its revenge on both Moi, who had mounted brutal police campaigns against the movement, and on Kenyatta, who represented the family widely blamed for the historical injustices that the movement and its followers claimed to have suffered.[89]

Furthermore, following this, the government 'launched a police crackdown on the movement and created special units to infiltrate its ranks'.[90] To add to the murkiness of distinguishing between real and simulated Mungiki action, Peter Kagwanja argues that Mungiki's allegations of state infiltration by police agents and even of state-sponsored pseudo gangs masquerading as Mungiki should not be taken lightly.[91] This is particularly so given that similar tactics were deployed by the British colonial state against the Mau Mau, which is the template followed here.[92] What is not seriously in doubt, however, is that the Mungiki commoditised their capacity to unleash real and symbolic violence for both commercial and political ends.

Resort to violence is essentially a Faustian pact by way of conceiving of violence as inherently evil, but nevertheless capable of achieving good when opposing violence. In Goethe's *Faust*, Faust asks Mephistopheles: 'Who are you then?' and is answered perhaps truthfully but not completely honestly: 'Part of that force which would do ever evil, and does ever good.'[93] As Walter Benjamin points out, distinguishing between law-making or law-preserving violence leaves the question of violence itself untouched and unquestioned.[94] The prevailing test is only violence as a means to an end; therefore, in this way, violence is only to be evaluated strictly as a means, a so-called necessary evil whose evil is undisputed but whose necessity is impossible to prove or disprove.

Agamben discusses two paradigms in Western ethical and political thought that are especially critical to the 'unwilling and unable' pairing in the ICC's complementary jurisdiction.[95] The first 'tragic' model is based on action and praxis, while the second is anti-tragic and based on knowledge and contemplation. The tragedy of Faust resolutely assigns the primacy to action.[96] Free will read as freedom is equivocal because the context in which it is used is not political freedom but rather moral and juridical freedom regarding the imputability of actions. The church fathers used 'it as a technical term to express the mastery of the will over actions in . . . the origin of evil and responsibility of sin'.[97] In that sense, it is found for the first time 'referring significantly to the devil'.[98] Indeed, per Agamben, God accuses Satan of accusation itself.[99]

For Agamben, it 'is an obvious fact' that 'the law is defined as an articulation of violence and justice'.[100] Agamben positions this definitive aspect of the law as a political theodicy – a justification of evil – stating that 'the law consists of essentially in the production of a permitted violence, which is to say in a justification of violence'.[101] He even references Kelsen's inclusion of the non-violence precept in the Sermon on the Mount as also based on sanction;[102] this is the same sermon that Weber analysed only to conclude that politicians 'must abide by its precise opposite lesson: 'You shall use force to resist evil.'[103] Agamben notes that this link between the law and sanction was considered as 'less than perfect' in Roman jurisprudence.[104] This approach is therefore comparable to Weber's answer to the question, 'Can the ethical demands made on politics really be quite indifferent to the fact that politics operates with a highly specific means, namely, power behind which *violence* lies concealed?'[105] This is why Weber includes in this the startling observation that 'the politician must abide by the opposite commandment ['resist not him that is evil with violence']: 'You shall use force to resist evil, for otherwise you will be *responsible* for its running amok.'[106] Weber arrived at that conclusion by identifying and distinguishing an ethic of responsibility versus an ethic of conviction. While the former holds that 'a Christian does what is right and leaves the outcome to God', the latter provides that you must answer for the (foreseeable) consequences of your actions.[107] What unites Weber and those who wrote in his wake is that violence is justified as being politically necessary, particularly with regard to resisting violence, and that this riddle is in the nature of a Faustian pact.

Conclusion

The Mungiki consciously utilise the etymological associations of their name with 'people' to promote a form of Kikuyu nationalism in a complex process of representation of the Kikuyu tribe onward to Kenyans as a whole and then all the way to Africa generally. This process of conflation is (but for defence counsel Khan's 'deal with the devil' observation above) neither adequately identified nor captured using the mechanism of international criminal trials. This form of Mungiki populism further pushes the distinction between victim and victimiser right to the limit and beyond. Mungiki's political and historical antecedents are based very much on control over women's bodies and sexuality, utilising both physical and structural forms of political violence as the springboard for their authority over the rest of society.

This chapter began by noting that 'Mungiki' literally means 'people' and then went on to identify the direct absence of 'people' in international law. It then looked at how Mungiki's theory and practice of female circumcision were a political act of symbolic violence. That violence perpetrated by the Mungiki against the Kenyan state was then contextualised with regard to the law by reference to the literary trope of the Faustian pact. Given these complexities, prosecution – whether domestic, hybridised or international – while necessary to redress the criminal violations committed, can only be one of the necessary responses to the political violence associated with the Mungiki.

Notes

1. International Criminal Court, Judge Silvia Fernández de Gurmendi President of the International Criminal Court: Keynote remarks at plenary session of the 16th Session of the Assembly of States Parties to the Rome Statute on the topic of the 20th anniversary of the Rome Statute, 13 December 2017, p. 4.

2. J. Dugard, 'Rome Statute 20 Years: Addressing Current and Future Challenges. Speech to Assembly of States Parties of the ICC', 7 December 2018, https://asp.icc-cpi.int/iccdocs/asp_docs/ASP17/20A.Dugard%20speech.pdf.

3. ICC, Transcript case *The Prosecutor v. William Samoei Ruto and Joshua Arap Sang*, ICC-01/09-01/11, 15 January 2016, at 63.

4. P. M. Kagwanja, 'Courting Genocide: Populism, Ethno-nationalism and the Informalisation of Violence in Kenya's 2008 Post-election Crisis', *Journal of Contemporary African Studies* 27, no. 3 (2009): 3.

5. Kagwanja, 'Courting Genocide', 366.

6. C. Mudde and C. R. Kaltwasser, *The Oxford Handbook of Political Ideologies* (Oxford: Oxford University Press, 2013).

7. *The Prosecutor vs Francis Kirimi Muthaura, Uhuru Muigai Kenyatta, and Mohammed Hussein Ali*, ICC Pre-Trial Chamber II, Confirmation of Charges Hearing, ICC-01/09-02/11, Court Transcript, p. 67.

8. UN Human Rights Council, Report of the Special Rapporteur on Extrajudicial, Summary or Arbitrary Executions Mr Philip Alston: Addendum – Mission to Kenya, A/HRC/11/2/Add.6, 26 May 2009, p. 7.

9. UN Human Rights Council, Report of the Special Rapporteur, p. 8, n 12.

10. J. Rasmussen, 'Outwitting the Professor of Politics? Mungiki Narratives of Political Deception and Their Role in Kenyan Politics', *Journal of Eastern African Studies* 4, no. 3 (2010): 435–49.

11. A. Harneit-Sievers and R. M. Peters, 'Kenya's 2007 General Election and Its Aftershocks', *Africa Spectrum* 43, no. 1 (2008): 136.

12. G. Wamue, 'Revisiting Our Indigenous Shrines Though Mungiki', *African Affairs* 100, no. 400 (2001): 451.

13. Wamue, 'Revisiting Our Indigenous Shrines Though Mungiki', 451.

14. Rasmussen, 'Outwitting the Professor of Politics?', 437.

15. G. Agamben, *Homo Sacer: Sovereign Power and Bare Life* (Stanford, CA: Stanford University Press, 1998), 24.

16. B. M. Ahlberg and K. M. Njoroge, '"Not Men Enough to Rule!" Politicization of Ethnicities and Forcible Circumcision of Luo Men During the Postelection Violence in Kenya', *Ethnicity & Health* 18, no. 5 (2013): 454–68.

17. Rasmussen, 'Outwitting the Professor of Politics?', 437.

18. S. Graf, 'To Regain Some Kind of Human Equality: Theorizing the Political Productivity of "Crimes Against Humanity"', *Law, Culture and the Humanities* 13, no. 3 (2017): 761.

19. M. Ruteere, 'Dilemmas of Crime, Human Rights and the Politics of *Mungiki* Violence in Kenya', Kenya Human Rights Institute (2008), 23–4, https://papers.ssrn.com/sol3/papers.cfm?abstract_id=1462685.

20. Rasmussen, 'Outwitting the Professor of Politics?', 437–8.

21. See Montevideo Convention on the Rights and Duties of States (1933), 165 LNTS 19 ('Montevideo Convention'), Article 1.

22. R. Wolfram, 'Preamble', in *The Charter of the United Nations: A Commentary*, 3rd ed., edited by B. Simma, D.-E. Khan, G. Nolte and A. Paulus (Oxford: Oxford University Press, 2012), 103.

23. Wolfram, 'Preamble', 103.

24. *Prosecutor v. Akayesu*, ICTR, Judgement, ICTR-96-4-T, 2 September 1998, para 516.

25. See Rome Statute for the International Criminal Court (1998), 2187 UNTS 90 ('Rome Statute'), Article 25.
26. G. Agamben, *Means Without End: Notes on Politics* (Minneapolis: University of Minnesota Press, 2000a), 29.
27. Agamben, *Homo Sacer*, 177.
28. Agamben, *Homo Sacer*; G. Agamben, *State of Exception* (Chicago: Chicago University Press, 2005); G. Agamben, *The Sacrament of Language: An Archaeology of the Oath* (Stanford, CA: Stanford University Press 2011).
29. Graf, 'To Regain Some Kind of Human Equality'.
30. Ahlberg and Njoroge, '"Not Men Enough to Rule!"'.
31. Ahlberg and Njoroge, '"Not Men Enough to Rule!"', 464.
32. Ahlberg and Njoroge, '"Not Men Enough to Rule!"', 460.
33. Ahlberg and Njoroge, '"Not Men Enough to Rule!"', 462.
34. Wamue, 'Revisiting Our Indigenous Shrines Though Mungiki', 466.
35. Agamben, *The Sacrament of Language*, 1.
36. Agamben, *The Sacrament of Language*, 2.
37. G. Agamben, *The Time That Remains: A Commentary on the Letter to the Romans* (Stanford, CA: Stanford University Press, 2005), 19, 21, 24, 165, 176.
38. Wamue, 'Revisiting Our Indigenous Shrines Though Mungiki', 461.
39. Wamue, 'Revisiting Our Indigenous Shrines Though Mungiki', 461.
40. Rasmussen, 'Outwitting the Professor of Politics?', 438.
41. W. N. Njambi, 'Dualisms and Female Bodies in Representations of African Female Circumcision: A Feminist Critique'. *Feminist Theory* 5, no. 3 (2004): 294.
42. Ahlberg and Njoroge, '"Not Men Enough to Rule!"', 464.
43. K. W. Stringer, '"A Household Divided": A Fragmented Religious Identity, Resistance and the Mungiki Movement Among the Kikuyu in Post-colonial Kenya', PhD thesis, Ohio State University, 117, https://etd.ohiolink.edu/!etd.send_file?accession=osu1395764314&disposition=inline.
44. Rasmussen, 'Outwitting the Professor of Politics?', 444.
45. K. Kyle, 'The Politics of the Independence of Kenya', *Contemporary British History* 11, no. 4 (1997): 50; J. Lonsdale, 'Mau Maus of the Mind: Making Mau Mau and Remaking Kenya', *The Journal of African History* 31, no. 3 (1990): 393–421. T. R. Mockaitis, 'Minimum Force, British Counter-Insurgency and the Mau Mau Rebellion: A Reply', *Small Wars & Insurgencies* 3, no. 2 (1992): 88.
46. G. Agamben, *Stasis: Civil War as a Political Paradigm (Homo Sacer II, 2)* (Edinburgh: Edinburgh University Press, 2015).
47. Agamben, *Stasis*, 1.
48. Agamben, *Stasis*, 1.
49. Agamben, *Stasis*, 3.
50. Agamben, *Stasis*, 12.
51. Agamben, *Stasis*, 12.
52. Agamben, *Stasis*, 13.
53. Agamben, *Stasis*, 15.
54. Agamben, *Stasis*, 16.
55. Agamben, *Stasis*, 18.
56. T. Hobbes, *Leviathan*, Richard Tuck ed. (Cambridge: Cambridge University Press, 2005).
57. Agamben, *Stasis*, 27.

58. Agamben, *Stasis*, 29.
59. Agamben, *Stasis*, 33.
60. Agamben, *Stasis*, 30–1, 35.
61. Agamben, *Stasis*, 4.
62. Agamben, *Stasis*, 30, 33, 36, 54, 56.
63. Agamben, *Stasis*,
64. Agamben, *Stasis*, 47.
65. Agamben, *Stasis*, 54.
66. G. Agamben, *Karman: A Brief Treatise on Action, Guilt, and Gesture* (Stanford, CA: Stanford University Press, 2018), 43–4.
67. Agamben, *Karmen*, 20.
68. M. Katumanga and L. Cliffe, *Armed Violence and Poverty in Nairobi: A Mini Case Study for the Armed Violence and Poverty Initiative* (Bradford: Bradford Centre for International Cooperation and Security. 2005), 17.
69. M. Weber, *The Vocation Lectures*, ed. D. S. Owen (Indianapolis, IN: Hackett, 2004), 33.
70. Weber, *The Vocation Lectures*, 33.
71. Weber, *The Vocation Lectures*, 33.
72. Weber, *The Vocation Lectures*, 33.
73. J. Derrida, 'Force de Loi: La "Fondement Mystique de L'Autorite"'/'Force of Law: the "Mystical Origin of Authority"', *Cardozo Law Review* 11, nos 5–6 (1990): 987.
74. Weber, *The Vocation Lectures*, 33.
75. Weber, *The Vocation Lectures*, 90.
76. Weber, *The Vocation Lectures*, 27, 91.
77. Agamben, *State of Exception*, 52–64.
78. W. Benjamin, *Reflections: Essays, Aphorisms, Autobiographical Writings* (San Diego, CA: Harcourt Brace Jovanovich, 1978), 277.
79. Benjamin, *Reflections*, 280–1.
80. C. Schmitt, *Political Theology: Four Chapters on the Concept of Sovereignty* (Chicago: Chicago University Press, 2005), 36.
81. Schmitt, *Political Theology*, 36.
82. *The Prosecutor vs Francis Kirimi Muthaura, Uhuru Muigai Kenyatta, and Mohammed Hussein Ali*, ICC Pre-Trial Chamber II, Public Redacted Version Decision on the Confirmation of Charges Pursuant to Article 61(7)(a) and (b) of the Rome Statute, at paras 289–95.
83. *The Prosecutor vs Francis Kirimi Muthaura, Uhuru Muigai Kenyatta, and Mohammed Hussein Ali*.
84. Rasmussen, 'Outwitting the Professor of Politics?', 438.
85. Rasmussen, 'Outwitting the Professor of Politics?', 435.
86. Rasmussen, 'Outwitting the Professor of Politics?', 440.
87. Rasmussen, 'Outwitting the Professor of Politics?', 440.
88. Rasmussen, 'Outwitting the Professor of Politics?', 441.
89. Rasmussen, 'Outwitting the Professor of Politics?', 440.
90. Rasmussen, 'Outwitting the Professor of Politics?', 444.
91. P. Kagwanja, 'Clash of Generations? Youth Identity, Violence and the Politics of Transition in Kenya, 1997–2002', in *Vanguards and Vandals: Youth, Politics and Conflict in Africa*, edited by J. Abbink and I. Kessel (Leiden: Brill, 2005), 41–2.

92. Kagwanja, 'Clash of Generations?'
93. J. Goethe, *Faust: A Tragedy: Interpretive Notes, Contexts, Modern Criticism*, 2nd ed. (New York: W.W. Norton, 2001), 36.
94. Benjamin, *Reflections*, 277.
95. Agamben, *Karman*.
96. Agamben, *Karman*, 35.
97. Agamben, *Karman*, 47.
98. Agamben, *Karman*, 47.
99. Agamben, *Karman*, 7.
100. Agamben, *Karman*, 20.
101. Agamben, *Karman*, 22.
102. Agamben, *Karman*, 22.
103. Weber, *The Vocation Lectures*, 81–2.
104. Agamben, *Karman*, 23.
105. Weber, *The Vocation Lectures*, 81.
106. Weber, *The Vocation Lectures*, 83.
107. Weber, *The Vocation Lectures*, 83.

10

War! What is it Good For? Law, Violence, the 'Laudes Regiae' and Laudatory Reggae

War is the father of all things, the king of all things.
Some he proves to be gods, others men;
some he makes slaves, others free.

Heraclitus's Fragmentum 53

Introduction

Whereas both law and music have provided justification for war as a necessary evil, the two are seldom considered together in that regard. Although they have both provided an explaining away of the evil of war (a lay theodicy), this remains unexplored and under-theorised. Furthermore, ironically it is more present for music and musicians than it is for law and lawyers.[1] Parker notes that, 'As a community of jurists, we have become deaf to law and to the problem of the acoustic.'[2] Lyrics link law to text, to poetry and sometimes, as we shall see, to violence. That confluence is the point of inquiry for this chapter. Is it really too simplistic, as Manderson critiques Derrida in *Songs Without Music: Aesthetic Dimensions of Law and Justice*, to understand 'law as a species of mandated force, of state-sanctioned violence'?[3] After all, Manderson agrees that 'War, like law, is not merely an exercise in brute force but rather a series of symbolic acts.'[4] Sykes observes the ambiguity or ambivalence in that 'music is a cultural force that may contest or enhance political and legal power'.[5]

Consequently, the chapter asks and attempts to answer several questions: What utility could there possibly be in war? What does the law have to say about it? And why is music relevant? The argument pursued is that the combination of music, law and violence aggregates and disaggregates the body politic. This chapter examines and stages encounters between war, law and music spanning from the 'Laudes Regiae' medieval acclamatory hymn and George Frideric Handel's 'The Lord is a Man of War' to Bob Marley's speech set to Reggae 'War' and Edwin Starr's 'War' in relation to the international law on the use of force. In this vein, a little-known war casualty was Starr's 1969 Vietnam-era protest song 'War', which gives this chapter its full title. Along with Culture Club's 1984 ironically titled 'War Song' among others, it was banned from radio playlists in the lead-up to the first Gulf War.[6] With lyrics like 'War . . . What is it good for? . . . Absolutely nothin', '[War] friend only to the undertaker/Oh, war it's an enemy to all mankind' in the case of Starr and 'war is stupid and people are stupid' for fighting wars in the case of Culture Club, these songs were not considered good for morale, either civilian or military, and were viewed as dangerously off message in an era of ever-more stringent control over messaging in times of war.

Be that as it may, stating that war is good for absolutely nothing is perhaps more about expressing dissent than factually reporting on an existing state of affairs. In a world of rational actors (and surely political leaders belong to this category as well), war is engaged with in a calculated fashion and entails risks and rewards, characterisations and consequences. Joel Baer agrees that the phrase 'enemy of all mankind' encountered as above in Starr's *War* or *hostis humani generis,* as it is rendered in international criminal law, is not metaphorical.[7] He adds that in the eighteenth century, the pirate was likened to Satan, in that one was in a state of enmity with humanity while the other similarly was at war with God, and both were doomed as a result.[8] Enter then Schmitt. He said at least three things relevant to war, enmity, Satan, piracy and literalness. First, and most famously, he maintains that, 'All significant concepts of the modern theory of the state are secularized theological concepts'.[9] Second, and quite infamously, he claims that, 'The specific political distinction to which political actions and motives can be reduced is that between friend and enemy.'[10] Furthermore, these 'concepts are to be understood in the concrete and existential sense, not as metaphors or symbols'.[11] This is why Sonja Schillings is then able to argue that the legal fiction of 'enemy of humanity' provides more than ample traction for legitimating violence in the name of the state.[12] Third, but not as famously, Schmitt said that, 'To me, the prosecutorial is even more sinister than the inquisitorial. Perhaps in my case this can be traced back to theological roots. For *Diabolus* means "the prosecutor".'[13]

The present discussion consequently looks into how war manipulates the applicability and non-applicability of rules in both time and space – more poetically, the mortal realm – as if by (and akin to) magic through law. Giorgio Agamben traces some rhetorical and grammatical aspects of language relevant to law in the present discussion. The first rhetorical aspect is the 'assertion', which is in the indicative mood, while the second is the 'commandment', which is in the imperative mood. One refers to what 'is' or exists; the other refers to 'be' or shall exist. One belongs to science and philosophy; the other to politics, law, religion and magic.[14] Therefore, the imperative mood defines the verbal mode proper to law and religion, which share a performative character. Words and phrases in those discourses do not refer to actual being but to having-to-be.[15] Furthermore, the capture of such trappings of law is more real than is apparent in the case of total war, which is why examining a cultural artefact, like music, in times of war along with law in a time of war can tell us something about what war is for and the role of music.

War in Domestic and International Law

The first Chief Justice of the High Court of Australia, Sir Samuel Griffith, had occasion to speak of the Australian Commonwealth Constitution's 'war power'.[16] This was in the early case of *Farey v. Burvett*, where he said, 'the words "naval" and "military" are not words of limitation, but rather of extension'.[17] In a time of war, such phrasing proved sufficient to set the price of bread in a way that would be outside the Commonwealth's power in times of peace.[18] Indeed, as Dixon J observed in *Andrew v. Howell*, the nature of the war power as defined in the Australian Constitution is expansive, with 'its application depend[ing] upon facts, and as those facts change so may its actual operation as a power'.[19] From wage[20] and share price fixing[21] to prohibiting advertising[22] and the curtailment of civil liberties,[23] the historical exercise of section 51(vi) has afforded the Commonwealth the opportunity to reach into every aspect of Australian society. To put it another way, the powers of government increase exponentially in a time of war to be able to, for instance, set the price of basic foodstuffs in Australia or curtail the playing of popular hits in more recent times in the United Kingdom, as discussed above, or in Kenya as seen below. According to Isaacs J in a minority judgment for *Farey v. Burvett*, when the existence of Australia was under threat, such as would be the case in a total war, then the defence power was virtually unlimited, 'bounded only by the requirements of self-preservation'.[24]

To illustrate this boundless expansion of power when faced with existential threats using an example, this time drawn from public international law, the International Court of Justice (ICJ) (which was evenly split with seven votes to seven, resolved by the President's casting vote)[25] had this to say on the legality of the threat or use of nuclear weapons:[26]

> However, in view of the current state of international law, and of the elements of fact at its disposal, the Court cannot conclude definitively whether the threat or use of nuclear weapons would be lawful or unlawful in an extreme circumstance of self-defence, in which the very survival of a State would be at stake.

This case is extraordinary in that the court essentially ruled that it was unable to answer a question before it, even after accepting jurisdiction. It reaffirmed the principle that 'necessity knows no law' in a way that meant, according to law, legal constraints do not extend to existential conflicts. That renders definition and decision impossible in the indistinct and uncertain boundary between lawful force and political violence at international law. This *non-liquet* or identification of a gap in the law that the law cannot answer illustrates a 'state of exception' contemplated by the law, whereupon the law is paralysed or rendered inapplicable and the sovereign is essentially free and left to their own devices, governed only by the exigencies of necessity.[27]

War and Peace

Now that is what the present discussion hypothesises is what war is good for: expanding governmental power through and with the sanction of law. Why the law, though? The argument is that the law is more than merely useful because it is necessary. The next section will demonstrate first that the law is useful in light of its application of binary distinctions before showing that it is necessary because some form of law is always indispensable to governing political communities, even of the most authoritarian types.

The opposition between what may be referred to as states of war and peace as distinct and separate realms of both law and fact has been axiomatic, particularly for international law. Increasingly, however, that distinction, once taken for granted, now seems outmoded, quaint, cast onto the rubbish heap of history. This is because the current international legal system, during both war and peace, constructs its principal actors in the form of an institutionalised state possessing certain attributes (including a monopoly on the legitimate use of violence) as the basis for participation in international politics.[28] Having said that, Charles Garraway notes that the war on terror 'has challenged the very framework of international law itself'.[29] Evidence for this can be found in the fact that while luminaries of the international law canon, such as Hugo Grotius and Lassa Oppenheim, divided international law into the law of war and the law of peace, contemporary textbooks do not follow the same dichotomy – indeed, the latest edition of Oppenheim's monumental work abandoned a planned volume updating the law of war as the law of armed conflict.[30]

The war–peace dichotomy and the resultant differentiation of applicable legal regime are exemplary of an exception/rule scheme. Peace is the rule and war (or, perhaps better, armed conflict) the exception. This is why, for example, United Nations Security Council (UNSC) Resolutions authorising the use of force do not do so explicitly but instead use the wording 'by all necessary means' to achieve their object.[31] Such wording is deemed sufficient to permit the use of force without specifically recommending it. In international law, therefore, armed conflict is the most radical state of affairs (being literally out of the norm where all that is necessary is permissible) in the most inclusive human society (the international community representative of universality). But what does any of this have to do with music?

Music, War and Law

James Parker offers a definition of acoustic jurisprudence as 'an orientation towards law and the practice of judgment attuned to questions of sound and listening'.[32] The present discussion builds upon that approach and adds paying attention to lyrics and librettos consistently with the terms and ambitions of acoustic jurisprudence. It uses what may very loosely be termed 'martial music' (music oriented along a spectrum between anti- and pro-war) as a cultural artefact to tell us something about the relationship of law to violence and violence to music, and consequently law's judgement of music via mass violence of the political variety. This is as a subset of a larger inquiry into what law means for culture and what culture means for war in a total war, which must perforce include cultural war.

It is somewhat gratifying to note in the pages of a law journal in 2018 that in 1942 Adolf Hitler would dearly have loved to see the advent of the end of law and the demise of the last lawyer. In that spirit, he vowed that, 'I shall not rest until every German sees that it is a shameful thing to be a lawyer.'[33] Notwithstanding all that, not even he could do without lawyers, as they were absolutely necessary to the general lawlessness that he and his regime perpetrated with the sort of Mephistophelean craftiness and diabolical irony that is evident, for instance, in placing a plaque stating 'work sets you free' on concentration camp gates. Hitler did learn, though, to use the forms of law and the force of law to achieve his lawless ends. As a matter of fact, members of his regime were held accountable upon this specific basis. The point to be made here, though, is that even an absolute dictator like Hitler, whose word was literally law, found the law (or at least its forms and force) necessary as he set about his task no matter how personally distasteful he found lawyers. If certain passages of the autobiographical *Mein Kampf* are anything to go by, that task had Hitler cast himself as a sort of artist painting with the medium of violence with his people as the paintbrush on the canvas of human life generally.

> All who are not of good race in this world are chaff. And all occurrences in world history are only the expression of the races' instinct of self-preservation, in the good or bad sense . . . What applies to work as the foundation of

human sustenance and all human progress is true to an even greater degree for the defense of man and his culture. In giving one's own life for the existence of the community lies the crown of all sense of sacrifice . . . Our own German language possesses a word which magnificently designates this kind of activity: Pflichterfullung (fulfilment of duty); it means not to be self-sufficient but to serve the community.[34]

In this, the law was for him a necessary evil. That 'necessity' as noted above is the same designation provided to signal the sanctioning of armed force in UN Security Council (UNSC) Resolutions under Chapter VII of the Charter.

War as a Necessary Evil, Allegedly

Utilising political violence as a means is a delicate process, somewhat akin to attempting the opening up of Pandora's box one trouble at a time at will. It only takes one slip-up to engulf the world in all sorts of troubles. For Walter Benjamin, 'it is clear that the most elementary relationship within any legal system is that of ends to means, and, further, that violence can first be sought only in the realm of means, not of ends'.[35] Additionally, for him, legality is the criterion of means.[36] This already encountered register of justifying violence as a necessary, but evil means for at least some legally justifiable ends is quite literally Mephistophelean. This is because it links evil and good in a causal relationship where evil is engaged in, and with, to produce something good. More specifically, in Goethe's *Faust*, Faust asks Mephistopheles: 'Who are you then?' and is answered perhaps truthfully but not completely honestly: 'Part of that force which would do ever evil, and does ever good.'[37] The irony here is inescapable: Moyn, for one, finds it 'is certainly worth worrying that the restraint of war has become the companion of forever war rather than the beginning of peace'.[38]

If we then turn to Bob Marley's 'War' song, we find him singing, 'That until the basic human rights/Are equally guaranteed to all/Without regard to race/Dis a war'. Some stanzas later we encounter:

And until that day
The African continent
Will not know peace
We Africans will fight
– we find it necessary –
And we know we shall win
As we are confident
In the victory
Of good over evil.

The last phrase is repeated five times to the end. Those lines do not just link the struggle for human rights to war as a justifiable means of attaining them, but they explicitly see any resulting victory as being one of good over evil. Once again, the 'necessary' as already noted above sanctions the use of violence.

Bob Marley was consequently not uniquely of that view. When we turn to the Preamble to the Universal Declaration of Human Rights (UDHR) we find the following paragraphs:

> Whereas recognition of the inherent dignity and of the equal and inalienable rights of all members of the human family is the foundation of freedom, justice and peace in the world,
>
>   Whereas it is essential, if man is not to be compelled to have recourse, as a last resort, to rebellion against tyranny and oppression, that human rights should be protected by the rule of law.

Clearly, the words of that Preamble (explaining recourse to rebellion as being precipitated by non-recognition of human rights) are not only expressed in the basic idiom of but could well have been the source material for Bob Marley's 'War'. That is hardly surprising because Marley merely set somebody else's words to music verbatim, but for the artistic licence of interpolating the phrase 'Dis a war'. The rest are taken from what must be the most resounding I-told-you-so speech ever delivered to the United Nations General Assembly (UNGA). In it, Haile Selassie Emperor of Ethiopia opened with:

> Twenty-seven years ago, as Emperor of Ethiopia, I mounted the rostrum in Geneva, Switzerland, to address the League of Nations and to appeal for relief from the destruction which had been unleashed against my defenseless nation, by the Fascist invader. I spoke then both to and for the conscience of the world. My words went unheeded, but history testifies to the accuracy of the warning that I gave in 1936.[39]

Marley's take on war is consequently perfectly poised between those who abhor war, like Starr and Culture Club above, and those who extol its virtues (as we shall see below) to justify it as a necessary evil – as a tool for justice against oppression for the purposes of advancing human rights. It is also quite precisely identical to the stance of both domestic and international law where political violence can be justified as a necessary if regrettable means for certain ends. This tacit justification for political violence was not lost on Kenyan authorities following an abortive military coup in August 1982, when they banned not just this song, nor even Marley's entire discography, but the entire genre of reggae from radio playlists.[40]

If we then somewhat shift the register from reggae to the medieval acclamatory hymn Laudes Regiae or royal acclamation, we encounter Ernst H. Kantorowicz's *Laudes Regiae: A Study in Liturgical Acclamations and Mediaeval Ruler Worship*, which also incorporates 'A Study of the Music of the Laudes and Musical Transcriptions by Manfred F. Bukofzer'. Kantorowicz's *Laudes Regiae*, just like the Haile Selassie speech (Selassie 1963), from which Bob Marley's *War* was derived, was born in the context of anti-fascism. This can be seen straight from the preface to his study, where Kantorowicz stated that: 'The modern revival of the laudes, here only touched upon, broaches the problem of acclamations, and their function, in modern dictatorial states in which they appear as an indispensable vehicle of political propaganda, pseudo-religious emotionalism, and public reac-knowledgment of power' (Kantorowicz 1957: ix–x). For Kantorowicz: 'To "acclaim" meant to "create" a new ruler and to recognize him publicly in his new dignity' (Kantorowicz 1957: 76–7). He adds 'that the acclaiming *vox populi*, represented by one group or another, had a distinctly constitutional effect. It was through the medium of acclamatory election that the *vox pop-ulii*, audible through the politically strongest group at the time, elevated the new monarch or assented to the fact of his elevation' (Kantorowicz 1957: 77). Not even where a throne had been achieved by violence, could a formal acclamation be lacking (Kantorowicz 1957: 77). Although origi-nally the inauguration of a ruler had originally nothing whatever to do with the Church in that it was a constitutive and purely 'civil' or 'military' act (Kantorowicz 1957: 77), for Kantorowicz, it was precisely the combined undifferentiated acclamation of the people, the army, and the senate that was legally constitutive while accompanying the physical act of crowning (Kantorowicz 1957: 82). This is why:

> the shouts of the Romans and the laudes, as they then followed one after the other without a break, seem to have formed one single tumultuous outburst of voices in which it is idle to seek the particular cry which was 'constitu-tive' and legally effective. In this case, the acclamation of the Church, as it intermingled with that of the people, or of 'those present,' for once had also a legally binding character (Kantorowicz 1957: 84).

Agamben, one of the most acute contemporary readers of Kantorowicz, states that:

> Recounting this new and extreme version of the laudes at the end of his book, Kantorowicz observes that acclamations are 'indispensable to the emo-tionalism of a Fascist regime' . . . And in a footnote on Nazi acclamations

he launches a final, ironic attack on [Erik] Peterson, writing that the acclamation Ein Reich, ein Volk, ein Fuhrer, declared in Vienna in 1938 on the occasion of the annexation of Austria, 'leads via Barbarossa . . . to the Heis theos so brilliantly discussed by Peterson' . . . The attempt to exclude the very possibility of a Christian 'political theology,' so as to found in glory the only legitimate political dimension of Christianity, comes dangerously close to the totalitarian liturgy (Agamben 2011a: 193, citing Kantorowicz 1957: 185).

Kantorowicz did not miss this possibility and legacy: 'And when the *laudes regiae* were sung at a mediaeval coronation or on festival days, both the text and the tune of this chivalrous responsory could remind the audience that it had once been the legions – Roman, Oriental, and Germanic – that raised the elect to the imperial throne' (Kantorowicz 1957: 31).

Kantorowicz again:

However, it was only in the 'twenties of our century that the laudes regiae, revived by learned musicologists and liturgiologists, began to reappear also on the political stage of postwar Europe, and, by the irony of which History is so fond, this chant made its reappearance along with what was believed the new lodestar of political life: totalitarianism and dictatorship . . . Political acclamations have been resuscitated systematically in the authoritarian countries. They are indispensable to the emotionalism of a Fascist regime (Kantorowicz 1957: 31).

To provisionally summarise the argument so far: the Laudes chants up empire (the monarch, elected to the throne by the senate and the army and by God), while reggae chants down empire (Babylon represented by the West, the Government, the Police and the Church). Music is indispensable to both and thus does both.

If we again shift register and period to Baroque Music, we find George Frideric Handel's oratorio *Israel in Egypt* provides the rather uncommon Duet for Bass 'The Lord is a Man of War'. Its libretto is straightforwardly drawn from the Bible – Exodus xv, 3, 4:

The Lord is a man of war: Lord is His name. Pharaoh's chariots and his host hath He cast into the sea; his chosen captains also are drowned in the Red Sea.

In setting it to music, however, Handel created an effect through tone painting whereby the 'drowned' above has its 'ow' lengthened so as to mimic derisive laughter 'ha-ha-ha-ha', in a way that mocks the dead in a famous victory for a martial God.

The following excerpted review of a past performance of the oratorio should illustrate this point:

> The choir, meticulously prepared as always by John Scott, the organist and music director at the church, seemed unusually energized. The boys especially, looking typically angelic in their red cassocks, sang with animated, almost bloodthirsty commitment.
>
> As well they might, responding to Handel's cheerleading and his incomparably vivid tone-painting. His music playfully taunts the suddenly hapless Egyptians even as the biblical text describes their mounting agonies: 'There came all manner of flies and lice in all their quarters'; 'He gave them hailstones for rain' 'He smote all the firstborn of Egypt.'
>
> In many encounters with the work, I've never heard the final words – 'the horse and his rider hath he thrown into the sea' – sound so savage, so definitive and so satisfying.[41]

Surely, 'bloodthirsty' and 'savage' being deemed 'satisfying' is rather unexpected with reference to a sacred Baroque Oratorio, but nor is it inaccurate, or inappropriate, or a figment of the reviewer's imagination. It is to do with a certain justification of violent means where the ends are sanctified or sanctioned by a god or, in more secular times, by the people as the voice of God.

Now let us turn to some East African music and the conviction of Rwandan musician Simon Bikindi of 'direct and public incitement to genocide' by the International Criminal Tribunal for Rwanda (ICTR). James Parker (2015) developed his acoustic jurisprudence at least partially on the basis of this case. In arriving at their decision, the trial court found that he had, among others, composed eight 'war songs' from 1991 onwards.[42] This materially contributed to the result of the case which turned substantially on the inflammatory lyrics of his songs. Their musical merit was needless to say neither here nor there.

The musical examples set out above transcend time, place and genre but all orient themselves somehow to war in either condemning it, or justifying it, or even extolling it or its virtuous use. The responses to the musicians extend from reverentially staging their works, to banning them from playlists, to convicting them of genocide-related offences. To summarise the argument, while the Laudes chants up empire (investing the monarch, who is elected to the throne by the senate and the army and by God) reggae chants down empire (with empire named as Babylon which is represented by the Government, the Police and the Church).[43]

Wide-ranging responses have been presented, mirroring the range of attitudes to war. But how far can music go in preventing war? Of all the examples, only Marley's song is in complete consonance with the law and consequently renders both the law and the song Mephistophelean in extolling the virtuous ends of vicious means. It must not be forgotten that as, an adherent of the Rastafari religion, Marley worshipped the Emperor Haile Selassie as God – a quite literal apotheosis of the human. In terms of moral clarity, until all of us opposed to political violence in principle collectively have the vision and courage of our convictions to change our lifestyles in consonance with our principles, we have as much integrity as can be mustered by chanting 'no war for oil' while setting a nylon flag on fire, doused with petrol, using a butane lighter, having driven to the demonstration, as we listen to anti-war music from a plastic CD. Which is to say not much integrity at all. Not even irony will save us. It is, after all, just another Mephistophelean trait.

Notes

1. S. Levinson and J. M. Balkin, 'Law, Music and Other Performing Arts', *University of Pennsylvania Law Review* 139 (1991): 1597–658.
2. J. Parker, 'The Soundscape of Justice', *Griffith Law Review* 20, no. 4 (2011): 989.
3. D. Manderson, *Songs Without Music: Aesthetic Dimensions of Law and Justice* (Berkeley, CA: University of California Press, 2000), 98.
4. Manderson, *Songs Without Music*, 145.
5. R. Sykes, 'Listening Back: Music, Cultural Heritage and Law', *International Journal for the Semiotics of Law* 31 (2018): 183.
6. M. Kirby, *Sociology in Perspective* (Portsmouth: Heinemann, 2000), 164; Slate, 'It's the End of the World as Clear Channel Knows It', 17 September 2001, www.slate.com/articles/news_and_politics/chatterbox/2001/09/its_the_end_of_the_world_as_clear_channel_knows_it.html.
7. J. Baer, '"The Complicated Plot of Piracy": Aspects of English Criminal Law and the Image of the Pirate in Defoe', *The Eighteenth Century* 23, no. 1 (1982): 3–26.
8. Baer, '"The Complicated Plot of Piracy"', 10.
9. C. Schmitt, *Political Theology: Four Chapters on the Concept of Sovereignty* (Chicago: Chicago University Press, 2005), 36.
10. Schmitt, *Political Theology*, 26.
11. C. Schmitt, *The Concept of the Political* (Chicago: University of Chicago Press, 2007), 27.
12. S. Schillings, *Enemies of All Humankind: Fictions of Legitimate Violence* (Lebanon, NH: Dartmouth College Press, 2016), 185.
13. C. Schmitt, *Ex Captivitate Salus* (Cambridge: Polity Press, 2017), 14.
14. C. Agamben, *State of Exception* (Chicago: University of Chicago Press, 2005), 114.
15. C. Agamben, *Opus Dei: An Archaeology of Duty* (Stanford, CA: Stanford University Press, 2013), 119.
16. Commonwealth of Australia Constitution Act 1900 (Imp) s 51(vi).
17. *Farey v Burvett* [1916] 21 CLR 433 at 440.
18. *Farey v Burvett*, 440–1. There are more recent cases on the scope of the war power, most notably *Thomas v Mowbray* [2007] HCA 33; 233 CLR 307; 81

ALJR 1414; 237 ALR 194, which address the extent of individual liberty in a way that tends to efface the distinction between war and peace with regard to the 'war on terror'.

19. *Andrews v Howell* [1941] 65 CLR 255 at 278.
20. *R v Foster* [1949] 79 CLR 43.
21. *Miller v Commonwealth* [1946] 73 CLR 187.
22. *Ferguson v Commonwealth* [1943] 66 CLR 432.
23. *Australian Communist Party v Commonwealth* [1951] 83 CLR 1; *Thomas v Mowbray* [2007] 233 CLR 307.
24. *Farey v Burvett* [1916] 21 CLR para. 455.
25. In favour were President Bedjaoui and Judges Ranjeva, Herczegh, Shi, Fleischhauer, Vereshchetin and Ferrari Bravo. Against were Vice-President Schwebel and Judges Oda, Guillaume, Shahabuddeen, Weeramantry. See Koroma and Higgins (1996).
26. *Legality of the Threat or Use of Nuclear Weapons, Advisory Opinion*, 8 July 1996, 226, para. 105. www.icj-cij.org/files/case-related/95/095-19960708-ADV-01-00-EN.pdf.
27. C. Agamben, *The Time That Remains: A Commentary on the Letter to the Romans* (Stanford, CA: Stanford University Press, 2005), 1.
28. G. Teubner, 'Alienating Justice: On the Surplus Value of the Twelfth Camel'. In *Consequences of Legal Autopoiesis*, edited by D. Nelken and J. Pribán (Aldershot: Ashgate, 2001), 21.
29. C. Garraway, 'Can the Law of Armed Conflict Survive 9/11?', in *Yearbook of International Humanitarian Law, Vol. 14*, edited by M. Schmitt and L. Arimatsu (Cambridge: Cambridge University Press, 2011), 383.
30. A. Watts, C. Greenwood and A. Oppenheim, *Oppenheim's International Law, Vol. 2*, 8th ed. (Harlow: Longman, 2009).
31. J. Baker, *The Politics of Diplomacy: Revolution, War and Peace* (New York: G.P. Putnam's Sons, 1995), 304–5; Freudenschuss, 'Between Unilateralism and Collective Security: Authorizations of the Use of Force by the UN Security Council', *European Journal of International Law* 5 (1994): 492.
32. J. Parker, *Acoustic Jurisprudence: Listening to the Trial of Simon Bikindi* (Oxford: Oxford University Press, 2015), 15.
33. J. Librett, 'From the Sacrifice of the Letter to the Voice of Testimony: Giorgio Agamben's Fulfillment of Metaphysics', *Diacritics* 37, nos 2–3: 11; R. Strickland and F. Reed, *The Lawyer Myth: A Defense of the American Legal Profession* (Athens, OH: Ohio University Press, 2008), 55.
34. A. Hitler, *Mein Kampf: Volume 1 – A Reckoning* (1924). www.hitler.org/writings/Mein_Kampf/mkv1ch11.html.
35. W. Benjamin, *Reflections: Essays, Aphorisms, Autobiographical Writings* (San Diego, CA: Harcourt Brace Jovanovich, 1978), 277.
36. Benjamin, *Reflections*, 278.
37. J. Goethe, *Faust: A Tragedy: Interpretive Notes, Contexts, Modern Criticism*, 2nd ed. (New York: W.W. Norton, 2001), 36.
38. S. Moyn, 'Tolstoy's Case Against Humane War', *Plough Quarterly*, 25 March 2000, www.plough.com/en/topics/justice/politics/tolstoys-case-against-humane-war.

39. H. Selassie, 'Haile Selassie's Address to the United Nations, 1963', 4 October 1963, https://en.wikisource.org/wiki/Haile_Selassie%27s_address_to_the_United_Nations,_1963.
40. K. Mutunga, 2007. 'The Devil in Music', *Daily Nation*, 24 August 2007, www.nation.co.ke/lifestyle/weekend/1220-203316-wlc25sz/index.html.
41. J. Oestreich, 'Review: St Thomas Choir and Concert Royal Perform Handel', *New York Times*, 14 May 2015, www.nytimes.com/2015/05/15/arts/music/review-st-thomas-choir-and-concert-royal-perform-handel.html.
42. *The Prosecutor v Simon Bikindi*, 2 December 2008, para. 201, www.unmict.unictr.org/sites/unictr.org/files/case-documents/ictr-01-72/trial-judgements/en/081202.pdf.
43. S. King and R. Jensen, 'Bob Marley's "Redemption Song": The Rhetoric of Reggae and Rastafari', *Journal of Popular Culture* 29: 17–36.

References

ABC News. 2016. 'South China Sea: US Warship Challenges Beijing's Territorial Claims with Freedom of Navigation Exercise'. 22 October. www.abc.net. au/news/2016-10-22/us-warship-challenges-chinas-claims-in-south-china-sea/7956826.

Abe, S. 2014. 'Message from Prime Minister Shinzo Abe on the occasion of "Marine May"'. http://japan.kantei.go.jp/96_abe/statement/201407/20140718 uminohi.html.

Abraham, W. 1964. 'The Life and Times of Anton Wilhelm Amo'. *Transactions of the Historical Society of Ghana* 7, 60–81.

Abraham, W. 2006. 'Anton Wilhelm Amo'. In *A Companion to African Philosophy*, edited by K. Wiredu. 191–9. London: Blackwell.

Agamben, G. 1990. *The Coming Community*, Stanford, CA: Stanford University Press.

Agamben, G. 1991. *Language and Death: The Place of Negativity*, Minneapolis: University of Minnesota Press.

Agamben, G. 1993a. *Infancy and History: The Destruction of Experience*, New York: Verso.

Agamben, G. 1993b. *Stanzas: Word and Phantasm in Western Culture*, Minneapolis: University of Minnesota Press.

Agamben 1993c. 'Bartleby'. In *The Coming Community*, 35–8. Minneapolis: University of Minnesota Press.

Agamben, G. 1995. *Idea of Prose*. Albany, NY: State University of New York Press.

Agamben, G. 1998. *Homo Sacer: Sovereign Power and Bare Life*. Stanford, CA: Stanford University Press.

Agamben, G. 1999a. *The End of the Poem: Studies in Poetics*. Stanford, CA: Stanford University Press.

Agamben, G. 1999b. *Potentialities: Collected Essays in Philosophy*. Stanford, CA: Stanford University Press.

Agamben, G. 2000a. *Means Without End: Notes on Politics*. Minneapolis: University of Minnesota Press.

Agamben, G. 2000b. *Remnants of Auschwitz: The Witness and the Archive*. New York: Zone Books.

Agamben, G. 2004. *The Open: Man and Animal*. Stanford, CA: Stanford University Press.

Agamben, G. 2005a. *State of Exception*. Chicago: University of Chicago Press.

Agamben, G. 2005b. *The Time That Remains: A Commentary on the Letter to the Romans*. Stanford, CA: Stanford University Press.

Agamben, G. 2009a. *The Signature of All Things: On Method*. New York: Zone Books.

Agamben, G. 2009b. *What is an Apparatus? And Other Essays*. Stanford, CA: Stanford University Press.

Agamben, G. 2011a. 'The Archaeology of Commandment'. European Graduate School Video Lectures, 21 May. www.youtube.com/watch?v=T4MjMj4S4B8.

Agamben, G. 2011b. *The Kingdom and the Glory: For a Theological Genealogy of Economy and Government*. Stanford, CA: Stanford University Press.

Agamben, G. 2011c. *The Sacrament of Language: An Archaeology of the Oath*. Stanford, CA: Stanford University Press.

Agamben, G. 2012. *The Church and the Kingdom*. London: Seagull Books.

Agamben, G. 2013. *Opus Dei: An Archaeology of Duty*. Stanford, CA: Stanford University Press.

Agamben, G. 2014. 'What is a Destituent Power?' (trans. S. Wakefield). *Environment and Planning D: Society and Space* 32, no. 1: 65–74.

Agamben, G. 2015a. *Pilate and Jesus*. Stanford, CA: Stanford University Press.

Agamben, G. 2015b. *Stasis: Civil War as a Political Paradigm (Homo Sacer II, 2)*. Edinburgh: Edinburgh University Press.

Agamben, G. 2016. *The Use of Bodies*. Stanford, CA: Stanford University Press.

Agamben, G. 2017a. *Mystery of Evil: Benedict XVI and the End of Days* (trans. A. Kotsko). Stanford, CA: Stanford University Press.

Agamben, G. 2017b. *What is Philosophy?* Stanford, CA: Stanford University Press.

Agamben, G. 2018a. *The Adventure*. Cambridge, MA: MIT Press.

Agamben, G. 2018b. *Karman: A Brief Treatise on Action, Guilt, and Gesture*. Stanford, CA: Stanford University Press.

Agamben, G. 2018c. *What is Real?* Stanford, CA: Stanford University Press.

Agamben, G. 2019. *Creation and Anarchy: The Work of Art and the Religion of Capitalism*. Stanford, CA: Stanford University Press.

Ahlberg, B. M. and K. M. Njoroge. 2013. '"Not Men Enough to Rule!" Politicization of Ethnicities and Forcible Circumcision of Luo Men During the Postelection Violence in Kenya'. *Ethnicity & Health* 18, no. 5: 454–68.

Akhtar-Khavari, A. et al. 2016. 'Open Letter on Nuclear Weapons'. https://uploads.guim.co.uk/2016/03/10/Open_Letter_on_Nuclear_Weapons_-_Defence_Minister.pdf.

Allain, J. 2007. 'The Definition of "Slavery" in General International Law and the Crime of Enslavement Within the Rome Statute'. Guest Lecture Series of the Office of the Prosecutor, The Hague, 26 April. https://asp.icc-cpi.int/iccdocs/asp_docs/library/organs/otp/ICC-OTP-20070426-Allain_en.pdf.

Alston, P. 1990. 'US Ratification of the Covenant on Economic, Social and Cultural Rights: The Need for an Entirely New Strategy'. *American Journal of International Law* 84, no. 2: 365–93.

Alston, P. 2009. *Putting Economic, Social, and Cultural Rights Back on the Agenda of the United States*. NYU School of Law, Public Law Research Paper 09-35. https://papers.ssrn.com/sol3/papers.cfm?abstract_id=1397703.

Alvarez, J. E. 2013. '*Tadić* Revisited: The Ayyash Decisions of the Special Tribunal for Lebanon'. *Journal of International Criminal Justice* 11, no. 2: 291–302.

Ambos, K., J. Large and M. Wierda. 2009. *Building a Future on Peace and Justice: Studies on Transitional Justice, Peace and Development. The Nuremberg Declaration on Peace and Justice* (2nd ed.). Dordrecht: Springer.

American Journal of International Law (AJIL). 1909. 'General Act of the Conference of Berlin Concerning the Congo'. *The American Journal of International Law* 3, no. 1, 7–25.

Anderegg, J. 2006. 'Unrecognized Modernity: Intertextuality and Irony in Goethe's *Faust*'. *Colloquia Germanica* 39, no. 1: 31–41.

Anderson, D. M. 2002. 'Vigilantes, Violence and the Politics of Public Order in Kenya'. *African Affairs* 101, no. 405: 531–55.

Aquinas, St Thomas 2013. *Summa Theologica*. New York: Benzinger Bros.

Arendt, H. 1949. 'The Rights of Man: What are They?', *Modern Review* 3: 4–37.

Arendt, H. 1973. *The Origins of Totalitarianism*. New York: Harcourt, Brace, Jovanovich.

Arendt, H. 2006. *Eichmann in Jerusalem: A Report on the Banality of Evil*. Harmondsworth: Penguin.

Aristotle. 1984. *The Rhetoric and the Poetics of Aristotle*. New York: Modern Library.

Associated Press. 2015. 'US Navy: Beijing Creating a "Great Wall of Sand" in South China Sea'. *The Guardian,* 31 March. www.theguardian.com/world/2015/mar/31/china-great-wall-sand-spratlys-us-navy.

Aurey, X. 2017. 'The Nuremberg Doctors' Trial: Looking Back 70 Years Later'. *International Criminal Law Review* 17, no. 6: 1049–69.

Austin, J. 1962. *How to Do Things with Words,* Cambridge, MA: Harvard University Press.

Austin, J. 1975. *How to Do Things with Words*, 2nd ed. Cambridge, MA: Harvard University Press.

Axe, D. 2009. '10 Things You Didn't Know About Somali Pirates'. *The Wall Street Journal,* 27 April, www.wsj.com/articles/SB124060718735454125.

Baer, J. 1982. '"The Complicated Plot of Piracy": Aspects of English Criminal Law and the Image of the Pirate in Defoe'. *The Eighteenth Century* 23, no. 1: 3–26.

Bahadur, J. 2011. 'Somali Pirates: "We're Not Murderers . . . We Just Attack Ships"'. *The Guardian*, 25 May. www.theguardian.com/world/2011/may/24/a-pioneer-of-somali-piracy.

Bailey, P. 1997. 'The Right to an Adequate Standard of Living: New Issues for Australian Law'. *Australian Journal of Human Rights* 4, no. 1: 25–50.

Baker, J. 1995. *The Politics of Diplomacy: Revolution, War and Peace*. New York: G.P. Putnam's Sons.

Baker, K. 2019. 'Eduard Pernkopf: The Nazi Book of Anatomy Still Used by Surgeons'. *BBC News*, 18 August. www.bbc.com/news/health-49294861.

Balfour, L. 2013, 'What Babo Saw: Benito Cereno and "The World We Live In"'. In A. Frank (ed.), *A Political Companion to Herman Melville*, Lexington, KY: University Press of Kentucky.

Balkin, J. M., and S. Levinson. 1998–99. 'Interpreting Law and Music: Performance Notes on "The Banjo Serenader" and "The Lying Crowd of Jews"'. *Cardozo Law Review* 20, nos 5–6: 1513–72.

Bantekas, I., and S. Nash. 2007. *International Criminal Law*. London: Routledge.

BBC News. 2010. 'China's Anti-Piracy Role Off Somalia Expands'. 29 January. http://news.bbc.co.uk/2/hi/asia-pacific/8486502.stm.

BBC News. 2015. 'China "Expanding Island Building" in South China Sea'. 8 May. www.bbc.com/news/world-asia-china-32666046.

BBC News. 2016. 'Q&A: South China Sea Dispute'. 12 July. www.bbc.com/news/world-asia-pacific-13748349.

Bechky, P. 2012. 'Lemkin's Situation: Toward a Rhetorical Understanding of Genocide'. *Brooklyn Law Review* 77, no. 2: 551–624.

Beebee, T. 2012. 'Carl Schmitt's Myth of Benito Cereno'. *Seminar: A Journal of Germanic Studies* 42: 114–34.

Bendersky, J. W. 1983. *Carl Schmitt: Theorist for the Reich*. Princeton, NJ: Princeton University Press.

Bendersky, J. W. 1987. 'Carl Schmitt at Nuremberg'. *Telos* 72: 91–6.

Benjamin, W. 1978. *Reflections: Essays, Aphorisms, Autobiographical Writings*. San Diego, CA: Harcourt Brace Jovanovich.

Benton, L. 2010. *A Search for Sovereignty: Law and Geography in European Empires, 1400–1900*. Cambridge: Cambridge University Press.

Berlin, I. 1980. 'The Originality of Machiavelli in Berlin'. In *Against the Current: Essays in the History of Ideas*, edited by H. Hardy, 25–79. New York: Viking.

Bess, R. 1989. 'A.W. Amo: First Great Black Man of Letters'. *Journal of Black Studies* 19, no. 4: 387–93.

Bignall, S. and M. G. Svirsky. 2012. 'Introduction: Agamben and Colonialism'. In *Agamben and Colonialism*, edited by S. Bignall and M. G. Svirsky, 1–14. Edinburgh: Edinburgh University Press.

Bilsky, L. 2001a. 'Judging Evil in the Trial of Kastner'. *Law and History Review* 19, no. 1: 117–60.

Bilsky, L. 2001b. 'Judging and Understanding'. *Law and History Review* 19, no. 1: 183–8.

Bilsky, L. 2002. 'Breaking the Acoustic Wall Between the Kastner and Eichmann Trials'. In *The History of Law in a Multicultural Society*, edited by R. Harris, S. Kedar, P. Lahav, and A. Likhovski, 123–45. Aldershot: Ashgate.

Binswanger, H. C. and K. R. Smith. 2000. 'Paracelsus and Goethe: Founding Fathers of Environmental Health'. *International Journal of Public Health* 78, no. 9: 1162–5.

Bisley, N. 2016. 'We Should Think Carefully About an Australian FONOP in the South China Sea'. *The Lowy Interpreter*, 4 February. www.lowyinstitute.org/the-interpreter/we-should-think-carefully-about-australian-fonop-south-china-sea.

Black, E. 2008. *The Transfer Agreement: The Dramatic Story of the Pact Between the Third Reich and Jewish Palestine*. New York: Dialog Press.

Blanchard, B. 2015. 'China Navy Carries Out More Drills in Disputed South China Sea'. Reuters, 13 December. www.reuters.com/article/us-southchinasea-china-idUSKBN0TW01D20151213#4lceWmQbXGhM3QvL.97.

Bloom, H. 1994. *The Western Canon: The Books and School of the Ages*. New York: Harcourt Brace.

Bodin, J. 1992. *On Sovereignty: Four Chapters from the Six Books of the Commonwealth*. Cambridge: Cambridge University Press.

Bossuyt, M. J. 1987. *Guide to the 'Travaux Préparatoires' of the International Covenant on Civil and Political Rights*. Leiden: Martinus Nijhoff.

Bourke, L. 2017. 'Neo-liberalism has Failed, Says Prominent British Labour Figure Ed Balls'. *Sydney Morning Herald*, 16 August. www.smh.com.au/federal-politics/political-news/neoliberalism-has-failed-says-prominent-british-labour-figure-ed-balls-20170815-gxwwe4.html.

Brown, J. K. 2002. *The Cambridge Companion to Goethe*. Cambridge: Cambridge University Press.

Buck-Morss, S. 2000. 'Hegel and Haiti'. *Critical Inquiry* 26, no. 4: 821–65.

Buck-Morss, S. 2009. *Hegel, Haiti and Universal History*. Pittsburgh, PA: University of Pittsburgh Press.

Buckland, W. 2010. *The Roman Law of Slavery: The Condition of the Slave in Private Law from Augustus to Justinian*. New York: Cambridge University Press.

Burchard, C. 2006. 'The Nuremberg Trial and Its Impact on Germany'. *Journal of International Criminal Justice* 4: 800–29.

Busch, F. 1986. 'Melville's Mail'. *The Iowa Review* 16, no. 2: 150–63.

Bush, G. W. 1990. 'Address Before a Joint Session of the Congress on the Persian Gulf Crisis and the Federal Budget Deficit'. https://en.wikisource.org/wiki/Address_Before_a_Joint_Session_of_the_Congress_on_the_Persian_Gulf_Crisis_and_the_Federal_Budget_Deficit.

Bush, G. W. 1991. 'After the War: The President: Transcript of President Bush's Address on the End of the Gulf War'. *New York Times*, 7 March. www.nytimes.com/1991/03/07/us/after-war-president-transcript-president-bush-s-address-end-gulf-war.html.

Butler, J. 1997. *Excitable Speech: A Politics of the Performative*. New York: Routledge.

Carter, A. 2016. 'SECDEF Carter Letter to McCain on South China Sea Freedom of Navigation Operation'. *UNSI News*, 5 January. https://news.usni.org/2016/01/05/document-secdef-carter-letter-to-mccain-on-south-china-sea-freedom-of-navigation-operation.

Cassese, A. 1999. '*Ex Iniuria Ius Oritur*: Are We Moving Towards International Legitimation of Forcible Countermeasures in the World Community?' *European Journal of International Law* 10: 25–30.

Cassese, A. 2008. *International Criminal Law*, 2nd ed. Oxford: Oxford University Press.

Cassese, A. 2012. 'The Nexus Requirement for War Crimes'. *Journal of International Criminal Justice* 10, no. 5: 1395–1417.

Cassese, A. and P. Gaeta. 2013. *Cassese's International Criminal Law*, 3rd ed. Oxford: Oxford University Press.

Charlton, C. 2015. 'Christians Escape Kenyan Terrorist Massacre After Muslim Passengers on Board Bus Say "Shoot Us All or Not at All"'. *Daily Mail*, 21 December. www.dailymail.co.uk/news/article-3369735/The-militants-threatened-shoot-Muslim-passengers-board-bus-defy-terrorists-demands-separate-Christians-deadly-terror-attack.html.

Charlesworth, H. 2002. 'International Law: A Discipline of Crisis.' *The Modern Law Review* 65: 377–92.

Charlesworth, H. 2005. 'Current Trends in International Legal Theory.' In *Public International Law: An Australian Perspective*, 2nd ed., edited by S. K. N. Blay, R. W. Piotrowicz and B. M. Tsamenyi, 402–11. Melbourne: Oxford University Press.

Chatham House. 2015. 'Challenges to the Rules-Based International Order'. www.chathamhouse.org/sites/default/files/London%20Conference%202015%20-%20Background%20Papers.pdf.

Cheng, D. 2016. 'US Conducts Freedom of Navigation Operation in South China Sea'. *The Daily Signal*, 3 February, http://dailysignal.com/2016/02/03/us-conducts-freedom-of-navigation-operation-in-south-china-sea.

Chesterman, S. and M. Byers. 1999. 'Has US Power Destroyed the UN?' *London Review of Books*, 21: 9.

Choi, T. 2015. 'Why the US Navy's First South China Sea FONOP Wasn't a FONOP'. *The Diplomat*, 4 November. www.thediplomat.com/2015/11/why-the-us-navys-first-south-china-sea-fonop-wasnt-a-fonop.

Christodoulidis, E. and S. Veitch. 2001. *Lethe's Law: Justice, Law and Ethics in Reconciliation*. Oxford: Hart.

Connelly, A. 2016. 'The Problem with American Assumptions About Australia'. *The Lowy Interpreter*, 17 May. www.lowyinterpreter.org/post/2016/05/17/The-problem-with-American-assumptions-about-Australia.aspx?utm_source=Lowy+Interpreter&utm_campaign=a23bcf2aaf-RSS_EMAIL_CAMPAIGN&utm_medium=email&utm_term=0_eed7d14b56-a23bc-f2aaf-59370029.

Conroy, S. 2016. 'Turnbull Government Adrift on Ambiguous South China Sea Rhetoric'. *The Interpreter*, 24 February, www.lowyinterpreter.org/author/Stephen%20Conroy.aspx.

Constable, M. 2005. *Just Silences: The Limits and Possibilities of Modern Law*. Princeton, NJ: Princeton University Press.

Constable, M. 2014. *Our Word is Our Bond: How Legal Speech Acts*. Stanford, CA: Stanford University Press.

Corten, O. and P. Klein. 2011. *The Vienna Conventions on the Law of Treaties: A Commentary*, Oxford: Oxford University Press.

Council for International Organizations of Medical Sciences (CIOMS) in collaboration with the World Health Organization (WHO). 2009. *International Ethical Guidelines for Epidemiological Studies*. https://cioms.ch/wp-content/uploads/2017/01/International_Ethical_Guidelines_LR.pdf.

Cover, R. M. 1975. *Justice Accused: Antislavery and the Judicial Process*. New Haven, CT: Yale University Press.

Craven, M. 2015. 'Between Law and History: The Berlin Conference of 1884–1885 and the Logic of Free Trade. *London Review of International Law* 3, no 1: 31–59.

Cryer, R. 2010. *An Introduction to International Criminal Law and Procedure*, 2nd ed. Cambridge: Cambridge University Press.

Dallaire, R. 2003. *Shake Hands with the Devil: The Failure of Humanity in Rwanda*, Toronto: Random House.

Davis, D. B. 1966. *The Problem of Slavery in Western Culture*. Ithaca, NY: Cornell University Press.

Davis, M. 2013. 'Should International Law Permit State-sanctioned Assassination of Non-state Enemies?' *Public Affairs Quarterly* 1, no. 27: 111–36.

Dennis, D. B. 2012. *Inhumanities: Nazi Interpretations of Western Culture*. Cambridge: Cambridge University Press.

Department of Defence. 2015. 'Australia–Indonesia 2+2: Joint Press Conference by Australian Foreign Minister Bishop and Australian Minister for Defence Payne', 21 December. www.minister.defence.gov.au/2015/12/21/minister-for-defence-transcript-joint-press-conference-by-australian-foreign-minister-bishop-and-australian-minister-for-defence-payne-australia-indonesia-22.

Department of Defence. 2016. *2016 Defence White Paper*. www.defence.gov.au/whitepaper/Docs/2016-Defence-White-Paper.pdf.

Derrida, J. 1990. 'Force de Loi: La "Fondement Mystique de L'Autorite"/Force of Law: the "Mystical Origin of Authority"'. *Cardozo Law Review* 11, nos 5–6: 920–1046.

Derrida, J. and G. Bennington. 2009. *The Beast and the Sovereign. Seminars of Jacques Derrida, Vol. 1*. Chicago: University of Chicago Press.

Donado, J. C. 2012. 'Heidegger's Letter to Schmitt'. *Telos*, 8 August. www.telospress. com/heideggers-letter-to-schmitt.

Donaldson, P. S. 1988. *Machiavelli and Mystery of State*. Cambridge: Cambridge University Press.

Douglas, L. 2001. 'Language, Judgment and the Holocaust'. *Law And History Review* 19, no. 1: 177–82.

Draper, N. 2010. *The Price of Emancipation: Slave-Ownership, Compensation and British Society at the End of Slavery*. Cambridge: Cambridge University Press.

Dugard, J. 2018. 'Rome Statute 20 Years: Addressing Current and Future Challenges. Speech to Assembly of States Parties of the ICC, 7 December. https://asp.icc-cpi. int/iccdocs/asp_docs/ASP17/20A.Dugard%20speech.pdf.

Dyzenhaus, D. 1998. The Morals of Modernity. *Canadian Journal of Philosophy* 28, no. 2: 269–86.

The Economist. 2016. 'Full Steam: If Long-standing Tensions ease in the South China Sea, China will Ensure They Rise Elsewhere', 20 August. www.economist.com/ news/asia/21705373-if-long-standing-tensions-ease-south-china-sea-chinawill-ensure-they-rise-elsewhere-full.

Emden, C. J. 2010. 'Constitutional Theory, 1928: Carl Schmitt and the Rechtsstaat'. *Telos* 153: 159–92.

Erickson, A. and J. Mikolay. 2009. 'Welcome China to the Fight Against Pirates'. *Proceedings Magazine*, 153 no. 3: 34–41.

Esposito, R. 2011. *Immunitas: The Protection and Negation of Life*. Cambridge: Polity Press.

Esposito, R. 2012. 'The *Dispositif* of the Person'. *Law, Culture and the Humanities* 8, no. 1: 17–30.

Esposito, R. 2013. *Terms of the Political: Community, Immunity, Biopolitics*, New York: Fordham University Press.

Farmer, S. 1995. 'Symbols that Face Two Ways: Commemorating the Victims of Nazism and Stalinism at Buchenwald and Sachsenhausen'. *Representations* 49: 97–119.

Fischer-Lescano, A. and G. Teubner. 2006. *Regime-Kollisionen*. Frankfurt: Suhrkamp.

Fiskesj, M. 2012. 'Outlaws, Barbarians, Slaves: Critical Reflections on Agamben's *Homo Sacer*. HAU: *Journal of Ethnographic Theory* 2, no. 1: 161–80.

Fletcher, G. P. and J. D. Ohlin. 2006. 'The ICC – Two Courts in One?' *Journal of International Criminal Justice* 4, no. 3: 428–33.

Fletcher, P. 2004. 'The Political Theology of the Empire to Come'. *Cambridge Review of International Affairs*, 17, no. 1: 49–61.

Fox, B. J. 2015. 'Carl Schmitt and Political Catholicism: Friend or Foe? *CUNY Academic Work*s 47. http://academicworks.cuny.edu/gc_etds/929.

Frankena, W. K. (1973). *Ethics*, 2nd ed. Upper Saddle River, NJ: Prentice Hall.

Freeman, M. D. A. and D. Lloyd. 2001. *Lloyd's Introduction to Jurisprudence*. London: Sweet & Maxwell.

Freud, S. 1953. 'The Moses of Michelangelo'. In *The Standard Edition of the Complete Psychological Works of Sigmund Freud*. London: Hogarth Press.

Foucault, M. 1976. *The History of Sexuality Vol. 1*. New York: Random House.

Foucault, M. 1977. *Discipline and Punish: The Birth of the Prison*. New York: Pantheon Books.

Freudenschuss, H. 1994. 'Between Unilateralism and Collective Security: Authorizations of the Use of Force by the UN Security Council'. *European Journal of International Law* 5: 492–531.

Fukuyama, F. 2006. *The End of History and the Last Man*. New York: The Free Press.

Fukuyama, F. 2016. 'One Belt, One Road: Exporting the Chinese Model to Eurasia'. *Project Syndicate*, 12 January. www.project-syndicate.org/commentary/china-one-belt-one-road-strategy-by-francis-fukuyama-2016-01#s7b-gUL8SCvH501Mf.99.

Garraway, C. 2011. 'Can the Law of Armed Conflict Survive 9/11?'. In *Yearbook of International Humanitarian Law*, Vol. 14, edited by M. Schmitt and L. Arimatsu, 383–90. Cambridge: Cambridge University Press.

Gattini, A. 2004. 'Kelsen's Contribution to International Criminal Law'. *Journal of International Criminal Justice* 2, no. 3: 795–809.

Geneva Convention for the Amelioration of the Condition of the Wounded and Sick in Armed Forces in the Field of 12 August 1949.

Geneva Convention Relative to the Treatment of Prisoners of War of 12 August 1949.

Gibbon, E. 1996. *The History of the Decline and Fall of the Roman Empire*. Harmondsworth: Penguin.

Gill, T. D. 1995. 'Legal and Some Political Limitations on the Power of the UN Security Council to Exercise Its Enforcement Powers Under Chapter VII of the Charter'. *Netherlands Yearbook of International Law* 26: 33–138.

Ginzburg, C. 1989. *Clues, Myths, and the Historical Method*. Baltimore, MD: Johns Hopkins University Press.

Goethe, J. 1995. *Scientific Studies* (D.E. Miller ed.). Princeton, NJ: Princeton University Press.

Goethe, J. 2001. *Faust: A Tragedy: Interpretive Notes, Contexts, Modern Criticism*, 2nd ed. New York: W.W. Norton.

Goethe, J. 2014. *Faust Volumes 1 and 2: Goethe's Collected Works*. Princeton, NJ: Princeton University Press.

Golder, B. 2015. *Foucault and the Politics of Rights*. Stanford, CA: Stanford University Press.

Goodrich, P. 2014. *Legal Emblems and the Art of Law: Obiter depicta as the Vision of Governance*. Cambridge: Cambridge University Press.

Gould, E. H. 2012. *Among the Powers of the Earth: The American Revolution and the Making of a New World Empire*. Cambridge, MA: Harvard University Press.

Graf, S. 2017. 'To Regain Some Kind of Human Equality: Theorizing the Political Productivity of "Crimes Against Humanity"'. *Law, Culture and the Humanities* 13, no. 3: 744–63.

Graham, E. 2016. 'US Navy Carries Out Third FONOP in South China Sea'. *The Interpreter*, 10 May. www.lowyinterpreter.org/post/2016/05/10/US-Navy-carries-out-third-FONOP-in-South-China-Sea.aspx?utm_source=Lowy+Interpreter&utm_campaign=da05f2f7bd-RSS_EMAIL_CAMPAIGN&utm_medium=email&utm_term=0_eed7d14b56-da05f2f7bd-59370029.

Gray, J. 2007. *Black Mass: Apocalyptic Religion and the Death of Utopia*. New York: Farrar Straus and Giroux.

Greenberg, K. J. and J. L. Dratel. 2005. *The Torture Papers: The Road to Abu Ghraib*. New York: Cambridge University Press.

Greene, A. and B. Birtles. 2015. 'South China Sea: Audio Reveals RAAF Plane Issuing Warning to Chinese Navy During "Freedom of Navigation" Flight'. *ABC News*, 15 December. www.abc.net.au/news/2015-12-15/audio-captures-raaf-challenging-chinese-navy-in-south-china-sea/7030076.

Guardian Africa. 2015. 'Muslims Hailed for Protecting Christians During Terror Attack on Kenyan Bus'. *The Guardian*, 22 December. www.theguardian.com/world/2015/dec/22/kenya-al-shabaab-attack-muslims-protect-christians-mandera.

Haiyang, L. 2016. 'The Lawfare Over South China Sea: Exceptional Rules vs General Rules'. *Opinio Juris*, 14 July. http://opiniojuris.org/2016/07/14/the-lawfare-over-south-china-sea-exceptional-rules-vs-general-rules.

Harneit-Sievers, A. and R. M. Peters. 2008. 'Kenya's 2007 General Election and Its Aftershocks'. *Africa Spectrum* 43, no. 1: 133–44.

Hawkes, D. 2016. *The Faust Myth: Religion and the Rise of Representation*. New York: Palgrave Macmillan.

Hell, J. 2009. 'Katechon: Carl Schmitt's Imperial Theology and the Ruins of the Future'. *The Germanic Review: Literature, Culture, Theory* 84, no. 4: 283–326.

Heller, K. J. 2015. '400+ Academics Sign an Open Letter in Support of Harold Koh'. *Opinio Juris*, 16 April. http://opiniojuris.org/2015/04/16/400-academics-sign-an-open-letter-in-support-of-harold-koh.

Heller-Roazen, D. 2009. *The Enemy of All: Piracy and the Law of Nations*. Cambridge, MA: Zone Books.

Henckaerts, J.-M. and L. Doswald-Beck. 2005. *Customary International Humanitarian Law, Volume I: Rules*. Cambridge: ICRC/Cambridge University Press.

Herrero, M. 2015. 'On Political Theology: The Hidden Dialogue Between C. Schmitt and Ernst H. Kantorowicz in *The King's Two Bodies*'. *History of European Ideas* 41, no. 8: 1164–77.

Hitler, A. 1924. *Mein Kampf: Volume 1 – A Reckoning*. www.hitler.org/writings/Mein_Kampf/mkv1ch11.html.

Hobbes, T. 2005. *Leviathan* (Richard Tuck ed.). Cambridge: Cambridge University Press.

Hoff, J. 2007. *A Faustian Foreign Policy from Woodrow Wilson to George W. Bush: Dreams of Perfectibility*. Cambridge: Cambridge University Press.

Hollerich M. J. 2011. 'Introduction', in *Theological Tractates*, edited by E. Peterson. Stanford, CA: Stanford University Press.

Honig, B. 2009. *Emergency Politics: Paradox, Law, Democracy*. Princeton: Princeton University Press.

Huang, Y. 2012. 'Universal Jurisdiction Over Piracy and East Asian Practice'. *Chinese Journal of International Law* 11: 623–55.

Huxley, T. H. 1869. 'Nature: Aphorisms by Goethe'. *Nature* 1: 9–11.

ICAN. 2017. 'Positions on the Treaty'. www.icanw.org/why-a-ban/positions.

ILC. 1996. 'Draft Code of Crimes Against the Peace and Security of Mankind with Commentaries 1996'. In *Yearbook of the International Law Commission*, Vol. II, Part Two.

ILC. 2017a. 'Summary of the Work of the International Law Commission: Crimes Against Humanity'. http://legal.un.org/ilc/summaries/7_7.shtml.

ILC. 2017b. 'About the Commission: Origin and Background'. http://legal.un.org/ilc/ilcintro.shtml.

ILC. 2018. 'Summary of the Work of the International Law Commission: Identification of Customary International Law'. http://legal.un.org/ilc/summaries/1_13.shtml.

Independent International Commission on Kosovo. 2000. *The Kosovo Report*. Oxford: Oxford University Press.

International Criminal Court. 2010. 'Kenya: Situation in the Republic of Kenya'. www.icc-cpi.int/kenya.

IOM. 2017. 'IOM Learns of "Slave Market" Conditions Endangering Migrants in North Africa'. Media Release, Libya, 4 November. www.iom.int/news/iom-learns-slave-market-conditions-endangering-migrants-north-africa.

Israeli Security Agency. n.d. 'The Kastner Affair'. www.shabak.gov.il/SiteCollection Images/english/Moreshet/kastnerAffair_en.pdf.

Jinyuan, S. 2015. 'The East China Sea Air Defense Identification Zone and International Law'. *Chinese Journal of International Law* 14: 271–303.

Joerges, C. and N. Singh Galeigh. 2003. *Dark Legacies of Europe*. Oxford: Hart.

Jorgensen, M. (2016). 'East Timor: Concession is the Price for a Rules Based Order. *The Interpreter*, 15 February. www.lowyinterpreter.org/post/2016/02/15/East-Timor-Concession-is-the-price-for-a-rules-based-order.aspx.

Joyce, R. 2017. 'Anarchist International Law(yers)? Mapping Power and Responsibility in International Law'. *London Review of International Law* 5, no. 3: 397–424.

Jun, A. 2015. 'China's Island Construction Facilitates Navigation Freedom'. *Global Times,* 17 September. www.globaltimes.cn/content/942948.shtml.

Kaes, A., M. Jay and E. Dimendberg. 1994. *The Weimar Republic Sourcebook*. Berkeley, CA: University of California Press.

Kagwanja, P. M. 2003. 'Facing Mount Kenya or Facing Mecca? The Mungiki, Ethnic Violence and the Politics of the Moi Succession in Kenya, 1987–2002'. *African Affairs* 102 no. 406: 25–49.

Kagwanja, P. M. 2005. 'Clash of Generations? Youth Identity, Violence and the Politics of Transition in Kenya, 1997–2002'. In *Vanguards and Vandals: Youth, Politics and Conflict in Africa*, edited by J. Abbink and I. Kessel, 83–111. Leiden: Brill.

Kagwanja, P. M. 2009. 'Courting Genocide: Populism, Ethno-nationalism and the Informalisation of Violence in Kenya's 2008 Post-election Crisis'. *Journal of Contemporary African Studies* 27, no. 3: 365–87.

Kant, I. 1887. *The Philosophy of Law: An Exposition of the Fundamental Principles of Jurisprudence as the Science of Right*. Edinburgh: T. & T. Clark.

Kant, I. 1957. *Perpetual Peace*. New York: Liberal Arts Press.

Kant, I. 1965. *The Metaphysical Elements of Justice*. Indianapolis, IN: Bobbs-Merrill.

Kantorowicz, E. 1931. *Frederick the Second: 1194–1250,* New York: Richard R. Smith.

Kantorowicz, E. 1957. *The King's Two Bodies*. Princeton, NJ: Princeton University Press.

Kantorowicz, E. 1958. *Laudes Regiae: A Study in Liturgical Acclamations and Mediaeval Ruler Worship*. Los Angeles: University of California Press.

Katumanga, M. and L. Cliffe. 2005. *Armed Violence and Poverty in Nairobi: A Mini Case Study for the Armed Violence and Poverty Initiative*. Bradford: Bradford Centre for International Cooperation and Security, https://bradscholars.brad.ac.uk/bitstream/handle/10454/996/AVPI_Nairobi.pdf?sequence=1&isAllowed=y.

Kelsen, H. 1994. *Peace Through Law*. Chapel Hill, NC: University of North Carolina Press.

Kemple, T. M. 1995. *Reading Marx's Writing: Melodrama, the Market and the 'Grundrisse'*. Stanford, CA: Stanford University Press.

Kempner, R. 1987. *Interrogation of Carl Schmitt (III)*. New York: Telos.

Kent, H. 1954. 'The Historical Origins of the Three Mile Limit'. *American Journal of International Law* 48: 537–55.

Kenyatta, J. 1938. *Facing Mount Kenya: The Tribal Life of Gikuyu*. London: Secker and Warburg.

Kershaw I. 2000. *Hitler, 1936–1945: Nemesis*. London: Allen Lane.

Keyuan, Z. 2002. 'Disrupting or Maintaining the Marine Legal Order in East Asia?' *Chinese Journal of International Law* 1: 449–98.

Ki-moon, B. 2011. 'Oceans and Law of the Sea', 14 April. www.un.org/depts/los/clcs_new/submissions_files/mysvnm33_09/chn_2011_re_phl_e.pdf.

King, S. and Jensen, R. 1995. 'Bob Marley's "Redemption Song": The Rhetoric of Reggae and Rastafari'. *Journal of Popular Culture*, 29: 17–36.

Kirby, M. 2000. *Sociology in Perspective*. Portsmouth: Heinemann.

Knust, H. 1983. 'From Faust to Oppenheimer: The Scientist's Pact with the Devil'. *Journal of European Studies*, 13(49–50): 122–41.

Kogon, E. 1979. *A Theory and Practice of Hell: The German Concentration Camps and the System Behind Them* (Trans. Heinz Norden). New York: Octagon Books.

Koroma, A. G. and R. Higgins. 1996. *Legality of the Threat or Use of Nuclear Weapons, Advisory Opinion*, 8 July. www.icj-cij.org/files/case-related/95/095-19960708-ADV-01-00-EN.pdf.

Koselleck, R. 2006. 'Crisis' (Trans. Michaela W. Richter). *Journal of the History of Ideas* 67: 397–400.

Koskenniemi, M. 2005. *From Apology to Utopia: The Structure of International Legal Argument*. New York: Cambridge University Press.

Koskenniemi, M. 2007. *The Gentle Civilizer of Nations: The Rise and Fall of International Law 1870–1960*. Cambridge: Cambridge University Press.

Koskenniemi, M. 2009. 'The Politics of International Law, 20 Years Later'. *European Journal of International Law* 20, no. 1: 7–19.

Kotsko, A. 2017. *The Prince of This World*. Stanford, CA: Stanford University Press.

Kyle, K. 1997. 'The Politics of the Independence of Kenya'. *Contemporary British History* 11, no. 4: 42–65.

Lacey, N. 2008. *Women, Crime, and Character: From Moll Flanders to Tess of the D'Urbervilles*. Oxford: Oxford University Press.

Lafer, G. 2004. 'Neoliberalism by Other Means: The "War on Terror" at Home and Abroad'. *New Political Science* 26, no. 3: 323–46.

LaGrone, S. 2016. 'China Upset Over "Unprofessional" US South China Sea Freedom of Navigation Operation'. *USNI News*, 31 January. www.news.usni.org/2016/01/31/china-upset-over-unprofessional-u-s-south-china-sea-freedom-of-navigation-operation.

Lahav, P. 1997. *Judgment in Jerusalem: Chief Justice Simon Agranat and the Zionist Century*. Berkeley, CA: University of California Press.

Lauterpacht, H. 1927. *Private Law Sources and Analogies of International Law (with Special Reference to International Arbitration)*. London: Pearson Longman.

Lengyel, O. 1983. *Five Chimneys: A Woman Survivor's True Story of Auschwitz*. New York: Howard Fertig.

Lesaffer, R. 2005. 'Argument from Roman Law in Current International Law: Occupation and Acquisitive Prescription'. *European Journal of International Law* 16: 25–8.

Levi, P. 1988. *The Drowned and the Saved*. New York: Summit Books.

Levinson, S. and J. M. Balkin. 1991. 'Law, Music and Other Performing Arts'. *University of Pennsylvania Law Review* 139: 1597–1658.

Lewis, H. 2007. '"New" Human Rights: US Ambivalence Toward the International Economic and Social Rights Framework'. In *Bringing Human Rights Home: A History of Human Rights in the United States*, edited by C. Soohoo, C. Albisa and M. F. Davis, 100–41. Santa Barbara, CA: Praeger.

Librett, J. 2007. 'From the Sacrifice of the Letter to the Voice of Testimony: Giorgio Agamben's Fulfillment of Metaphysics'. *Diacritics* 37, nos 2–3: 11–33.

Lifton, R. J. 1986. *The Nazi Doctors: Medical Killing and the Psychology of Genocide*. New York: Basic Books.

Linder, C. 2016. 'Carl Schmitt in Plettenberg'. In *The Oxford Handbook of Carl Schmitt*, edited by J. Meierhenrich and O. Simons, 147–70. Oxford: Oxford University Press.

Loewenstein, K. 1945. 'Observations on the Personality and Work of Professor Carl Schmitt'. Karl Loewenstein Papers, Box 46, Folder 46, Amherst College Archives and Special Collections, Amherst, MA.

Lonsdale, J. 1990. 'Mau Maus of the Mind: Making Mau Mau and Remaking Kenya'. *The Journal of African History* 31, no. 3: 393–421.

Lowy Institute for International Policy. 2016. 'South China Sea: Conflicting Claims and Tensions'. Lowy Institute for International Policy, 20 May. www.lowyinstitute.org/issues/south-china-sea.

Luban, D. 2001. 'A Man Lost in the Gray Zone'. *Law and History Review*, 19, no. 1: 161–76.

McCall, D. 1989. *The Silence of Bartleby*. Ithaca, NY: Cornell University Press.

Machiavelli, N. 2003. *The Prince*. New York: Penguin.

Mackinder, H. J. 1904. 'The Geographical Pivot of History'. *The Geographical Journal*, 23, no. 4: 421–37.

McLeod, C. 2010. 'Towards a Philosophical Account of Crimes Against Humanity'. *European Journal of International Law* 21, no. 2: 280–308.

Maitland, F. 1901. *English Law and the Renaissance*. Cambridge: Cambridge University Press.

Manderson, D. (2000). *Songs Without Music: Aesthetic Dimensions of Law and Justice*. Berkeley, CA: University of California Press.

Marcus, J. 2015. 'US–China Tensions Rise Over Beijing's "Great Wall of Sand"'. *BBC News*, 29 May. www.bbc.com/news/world-asia-32913899.

Marks, S. 2009. 'False Contingency'. *Current Legal Problems* 62, no. 1: 1–21.

Martel, J. R. 2017. 'Book Review: *Decolonizing Democracy: Power in a Solid State*'. *Law, Culture and the Humanities* 13, no. 2: 309–11.

Marx, K. 2005. *The Communist Manifesto: A Road Map to History's Most Important Political Document*. London: Haymarket Books.

Matwijkiw, A. and B. Matwijkiw. 2013. 'Post-conflict Justice: Legal Doctrine, General Jurisprudence, and Stakeholder Frameworks'. In *Global Trends: Law, Policy & Justice: Essays in Honour of Professor Giuliana Ziccardi Capaldo*, edited by M. Bassiouni, 345–70. Oxford: Oxford University Press.

Mégret, F. 2013. 'Practices of Stigmatization'. *Law and Contemporary Problems* 76(3): 287–313.

Mehring, R. 2014. *Carl Schmitt: A Biography*. Cambridge: Polity Press.

Meierhenrich, J. and Simons, O. 2016. *The Oxford Handbook of Carl Schmitt*. Oxford: Oxford University Press.

Melville, H. 2001. 'Benito Cereno'. In *Melville's Short Novels: Authoritative Texts, Contexts, Criticism*, edited by D. McCall. New York: W.W. Norton.

Melville, H. 2008. *Benito Cereno*. Raleigh, NC: Freebook.

Menya, W. 2014. 'Fresh Push to Save Uhuru, Ruto from ICC'. *Daily Nation*, 14 June. www.nation.co.ke/news/politics/Fresh-push-to-save-Uhuru-and-Ruto-from-ICC/-/1064/2348938/-/k6ecsoz.

Mettraux, G. 2009. 'Nexus with Armed Conflict'. In *The Oxford Companion to International Criminal Justice*, edited by A. Cassese, 435. Oxford: Oxford University Press.

Meyer, E. 2018. 'Philosophy in the Contemporary World: After September 11, a Permanent State of Exception?'. Blog of the APA. https://blog.apaonline.org/2018/02/01/philosophy-in-the-contemporary-world-after-september-11th-a-permanent-state-of-exception.

Michelman, F. 1996. 'Parsing "a Right to Have Eights"'. *Constellations* 3, no. 2: 200–8.

Mitchell, C. 1968. 'Melville and the Spurious Truth of Legalism'. *The Centennial Review*, 12, no. 1: 110–26.

Mockaitis, T. R. 1992. 'Minimum Force, British Counter-Insurgency and the Mau Mau Rebellion: A Reply'. *Small Wars & Insurgencies* 3, no. 2: 87–89.

Morgan, E. 2020. *The Aesthetics of International Law*. Toronto: University of Toronto Press.

Morton, S. 2012. 'Reading Kenya's Colonial State of Emergency After Agamben'. In *Agamben and Colonialism*, edited by M. Svirsky and S. Bignall, 110–27. Edinburgh: Edinburgh University Press.

Moyn, S. 2020. 'Tolstoy's Case Against Humane War'. *Plough Quarterly*, 25 March. www.plough.com/en/topics/justice/politics/tolstoys-case-against-humane-war.

Mudde, C., and C. R. Kaltwasser. 2013. *The Oxford Handbook of Political Ideologies*. Oxford: Oxford University Press.

Müller, J. 2003. *A Dangerous Mind: Carl Schmitt in Post-War European Thought*. New Haven, CT: Yale University Press.

Mutunga, K. 2007. 'The Devil in Music'. *Daily Nation*, 24 August. www.nation.co.ke/lifestyle/weekend/1220-203316-wlc25sz/index.html.

Muvangua, N. and D. Cornell. 2012. *uBuntu and the Law: African Ideals and Post-Apartheid Jurisprudence*. New York: Fordham University Press.

Negri, A. 2007. 'Giorgio Agamben: The Discreet Taste of the Dialectic'. In *Sovereignty and Life*, edited by M. Calarco and S. De Caroli, 165–70. Stanford, CA: Stanford University Press.

Neumann, F. 1943. *Behemoth: The Structure and Practice of National Socialism 1933–1944*, Chicago: Ivan R. Dee.

Neumann, F., H. Marcuse and O. Kirchheimer. 2013. *Secret Reports on Nazi Germany: The Frankfurt School Contribution to the War Effort*. Princeton, NJ: Princeton University Press.

Njambi, W. N. 2004. 'Dualisms and Female Bodies in Representations of African Female Circumcision: A Feminist Critique'. *Feminist Theory* 5, no. 3: 281–303.

Nobel Media 2017. 'The Nobel Peace Prize 2017'. Media release, 6 October. www.nobelprize.org/nobel_prizes/peace/laureates/2017/press.html.

Noll, G. 2008. 'The Miracle of Generative Violence: René Girard and the Use of Force in International Law'. *Leiden Journal of International Law* 21, no. 3: 563–80.

Nouwen, S. and W. Werner. 2010. 'Doing Justice to the Political: The International Criminal Court in Uganda and Sudan'. *The European Journal of International Law* 21: 941–96.

Nuremberg Military Tribunals Under Control Council Law No. 10, *United States v. Karl Brandt, et al.* (Case No. 1) '*The Medical Case*' in *Trials of War Criminals Before the Nuremberg Military Tribunals Under Control Council Law No. 10* Vols I and II Nuremberg, October 1946–April 1949, Vol I and Vol II.

Nussbaum, A. 1952. 'The Significance of Roman Law in the History of International Law'. *University of Pennsylvania Law Review* 100, no. 5: 678–87.

O'Brien, D. and V. Carter. 2002–03. 'Chant Down Babylon: Freedom of Religion and the Rastafarian Challenge to Majoritarianism', *Journal of Law and Religion*, 18, no. 1: 219–48.

O'Donnell, G. 2004. 'The Quality of Democracy: Why the Rule of Law Matters'. *Journal of Democracy* 15, no. 4: 32–46.

O'Donnell, G. 2007. 'The Perpetual Crises of Democracy'. *Journal of Democracy*, 18, no. 1: 5–11.

Oestreich, J. 2015. 'Review: St Thomas Choir and Concert Royal Perform Handel'. *New York Times*, 14 May. www.nytimes.com/2015/05/15/arts/music/review-st-thomas-choir-and-concert-royal-perform-handel.html.

Oomen, B. 2010. 'Justice Mechanisms and the Question of Legitimacy: The Example of Rwanda's Multi-layered Justice Mechanisms'. In *Building a Future on Peace and Justice: Studies on Transitional Justice, Peace and Development. The Nuremberg Declaration on Peace and Justice* (2nd ed.), edited by K. Ambos, J. Large and M. Wierda, 175–202. Dordrecht: Springer.

Oppenheim, L. and R. Roxburgh. 2005. *International Law: A Treatise*. Clark, NJ: Lawbook Exchange.

Panda, A. 2016. 'Everything You Wanted to Know About the *USS Lassens* FONOP in the South China Sea'. *The Diplomat*, 6 January. www.thediplomat.com/2016/01/everything-you-wanted-to-know-about-the-uss-lassens-fonop-in-the-south-china-sea.

Parker, J. 2011. 'The Soundscape of Justice'. *Griffith Law Review* 20, no. 4: 962–93.

Parker, J. 2015. *Acoustic Jurisprudence: Listening to the Trial of Simon Bikindi*. Oxford: Oxford University Press.

Pennington, K. 1993. *The Prince and the Law 1200–1600: Sovereignty and Rights in the Western Legal Tradition*. Berkeley, CA: University of California Press.

Pflanz, M. 2014. 'Uhuru Kenyatta's ICC Prosecution Close to Collapse as Lawyers Demand Acquittal'. *The Telegraph*, 8 October. www.telegraph.co.uk/news/worldnews/africaandindianocean/kenya/11149256/Uhuru-Kenyattas-ICC-prosecution-close-to-collapse-as-lawyers-demand-acquittal.html.

Phelps, L. R. 1959. 'The Reaction to Benito Cereno and Billy Budd in German'. *Symposium: A Quarterly Journal in Modern Literatures* 13, no. 2: 294–9.

Prawer, S. 1975. 'Mephisto and Old Nick'. *Publications of the English Goethe Society* 45, no. 1: 23–63.

Preece, R. 2003. 'Darwinism, Christianity, and the Great Vivisection Debate'. *Journal of the History of Ideas* 64, no. 3: 399–419.

Protocol Additional to the Geneva Conventions of 12 August 1949, and Relating to the Protection of Victims of International Armed Conflicts of 8 June 1977.

Ramshaw, S. 2016. 'The Paradox of Performative Immediacy: Law, Music, Improvisation. *Law, Culture and the Humanities* 12, no. 1: 6–16.

Rapp-Hooper, M. 2016. 'Confronting China in the South China Sea'. *Foreign Affairs*, 8 February. www.foreignaffairs.com/articles/china/2016-02-08/confronting-china-south-china-sea.

Rasmussen, J. 2010. 'Outwitting the Professor of Politics? Mungiki Narratives of Political Deception and Their Role in Kenyan Politics'. *Journal of Eastern African Studies* 4, no. 3: 435–49.

Reagan, R. 1982. 'President Ronald Reagan's Statement on United States Participation in the Third United Nations Conference on the Law of the Sea'. US Navy Judge Advocate General's Corps, 10 March. www.jag.navy.mil/organization/documents/Reagan%20Ocean%20Policy%20Statement.pdf.

Redfern, W. D. 1985. *Puns*. Oxford: Blackwell.

Roberts W. R. 1984. *The Rhetoric and the Poetics of Aristotle*. New York: Random House.

Robertson, P. 2010. 'Pat Robertson Says Haiti Paying for "Pact to the Devil"'. http://edition.cnn.com/2010/US/01/13/haiti.pat.robertson/index.html.

Rogin, M. P. 1979. 'The King's Two Bodies: Abraham Lincoln, Richard Nixon & Presidential Self-Sacrifice'. *The Massachusetts Review* 20, no. 3: 553–73.

Rovere, C. 2016. 'Defence White Paper 2016: Eight Strategic Observations'. *The Interpreter*, 29 February. www.lowyinterpreter.org/post/2016/02/29/Defence-White-Paper-2016-Eight-strategic-observations.aspx?utm_source=Lowy+Interpreter&utm_campaign=69e96e8a4f-RSS_EMAIL_CAMPAIGN&utm_medium=email&utm_term=0_eed7d14b56-69e96e8a4f-59370029.

Ruteere, M. 2008. 'Dilemmas of Crime, Human Rights and the Politics of *Mungiki* Violence in Kenya'. Kenya Human Rights Institute. https://papers.ssrn.com/sol3/papers.cfm?abstract_id=1462685.

Safranski, R. 2017. *Goethe: Life as a Work of Art*. New York: W.W. Norton.

Salter, M. 2012a. 'Law, Power and International Politics with Special Reference to East Asia: Carl Schmitt's Grossraum Analysis'. *Chinese Journal of International Law* 11, no. 3: 393–427.

Salter, M. 2012b. *Carl Schmitt: Law as Politics, Ideology and Strategic Myth*. London: Routledge-Cavendish.

Sartori, G. 1989. 'The Essence of the Political in Carl Schmitt'. *Journal of Theoretical Politics* 1, no. 1: 63–75.

Schabas, W. 2010. *The International Criminal Court: A Commentary on the Rome Statute.* Oxford: Oxford University Press.

Schabas, W. (ed.). 2013. *The Universal Declaration of Human Rights: The Travaux Préparatoires.* Cambridge, MA: Cambridge University Press.

Schatz, A. 2017. 'The President and the Bomb'. *London Review of Books*, 16 November. www.lrb.co.uk/v39/n22/adam-shatz/the-president-and-the-bomb.

Schillings, S. 2016. *Enemies of All Humankind: Fictions of Legitimate Violence.* Lebanon, NH: Dartmouth College Press.

Schmid, E. 2015. *Taking Economic, Social and Cultural Rights Seriously in International Criminal Law.* Cambridge: Cambridge University Press.

Schmitt, C. 1985. *Political Theology: Four Chapters on the Concept of Sovereignty* (trans. G. Schwab), 4th ed. Chicago: University of Chicago Press.

Schmitt, C. 1993. 'Age of Neutralisations and Depoliticisations'. *Telos* 96: 119–29.

Schmitt, C. 1996. *The Leviathan in the State Theory of Thomas Hobbes.* Chicago: University of Chicago Press.

Schmitt, C. 2004. *Legitimacy and Legality.* Durham, NC: Duke University Press.

Schmitt, C. 2005. *Political Theology: Four Chapters on the Concept of Sovereignty.* Chicago: Chicago University Press.

Schmitt, C. 2006. *The Nomos of the Earth in the International Law of the Jus Publicum Europaeum.* New York: Telos.

Schmitt, C. 2007a. *The Concept of the Political.* Chicago: University of Chicago Press.

Schmitt, C. 2007b. *Theory of the Partisan: Intermediate Commentary on the Concept of the Political.* New York: Telos.

Schmitt, C. 2008. *Political Theology II: The Myth of Closure of Any Political Theology.* Cambridge: Polity Press.

Schmitt, C. 2011a. 'The Concept of Piracy'. *Humanity* 2: 27–9.

Schmitt, C. 2011b. *Writings on War* (Trans. T. Nunan). Cambridge: Polity Press.

Schmitt, C. 2014. *Dialogues on Power and Space.* Cambridge: Polity Press.

Schmitt, C. 2015. *Land and Sea: A World-Historical Mediation.* New York: Telos.

Schmitt, C. 2017. *Ex Captivitate Salus.* Cambridge: Polity Press.

Schmitt, C. and H. Kelsen (2015). *The Guardian of the Constitution.* Cambridge: Cambridge University Press.

Schotel, B. 2009. 'Reviews: Defending Our Legal Practices: A Legal Critique of Giorgio Agamben's *State of Exception*'. *Amsterdam Law Forum.* http://ojs.ubvu.vu.nl/alf/article/view/68/124.

Scott, S. V. 2016. 'China's Nine-Dash Line, International Law, and the Monroe Doctrine Analogy'. *China Information*, 30, no. 3: 296–311.

Selassie, H. 1963. 'Haile Selassie's Address to the United Nations, 1963', 4 October. https://en.wikisource.org/wiki/Haile_Selassie%27s_address_to_the_United_Nations,_1963.

Sentas, V. and J. Whyte. 2009. 'Law, Crisis, Revolution: An Introduction'. *Australian Feminist Law Journal* 31: 3–14.

Shapiro, M. J. 2012. 'The Micropolitics of Justice: Language, Sense and Space'. *Law, Culture and the Humanities* 8, no. 3: 466–84.

Shen, J. 2002. 'China's Sovereignty Over the South China Sea Islands: A Historical Perspective'. *Chinese Journal of International Law* 1, no. 1: 94–157.

Sherratt, Y. 2013. *Hitler's Philosophers.* New Haven, CT: Yale University Press.

Simma, B. 1999. 'NATO, the UN and the Use of Force: Legal Aspects'. *European Journal of International Law* 10: 1–22.

Simma, B., D.-E. Khan, G. Nolte and A. Paulus. 2012. *The Charter of the United Nations: A Commentary*, 3rd ed. Oxford: Oxford University Press.

Simpson, G. J. 2007. *Law, War and Crime: War Crimes Trials and the Reinvention of International Law*. Cambridge: Polity Press.

Sitze, A. 2014. 'Carl Schmitt: An Improper Name'. https://infrapolitica.files.wordpress.com/2014/10/carl-schmitt-an-improper-name.pdf.

Slate. 2001. 'It's the End of the World as Clear Channel Knows It', 17 September. www.slate.com/articles/news_and_politics/chatterbox/2001/09/its_the_end_of_the_world_as_clear_channel_knows_it.html.

Slaughter J. R. 2007. *Human Rights, Inc: The World Novel, Narrative Form, and International Law*. New York: Fordham University Press.

Smith, P. D. 2006. '"Was die Welt im Innersten zusammenhält": Scientific Themes in Goethe's *Faust*'. In *A Companion to Goethe's Faust: Parts I and II*, edited by P. Bishop, 194–220. Rochester, NY: Camden.

Steiner, G. 1971. *In Bluebeard's Castle: Some Notes Towards the Redefinition of Culture*. New Haven, CT: Yale University Press.

Strauss, L. 1958. *Thoughts on Machiavelli*, Glencoe, IL: The Free Press.

Strickland, R. and F. Reed. 2008. *The Lawyer Myth: A Defense of the American Legal Profession*. Athens, OH: Ohio University Press.

Stringer, K. W. 2014. '"A Household Divided": A Fragmented Religious Identity, Resistance and the Mungiki Movement Among the Kikuyu in Post-colonial Kenya'. PhD thesis, Ohio State University, https://etd.ohiolink.edu/!etd.send_file?accession=osu1395764314&disposition=inline.

Sunstein, C. R. 1996. 'On the Expressive Function of Law'. *University of Pennsylvania Law Review* 144, no. 5: 2021–53.

Sykes, R. 2018. 'Listening Back: Music, Cultural Heritage and Law'. *International Journal for the Semiotics of Law* 31: 183–6.

Teubner, G. 2001. 'Alienating Justice: On the Surplus Value of the Twelfth Camel'. In *Consequences of Legal Autopoiesis*, edited by D. Nelken and J. Pribán, 21–44. Aldershot: Ashgate.

Thompson, E. P. 1981. 'Overthrowing the Satanic Kingdom'. *The Nation*, 24 January, 87–93.

Thompson, K. 2016. 'In Our Best Interest: Treaty Scrutiny in a Connected World: Session 1'. In *Proceedings of the Joint Standing Committee on Treaties: 20th Anniversary Seminar*, www.aph.gov.au/Parliamentary_Business/Committees/Joint/Treaties/20th_Anniversary?

Tomuschat, C. 2006. 'The Legacy of Nuremberg'. *Journal of International Criminal Justice*, 4, no. 4: 830–44.

Ulmen, G. L. (1987). 'Return of the Foe'. *Telos* 72: 187–93.

United Nations. 1998a. UN Press Release SG/SM/6470 Transcript of Press Conference by Secretary-General Kofi Annan at United Nations Headquarters, 24 February 1998. www.un.org/News/Press/docs/1998/19980224.SGSM6470.html.

United Nations. 1998b. Diplomatic Conference of Plenipotentiaries on the Establishment of an International Criminal Court Rome, 15 June–17 July 1998. *Official Records Volume II: Summary Records of the Plenary Meetings and of the*

Meetings of the Committee of the Whole. http://legal.un.org/icc/rome/proceedings/E/Rome%20Proceedings_v2_e.pdf.

United Nations. 1998c. Diplomatic Conference of Plenipotentiaries on the Establishment of an International Criminal Court Rome, 15 June–17 July 1998. *Official Records Volume III: Reports and Other Documents.* http://legal.un.org/icc/rome/proceedings/E/Rome%20Proceedings_v3_e.pdf.

UNSC. 1993. UNSC Resolution 808/1993. www.icty.org/x/file/Legal%20Library/Statute/statute_808_1993_en.pdf.

van der Wilt, H. 2012. 'War Crimes and the Requirement of a Nexus with an Armed Conflict'. *Journal of International Criminal Justice* 10, no. 5: 1113–28.

Verini, J. 2016. 'The Prosecutor and the President'. *New York Times,* 26 June www.nytimes.com/2016/06/26/magazine/international-criminal-court-moreno-ocampo-the-prosecutor-and-the-president.html.

Virno, P. 2008. *Multitude: Between Innovation and Negation.* Los Angeles: Semiotext(e).

Wamue, G. 2001. 'Revisiting Our Indigenous Shrines Though Mungiki'. *African Affairs* 100, no. 400: 453–67.

Watts, A., C. Greenwood and A. Oppenheim (eds). 2009. *Oppenheim's International Law, Vol. 2,* 8th ed. Harlow: Longman.

Weber, M. 2004. *The Vocation Lectures* (Edited by David S. Owen). Indianapolis, IN: Hackett.

Wedgwood, R. 2000. 'Unilateral Action in the UN System'. *European Journal of International Law* 11, no. 2: 349–59.

Weeramantry, C. G. 2004. *Universalising International Law.* Leiden: Martinus Nijhoff.

Weigend, T. 2012. '"In General a Principle of Justice": The Debate on the "Crime Against Peace" in the Wake of the Nuremberg Judgment'. *Journal of International Criminal Justice* 10, no. 1: 41–58.

Weisberg, R. H. 1984. *The Failure of the Word.* New Haven, CT: Yale University Press.

Weisberg, R. H. 2014. *In Praise of Intransigence: The Perils of Flexibility.* Oxford: Oxford University Press.

Weiss, T. G. 2011. *Thinking About Global Governance: Why People and Ideas Matter.* New York: Routledge.

Wells, G. A. 1967. 'Goethe and the Inter Maxillary Bone'. *The British Journal for the History of Science* 3 no. 4: 348–61.

Werle, G. and F. Jessberger. 2014. *Principles of International Criminal Law,* 3rd ed. Oxford: Oxford University Press.

West, R. 1985. 'Authority Autonomy and Choice: The Role of Consent in the Moral and Political Visions of Franz Kafka and Richard Posner'. *Harvard Law Review* 99, no. 2: 384–428.

West, R. 1996. 'Invisible Victims: A Comparison of Melville's *Bartleby the Scrivener* and Glaspell's *A Jury of Her Peers'. Cardozo Studies in Law and Literature* 8: 203–52.

White, J. B. 1985. *Heracles' Bow: Essays on the Rhetoric and Poetics of the Law.* Madison, WI: University of Wisconsin Press.

White J. B. 1990. *Justice as Translation: An Essay in Cultural and Legal Criticism.* Chicago: University of Chicago Press.

Williams, R. 1977. *Marxism and Literature*. Oxford: Oxford University Press.

Wingfield-Hayes, R. 2014. 'China's Island Factory'. *BBC News*, 9 September. www.bbc.co.uk/news/resources/idt-1446c419-fc55-4a07-9527-a6199f5dc0e2.

Wolfram, R. 2012. 'Preamble', in *The Charter of the United Nations: A Commentary*, 3rd ed., edited by B. Simma, D.-E. Khan, G. Nolte and A. Paulus. Oxford: Oxford University Press.

World Medical Association. 1964. *World Medical Association Declaration of Helsinki Ethical Principles for Medical Research Involving Human Subjects*. www.who.int/bulletin/archives/79%284%29373.pdf.

Wright, Q. 1961. *The Role of International Law in the Elimination of War*. Manchester: Manchester University Press.

Xinhua. 2013. 'China Continues Fighting Somali Piracy'. *China Daily*, 27 December. www.chinadaily.com.cn/china/2013-12/27/content_17200695.htm.

Yoon, S. 2014. 'Xi Jinping's "True Maritime Power" and ESCS Issues'. *Chinese Journal of International Law* 13, no. 4: 887–89.

Zahar, A. and G. Sluiter. 2008. *International Criminal Law: A Critical Introduction*. New York: Oxford University Press.

Zartaloudis, T. 2010. *Giorgio Agamben: Power, Law and the Uses of Criticism*. New York: Routledge.

Zhang, H. 2010. 'Is it Safeguarding the Freedom of Navigation or Maritime Hegemony of the United States? Comments on Raul (Pete) Pedrozo's Article on Military Activities in the EEZ'. *Chinese Journal of International Law* 9: 31–47.

Zhukova, O. A. 2016. 'The Philosophy of New Spirituality: The Creative Manifesto of Nikolai Berdyaev'. *Russian Social Science Review* 57, no. 4: 260–74.

Zolo, D. 1998. 'Hans Kelsen: International Peace Through International Law'. *European Journal of International Law* 9, no. 2: 306–24.

Zolo, D. 2009. *Victors' Justice: From Nuremberg to Baghdad*. London: Verso.

Index

References to a page number followed by a note number (14n10) indicate material contained in the text at the page in question rather than in the note itself.

EU representative:
Easy Access System Europe
Mustamäe tee 50, 10621 Tallinn, Estonia
Gpsr.requests@easproject.com

www.ingramcontent.com/pod-product-compliance
Lightning Source LLC
Chambersburg PA
CBHW061211220326
41599CB00025B/4608